A Crisis of Conscience
A Catholic Doctor Speaks Out for Reform

A Crisis of Conscience

A Catholic Doctor Speaks Out for Reform

Hugh R. K. Barber, M.D.

A BIRCH LANE PRESS BOOK
Published by Carol Publishing Group

A Birch Lane Press Book
Published by Carol Publishing Group
Birch Lane Press is a registered trademark of Carol Communications, Inc.
Editorial Offices: 600 Madison Avenue, New York, N.Y. 10022
Sales and Distribution Offices: 120 Enterprise Avenue, Secaucus, N.J. 07094
In Canada: Canadian Manda Group, P.O. Box 920, Station U, Toronto, Ontario M8Z 5P9
Queries regarding rights and permissions should be addressed to
Carol Publishing Group, 600 Madison Avenue, New York, N.Y. 10022

Carol Publishing Group books are available at special discounts for bulk purchases, for
sales promotion, fund-raising, or educational purposes. Special editions can be created
to specifications. For details, contact: Special Sales Department, Carol Publishing
Group, 120 Enterprise Avenue, Secaucus, N.J. 07094

Manufactured in the United States of America
10   9   8   7   6   5   4   3   2   1

Library of Congress Cataloging-in-Publication Data

Barber, Hugh R.K., 1918–
      A crisis of conscience : a Catholic doctor speaks out / by Hugh R.
   K. Barber.
         p.   cm.
      "A Birch Lane Press book."
      ISBN 1-55972-162-6
      1. Catholic Church—Controversial literature.   2. Barber, Hugh R.
   K., 1918-   .   I. Title.
   BX1779.5.B38   1993
   282—dc20   92-39827
                                                        CIP

DEDICATION
To those who have suffered by the Church in the
past and to those who will rise to lead it into a
new era of greatness

Contents

Acknowledgments

I am most appreciative of the help given to me by many people. Most of the help came from productive discussions. I would like to acknowledge some of these people without burdening them with responsibility for the views expressed by me.

To my wife, Mary Louise, I am grateful for the patience she showed during the time that I was researching and then writing this book. She spent a great deal of time scanning newspapers and magazines for articles that would improve the quality of this book. Her support sustained me in this project.

Bridie McGuire and Ann McGuire do such a magnificent job in organizing my private practice and allowed me to write this book, although they had no knowledge of what I was writing. I want to thank them for their help.

To Dr. Irving Buterman, I want to express my thanks for the continued support and help that he has given me in providing care for my private patients.

To Ruzena Danek, I am most grateful for her help, encouragement, and many suggestions, as well as for her incisive manner in helping to make decisions on what would be valuable for the structure of this book. Her enthusiasm made this a labor of love and relieved the tediousness of writing on such a controversial subject. Her skill with the word processor and her editorial ability were invaluable to me. It is difficult to express my gratitude adequately. However, I am sure that those who read the book will appreciate what she has helped achieve.

To Marcia Miller, I am most grateful for her help in organizing the administrative office of the department of obstetrics and gynecology of Lenox Hill Hospital in New York City. Her dedication and untiring labor relieved me of a great deal of the administrative responsibility during the time that I was preparing and writing this book.

I want to express my deep gratitude to Elizabeth Armour for her skill in working with the word processor and for her immense help in bringing this book to fruition.

Among those who made suggestions were Catholics and non-

Catholics, clergy and laymen dedicated to updating the Catholic Church. The stimulus for this book came from the enthusiastic support that I received from many letters and phone calls that followed an interview by Dena Kleiman in the *New York Times*, which was called "For a Catholic Doctor, a Crisis of Conscience."

I am most grateful to a Protestant colleague and classmate, Stanley Bedford, whom I admire so much. Blackie, as I called him (black Protestant), taught me so much and helped me develop another point of view. I would also like to acknowledge Harry Dweck, an Orthodox Jew, and Alfred Tanz, who, by their loyalty, became trusted friends, and my good and dearest friend, recently called to heaven, James J. O'Rourke, a role model for all.

For his assistance in preparing the book I want to thank W. Watts Biggers.

I want to thank David James for the help he gave me by suggesting methods for contacting people in the field of publishing.

I want to thank my friend Harvey Schwaid for introducing me to Len Franklin, who is a legal expert in the field of publishing. Len Franklin in turn introduced me to Olga and George Weiser, book producers and author representatives who, through their many contacts, arranged for the publication of this book.

I also express my gratitude to Hillel Black of the Carol Publishing Group for his professional editing of the book and to Steven Schragis, the president of that company.

I want to express my appreciation to the Chaplaincy Society of New York City (Catholic, Protestant, and Jewish), which honored me with its Wholeness of Life Award, and to the United Jewish Appeal Federation for its award for "Outstanding Leadership and Compassion to Humanity." They gave me insight into the values of a pluralistic society.

I also want to express appreciation to my late uncle John C. Kilroe, who stimulated me to think about and analyze the complexities of life and taught me to be guided by my conscience.

My mother was great. She taught me that there were no blacks, whites, Asians, or others, but only human beings, and that I must respect their beliefs and intrinsic goodness.

A *Personal* Statement

A *Crisis of Conscience* represents my own views on my religion. I have tried to make it constructive rather than destructive. I have interpreted my Catholicism by analyzing the Church's doctrines, hierarchy, philosophy, and theology from a variety of experiences that I have had, mostly in my own dealings with the Church.

It is my fervent wish that it will start Catholics asking why and why not. A challenge by Catholics will erode the power of the Church and its male hierarchy, enhance the glory and mysticism of the Catholic religion, and hasten the changes that are needed. The time is now and it is the duty and responsibility of all Catholics to update their Church.

The Catholic Church has always ruled by fear and by making its members feel guilty and all too often inferior. It is my hope that my "crisis of conscience" and my solutions will help other Catholics dispel their sense of guilt as they follow their conscience. Many of the teachings of the Catholic Church reflect the interpretation of the Catholic religion by a reactionary male hierarchy. Therefore, the Church and its hierarchy are arbitrary and self-perpetuating. It is time for Catholics of goodwill to challenge these interpretations, change them as needed, and have a meaningful dialogue and progress regarding, among many things, the role of women in the Church, women clergy, marriage for its priests (both women and men), birth control, collegiality, ecumenism, religious freedom, theological and cultural pluralism, personalist approaches to moral issues, and the use of biblical and historical criticism. We must carry out the gains of Vatican II and address in depth the important issues, if not the most significant problems, that the Council failed to address. The Catholic Church will then not only survive, but will prevail.

I am not a disgruntled clergyman or a theologian who has been silenced by the Vatican, but I write as a dedicated Catholic and therefore I know that I speak for a great number of the 600 million Catholics who are denied a dialogue with the male hierarchy of the Church. If there is to be collegiality with bishops and the Vatican,

[xi]

then the same expression of goodwill must be shown to the grass-roots members of the Church.

Historically, the Church did not start with the hierarchy, but with poor and humble people. In the beginning the Church was scorned as the church of slaves and women. The male hierarchy came later. The poor and the humble are truly "the people of God." They are again taking the initiative as in the early days of the Church and are creating true communities—the base communities. Those who would lead must respect their hegemony and work with them as part of the community and not over them.

It is a voice of conscience that compelled me to express views, opinions, and interpretations of the arbitrary and self-perpetuating laws and doctrines of the Catholic Church. It was the same voice of conscience that compelled me to offer reforms that are necessary.

I hope that I shall injure none of my friends—Catholics and non-Catholics alike—nor the grass-roots clergy, both men and women, who are the backbone of the Church. If by chance I do so, inadvertently, I hope that I am forgiven.

A Crisis of Conscience
A Catholic Doctor Speaks Out for Reform

ONE

Faith and Life

I am writing this book to ask for your help in bringing about change in the Catholic Church, but let me admit at the very beginning that many people will find me an unlikely choice for that job. When a good friend whom I had not seen for some time learned about this book, his first reaction was astonishment.

"You?" he exclaimed. "I can't believe it. Of all the people in the world, you're the last one I'd ever expect to write anything critical of the Church." Then he stopped and his expression changed. "But maybe that's good," he added thoughtfully. "Maybe it will take a 100 percent Catholic like yourself to make other Catholics see how important change is."

Well, if a "100 percent Catholic" is what it takes, perhaps I am the right man for the job after all. I daresay that few people other than members of the clergy have had religion play so important a role in their lives.

"We're very good Catholics," I recently overheard one woman say to another in a restaurant. "It isn't easy, I can tell you, but I get my brood to Mass every Sunday."

"Kicking and screaming, I'll bet," said her friend.

The first woman nodded. "Oh, yes. But I get them there just the same."

I could not help but smile as I thought of my own childhood. I not only went to Mass every Sunday, I attended every single day of the week. What's more, I loved it.

I was born upstairs over a grocery store in Erie, Pennsylvania, only four blocks from a hospital. Yet my mother insisted on giving birth at home, an ironic decision since her son would grow up to be a doctor and a director of obstetrics and gynecology.

Within two weeks, I was baptized at St. Patrick's, a beautiful Catholic church only three blocks from our home. I was named after my mother's favorite brother, Hugh. He had graduated from high school at the age of fourteen as the valedictorian of his class. He was working to earn money for college when he developed diphtheria and died. My mother often told me of his dedication and integrity and tried to inspire me to follow his work ethics and lifestyle.

When my uncle Hugh was confirmed, he looked up the name of the saint that was honored on the day that he was born and found that it was St. Remegius, who was the bishop of Rheims, France. My mother often related the story of St. Remegius, who converted Clovis to Christianity and, therefore, the whole French empire. I always felt proud to have these names.

As some indication of the importance religion has played in my life, you might notice that I have four initials (H.R.K.B.) while most people have only three. I have always included my mother's maiden name, Kilroe, and, having been named for my uncle, I have always used my saint's name too—making me Hugh Remegius Kilroe Barber.

While I was still an infant, my father moved the family to a new section of Erie. He opened a grocery store diagonally across from the spot where a new Catholic church and school, Holy Rosary, would soon be built. It was in this school that I began my education, taught by the Sisters of St. Joseph from the Villa Maria Convent, wonderful teachers whose lessons would remain with me and my classmates all our lives.

Recently I received word that one of my classmates, a dear friend of mine, died in Florida. His name was Victor Camp and his passing brought to mind a flood of memories extending all the way back to a special episode in the first grade of Holy Rosary. In that grade, religious instruction was given and, if we qualified, we would receive First Communion. It was a great event. To be acknowledged as qualified meant everything to us. Well, not only did Victor and I qualify, we managed to be the very first to receive First Communion. You see, we were the two *smallest* members of our class, and therefore we were the first in line to go to the altar for First Communion. It began a lifelong friendship, ending only with Victor's death.

Father Joseph Leo Hurley was our parish priest and all of the children in church and school looked up to him. I felt he was the most brilliant and saintly man I had ever known and he became my role model. I wanted to grow up to be a priest just like Father Hurley. Not only did I go to Mass every day, I also spent much of my free time around the church and school. Father Hurley, impressed with my interest and enthusiasm, soon paid me the highest compliment of my young life: he asked me to be an altar boy. With great delight, I was fitted with a white cassock and red belt and invited to be present on the altar for midnight Mass. Even today, I can recall vividly the emotion I felt, the great sense of pride. Later, I would win a prize as outstanding altar boy.

If much of this seems a bit too easy because we lived so close to Holy Rosary, my fervor remained when, as I entered the third grade, my father moved us to a farm twelve miles out of town. I was forced to make a fourteen-mile round trip every day so that I could continue to attend Holy Rosary School and learn from the sisters. In the morning, I usually rode with the milkman to the trolley line, which would take me within eight blocks of school. The process was reversed when returning home in the evening. After getting off the trolley I would catch a ride home with someone, perhaps a man from the paper mill or the electric plant. But there were many days when most of the trip took place on foot. Yet, even during these years, I attended Mass every morning. And to this very day, I cherish the memory of those wonderful years.

The training at Holy Rosary was so superb that all of the students, no matter which school they went to afterward, graduated high in their class. That was true for me, even though I went to Wilson Junior High School, where I was one of the first to come from a Catholic school and where I experienced tension with the Protestants. I took much razzing because my Catholicism came across with great strength and I would not soft-pedal it. The kids knew I would rather die than eat meat on Friday—they called me a "mackerel snapper"— and that I went to Mass no matter what, more than once with a temperature of 103. Despite these idiosyncratic differences in our religions, the class elected me president.

The same sort of thing happened when I went to Academy High School. Playing football proved very important to me. A couple of the youngsters told me that if I wanted to make the team, I ought to keep hidden my beliefs as a practicing Catholic. Why? Because, they said, the coach was a thirty-third-degree Mason who was not about to let a

Catholic play. Well, I did not soft-pedal my Catholicism at all. I just tried to tackle and block better and catch passes better than anybody else. And I made the team. What's more, the coach turned out to be a great guy and a role model because of his high moral values and exemplary lifestyle.

During this time, and while I was in prep school in Cheshire, Connecticut, I kept in touch with my teachers from the Holy Rosary School, letting the sisters know that the lessons they had taught me were indelibly imprinted on my mind and in my heart. Thanks to them and the moral code they had taught me, I did not succumb to the many temptations I witnessed, especially as an athlete. I did not smoke or drink and I had such respect for women that everybody— female friends as well as male—teased me, calling me bashful. That was okay. I was proud of being able to live up to the code I had learned at Holy Rosary School.

Recently, my sixth-grade teacher, Sister Mary Cherubin, saw that I was listed among the best doctors chosen by *New York* magazine, and she wrote to congratulate me. The minute I saw her handwriting and name, it brought back a wave of nostalgia.

I remember when, at the age of nine years, I proudly showed her my new rosary beads and said that I was going to have the priest bless them. She replied to me that she would bless them and, with that, there was great joy in my heart until she added, "I would be a priest too except I am not a man and therefore will never have that power." Many times later, this has been replayed in my mind, and I feel that it has influenced me in how I will evaluate women in the Church later in this book.

At Columbia, where I attended college, religion played a more unexpected role. I eventually became captain of the football team, but there was a moment at the beginning when I was about to be rejected. Our coach was the great Lou Little, now in the Hall of Fame. A tough disciplinarian, his word was law and he had a rule that no one could wear any kind of jewelry during practice or a game. There was good reason because a ring might be locked on a swollen finger and chains might damage the trachea. However, my mother worried I might get hurt. She insisted that I wear the St. Christopher medal, which had been blessed by her favorite clergyman.

In our first practice session, we were in shorts and T-shirts and there I was with my religious medal hanging on a chain around my neck.

"Take that off," said Coach Little, pointing at the medal. "Didn't they tell you about the rule against wearing jewelry?"

I admitted that they had, but I told him, "This is very important, Coach, to me and to my mother. It's a St. Christopher medal and I'm very religious." I shook my head, adding, "I guess either I wear the medal or I don't play football."

Coach Little finally acquiesced, even though it was against his better judgment. Well, everything was fine until we were in a tough game with the University of Georgia. Heisman Trophy-winner Frankie Sinkwich was their running back. I had gone downfield under a punt and, when I returned to the huddle, I told the guys, "I think somebody in the stands threw a rock at me and hit my lip."

But one of my teammates saw that my medal had come out from under my shoulder pads and was covered with blood. "There's your rock," he said. The medal had flipped up and broken my front tooth!

When I called my mother and told her what had happened, she said to me, "Hugh, you were probably due for an injury. Just think how bad it might have been if you *hadn't* been wearing the medal. Don't you dare take it off or I'll be worried to death."

Who could argue with that kind of logic? Nevertheless, I took the precaution of taping the medal to my chest.

At the end of my college football days, I was selected for the College All-Star Team to play against the professional teams. I had the honor of playing against the great Chicago Bears, who beat Washington 73–0, and also against the Giants. During football camps preparing for these games, my religion still served as a major part of my life. At camp, I was impressed by the number of Catholic boys, some from Catholic schools and some from non-Catholic schools, who had a deep sense of religion. Although they were not as evangelistic as I was, nevertheless their faith was deep and abiding.

Our Catholic chaplain at Columbia was Father George Barry Ford, a remarkable man who became my good friend as well as my chaplain. I had never met anyone with such progressive ideas. For example, he would not allow money to be taken at the church door, as many Catholic churches did then, because he felt this was beneath the dignity of a great religion; he had great respect for Harry Emerson Fosdick, the Baptist minister famous for his books and sermons, and he encouraged me and other Catholic students to visit the Union Theological Seminary (Protestant) and the Jewish Theological Seminary, both adjacent to Columbia University. Father Ford felt strongly that ecumenism would be the salvation of humanity and Christianity.

Although I greatly admired Father Ford, I balked at any point where his ideas appeared to come into direct conflict with Church law. He in turn suggested that I was too unyielding in my beliefs and that they were often arbitrary. I did not agree and, despite our deep friendship, my belief in the absolute correctness of the Church remained unshaken. This became known around the college, and those students who came from strong Catholic backgrounds as I did began to look to me as their spokesman and defender.

Even during my demanding days at Columbia Medical School, I went to Mass every Sunday and as many weekdays as my class hours allowed. Wanting to do even more, I joined the Knights of Columbus and began advancing through the ranks. Such religious dedication caused great arguments with my Protestant colleagues in medical school. Although we were all friends, this did not prevent us from entering into very spirited, often belligerent, discussions about subjects such as contraception, abortion, and tubal ligation. I could not accept any of their views, no matter what reasoning my fellow students offered me.

So inflexible was my approach that one of those friends told me, "Even the Empire State Building bends a few feet in the wind, Hugh. Otherwise it would crack. Can't you do the same?"

When I entered Columbia College, there were remnants of discrimination against Jews and Irish Catholics. This forged a bond among us that has developed into many lasting friendships. Now I truly appreciate those friendships as the years have gone by. I am a better person for these loyal and lasting relationships. My association with my Jewish classmates has made me often think of the statement, "You cannot be a good Catholic unless you are first a good Jew."

There is one classmate who stands out above all others. Stanley Bedford, a dedicated Protestant, and I became close friends. One day I called him a black Protestant, a term Catholics used when referring to all Protestants, and, affectionately, I have called him "Blackie" ever since. He taught me a great deal and has played a significant part in my life, and our abiding friendship has carried through time. Each year we spend a very happy and merry Christmas together at his house. Stanley Bedford was an excellent student, a loyal friend, a person with many talents and interests who eventually became a judge of the superior court of New Jersey. I have always been grateful for his friendship and that of his family. Perhaps it was my many conversations with Stanley that convinced me that there was another logical and sincere approach to life and religion.

Father Ford suggested that in view of my religious rigidity, I might be happier becoming a medical missionary in some far-off land. I actually considered that idea, but I knew deep in my heart I wanted to be a doctor and practice in this country. Still, I had no intention of letting this ambition cause me to stray from my Church. I would be a doctor, but a *Catholic* doctor.

When I began my internship, I refused to work in the contraception clinic and would not scrub on any abortions. In those days, abortions had to be put through a committee and were approved only if, without abortion, the mother's life would clearly be jeopardized. Nor would I scrub with a doctor who was doing a tubal ligation. Colleagues tried to change my unwavering beliefs, and I often had bitter arguments with nurses that left scars and marred friendships.

Occasionally a young woman suffering from the results of a "back-alley abortion" would come in dying of sepsis. There was little we could do medically to help her, and my colleagues pointed out that if her abortion had been properly performed in a hospital, this young woman would not be near death. Although I felt great sadness for the young woman, I reminded them that though tragic, there was such a thing as retribution and justice and that the wages of sin were often death.

Upon completion of my initial residency, I was appointed assistant professor at the University of Oregon Medical School in the Department of Obstetrics and Gynecology. There was a tuberculosis hospital connected to the university and the physicians in charge felt that unless pregnant women with tuberculosis had abortions, they would die. I did not agree and spent much of my time arguing with these doctors, even offering to take their patients safely through pregnancy. I became very aggressive when some of the doctors questioned my motives.

But I stood my ground, and as a result changes were made and far fewer abortions were performed. It was a minor triumph for me, but it was also a moment for deep concern. Had there been deaths among these tubercular women—deaths caused by my stand—these lost lives would have troubled my conscience deeply. Fortunately, this did not happen and years later my approach proved to be medically correct. Abortion is no longer considered therapeutic for women with this illness. Modern medical therapy can now quickly control tuberculosis.

In 1951 I was appointed a fellow for the Cancer Program at Memorial Hospital in New York City. My fight concerning abortion would begin again. I did not believe abortion was therapeutic for cancer patients, and when one doctor insisted that the breast cancer patients he had aborted had fared better than those who were not pregnant, I rose and said angrily that on this basis we should encourage all women with breast cancer to get pregnant so we could abort them and provide a better chance for survival! Of course, this argument was not well received. Years later, I came to realize my view was fueled by religious fervor, not logic. However, I battled so strongly that even my most severe critics and adversaries began to soften their positions and my chief at Memorial Hospital became far less willing to allow abortion.

Before I completed my fellowship in oncology in the fall of 1954 at the Memorial Sloan-Kettering Institute, I married Mary Louise McAuley in July. The Catholic Church required that the banns of marriage be published in our mutual churches for three consecutive Sundays. This gave the parishioners the opportunity to raise any questions about whether the marriage should take place. We were both disturbed when we heard that my good friend Father Ford, whom we had asked to perform the ceremony, would not be available. He was scheduled to go to Japan and the Orient with his much-admired friend Eleanor Roosevelt. Father George Barry Ford presented the dilemma to the Archdiocese of New York. It graciously waived the banns of marriage and we were able to be married by Father Ford.

In 1962, following my appointment as director of obstetrics and gynecology at Lenox Hill Hospital in New York City, the debate about abortions being legalized in New York State was being championed by consumer advocates and the pro-choice faction. I was shocked and immediately strongly opposed changing the law. I accepted many speaking engagements to express my views and deep concern about what I perceived would happen to society if abortion on demand was voted into law. Most of these talks were to groups sympathetic to my views, but there was an occasional one that wasn't and, as you might expect, they always ended in confrontation. As in any emotional dispute, no opinions were changed on either side and, as I look back, the only thing that I accomplished was to help widen the gap and prevent any sensible dialogue that may have resulted in a program mutually acceptable to all. During this time I was criticized repeatedly by colleagues about my rigid position and, as word of my stand spread, I was challenged and picketed and even slandered. Bernard Nathanson was one of the pro-abortionists who led the attacks on me. As he later recalled in his book, *Aborting America*:

> The Department of Obstetrics and Gynecology was headed by Hugh Barber, a former All-American football player at Fordham [actually I was at Columbia College] who had established a national reputation in gynecology cancer . . . Barber was a practicing Catholic who stood adamantly against widening psychiatric indications for abortion in his department. So we struck him.

Indeed they did. I remember that day very well. It was Thursday, May 8, 1969, and the mob scenes started at noon. I was told that they were coming. I had visions of the march on Versailles. They came thirty or so strong and marched on a picket line in front of the hospital for an hour or so, chanting a few slogans, such as "Children by Choice," and carrying signs. I was told that a few nurses, residents, and interns from the hospital had joined the line, which did not surprise me, and was reassured when I was told by some of my colleagues that they did not represent the elite of our hospital. The media was assembled in force while a great number of pro-abortionist groups picketed not only my hospital, but my home as well.

I faced that mob alone, no one there to help me. There was no support from the Archdiocese of New York or from any of the Catholic doctors. What a disgrace that the Archdiocese of New York did not speak out. The protest was on the six o'clock news and although the archdiocese had a great opportunity to support my position, the silence on its part was deafening.

Have you ever stood before a howling mob of people who have been whipped into an emotional frenzy for a cause? It's a bit of a frightening experience, but at that time I had confidence in my decision and was proud of my courage. I admit, years later, that my rigidity has softened.

The pro-abortionists were able to arrange a meeting with the hospital authorities. I was asked to appear and, as you might expect, was subjected to some verbal abuse by those supporting the passage of a law permitting abortion on demand. One thing that I remember being said was that if Mickey Mantle skins his knee the whole hospital turns out, but if a woman wants an abortion it is denied. However, I stood my ground. I was rather sarcastic when I looked around and said, "If your mother had come to me and I would have seen what she produced, if the law could be made retroactive, I would accept it." It was in keeping with my personality, and my friends have often referred to me as Hugh the Barb. I do not know who won the battle, but I know I lost the war. In 1970 New York enacted a law that did not specify the grounds on which a pregnancy could be terminated, thus in effect authorizing abortion on demand.

It is interesting that in Nathanson's book, *Aborting America*, he states, "The choice [Lenox Hill Hospital—mine] was wise in terms of our publicity plan, but it turned out to be ironic." Bernard Nathanson in *Aborting America* also wrote, "Two years later I was desperately to need a favor from Lenox Hill Hospital." I, as director of obstetrics and gynecology, must add that, since it concerned the safety of young women who had complications following abortion, I streamlined their admission and their care, and established support groups to help them by giving them a number they could call day or night for advice and help.

Women of all ages and from all walks of life poured into New York State by train, bus, car, and plane. Abortions were performed without regard to need. Some of my fellow physicians, I am ashamed to admit, bragged about the unexpected windfall of funds they were receiving by way of these abortions, but not at Lenox Hill Hospital. I refused to allow abortions on demand on my service. Many doctors who would normally have opposed this ruling respected the depth of my religious feelings and decided not to perform abortions, at least not while I served as director.

Throughout my career there had been many reasons for me to question my religion, and some have asked why I remain in a Church that has been less than kind to me and my family. I shall present another example. My uncle Edwin Patrick Kilroe, who was the head of the legal department for Fox Film Corporation, had poured his money into the farm where he had been raised. He built buildings, improved the landscape, planted trees, constructed a dam, and made it a showplace in the heart of Wayne County, Pennsylvania.

The large Kilroe family had repeatedly showed their dedication to the Church by contributing their money, their time, their effort, and their love to the Catholic religion and many churches in Honesdale, Pennsylvania, and New York City. It was decided that the farm in Honesdale, which had served as the Kilroe homestead for generations, should be given to a religious order so that the good work the family had done could be continued.

All of us, including me, poured our energy into making it a beautiful and peaceful place. Finally the farm was given to the priests of the Sacred Heart with the understanding that the property would revert to the family, if it was not used for a religious purpose. The priests built a beautiful seminary and called it Kilroe Seminary, honoring the family name.

Everything went well until marked changes occurred in the Catholic Church and the number of novices declined. The clergy decided that they would sell the farm, which consisted of several hundred acres, despite the fact that this was in violation of the original contract. By that time I only had one living uncle from that large family and he was unable to stop them from selling the place.

The callous and indifferent approach of the male hierarchy of that order not only shocked me, but the entire community, because they knew about the altruism that went into this gift from the Kilroe family to the priests of the Sacred Heart. It jolted my belief in the Catholic Church and the male hierarchy, but the greatness of the Catholic religion itself helped me maintain my stability and continue to hold it in reverence.

However, the event did teach me a lesson: that the male hierarchy, which, in my judgment, is synonymous with the Catholic Church, was mainly interested in wealth and power and not in its fellow human beings.

Time and time again I have had to reaffirm my belief in the principles laid down by the Church as they came in conflict with society's shifting ideas on abortion. As a Catholic doctor whose chosen field is obstetrics and gynecology, it is not surprising that abortion was the challenge which most tested my religious mettle. What is surprising, however, is the fact that when my personal beliefs at last came into unresolved conflict with Church law, abortion played only a minor role. The key area of disagreement was something quite different.

T W O

Doubts and Crisis

I realize now that the basic mistake I made throughout most of my life was equating religion with the institutional Church. Simply because they had taken vows and mounted the altar, I attributed Christ-like wisdom to members of the clergy and I treated Church law as if it were an extension of Christ's Sermon on the Mount. No matter what the subject—birth control, divorce, women's ordination, abortion—I left no room for argument against Church rules, no room for flexibility. I would not bend and I refused to break. The Church was always right.

But there *were* moments of doubt. They were dealt with. They were controlled. But doubt was present nonetheless. Even as a small boy, for example, I wondered about the second-class status of women in the Church. You must understand that my world and that of my classmates often revolved around those wonderful nuns from the Villa Maria Convent in Erie, Pennsylvania. All my life I have had such respect for these nuns that to show my appreciation I established three awards to be given to students graduating from the eighth grade of Holy Rosary School. One award is given to honor my mother, Elizabeth Frances Barber, one to honor my wife, Mary Louise Barber, and the third to honor my sister, Mary Cecelia Barber Nugent.

In many ways and in many times, these nuns were all things to myself and my classmates. They took care of us when we were cold or hungry or lonely, dried our tears, and helped us smile when we were hurt. More important, they taught us the basic principles of humanity and social justice, at least to the extent that our young minds could understand.

And yet, after hours of tiring work with children, these nuns were forced to walk two blocks to the streetcar, then take the long ride to the convent where they lived in very hard, very meager circumstances. Meanwhile, our parish priest, Father Hurley, who did far less for us than any one of the nuns, had much shorter working hours, lived in a handsome house next to the church with someone to take care of his needs, had many social gatherings, and enjoyed his leisure at every opportunity. What a contrast. Although I greatly admired the priest, the disparity in lifestyles bothered me greatly. Women in the Church seemed to be treated as if they were inferior.

In high school, where I had my first relationships with non-Catholics, I found myself wondering about the Church law that said my religion was the only way to God. Although very proud that birth had allowed me to be one of the chosen few by my standards, I could not help but wonder about some of my classmates. Even as they teased me about fish on Friday and Mass every day, they elected me class president. Were they all really doomed to burn in hell? And what about my first football coach, the thirty-third degree Mason who might have, as expected, shown prejudice toward me as I tried to make the team? Instead, he tried to make me a better young man, as well as a better athlete. Was he another hopeless sinner?

While I was at Columbia, it was the Church's treatment of Father Ford that caused my most serious questioning. Bear in mind that Father Ford was a brilliant priest, well liked throughout the university community. Religion for him was something that one *lived*, and for Father Ford that meant respect for all human beings regardless of race, color, creed, or differential views. Although he was extraordinarily well informed, he was so witty that it took some time to appreciate his depth of knowledge and the remarkable impression he was making on the university and its students.

He encouraged the students at his parochial school to run the government of the school, including banking their own money, and he had them actively participating in the Mass. I was stunned to find students and parishioners reading parts of the Mass in English. Remember, this was back in 1940. I began to feel part of this new movement and with pride I started inviting my friends of other persuasions, including Protestants and Jews, to visit the Corpus Christi Church.

Not surprisingly, they were reluctant to come, knowing as they did that Catholics were forbidden to attend any of *their* services. But finally they accepted the invitation and one Sunday each month a group of non-Catholics was invited by Father Ford to gather in the rectory of the church's meeting room for a discussion over coffee. From these meetings, we developed warm friendships and mutual respect. Although few of these visitors were converted to Catholicism, each came away with a better understanding of the Catholic religion, as well as their own.

Father Ford took an active part in many organizations that had no direct connection with the Church or with Columbia University, organizations such as the Committee for Harlem Freedom House, the Bureau for Intercultural Education, and the Manhattanville Community Center, of which he was a founder. Through these and other ecumenical endeavors, he became widely recognized by New Yorkers of many faiths as one of the most beloved figures in the city.

Knowing all this about Father Ford, you can imagine how shocked I was to learn that he had been "silenced" by the Archdiocese of New York and sent away for one year to do penance. Why? The trouble began in 1945 with the start of what amounted to a feud between Bishop Garfield Oxnam of the Methodist Church in New York and Francis Cardinal Spellman of the Catholic Church in the New York Archdiocese. Bishop Oxnam had made a speech assailing the politics of the Catholic Church. Cardinal Spellman retaliated with a personal attack on Bishop Oxnam, calling him an "unhooded Klansman." Father Ford tried to calm the waters. Taking a neutral position, he told both men that their speeches were divisive, serving only to widen the gulf that already separated the many religious groups of New York. Father Ford was quoted in a news magazine as saying something to the effect that mediocrity is a quality shared by bishops of various denominations.

Father Ford told me that Cardinal Spellman flew into a rage because he, Father Ford, had taken a neutral position rather than siding with the cardinal. Father Ford was called to the chancery office and forbidden to speak any place except in his church, Corpus Christi. This was not the end of it. From this point on, Father Ford could do no right in Cardinal Spellman's eyes, which led to the silencing. Father Ford had to travel to a designated area in California, and for one year he could have little or no contact with the outside world.

At this time, I was only a young man struggling to become a physician, but I found the Church's role very difficult to accept. I was torn by my respect for and admiration of Father Ford and my deep feeling and awesome fear and respect for my religion. It seemed to me that any organization that found it necessary to silence someone of Father Ford's caliber might well be in trouble. Why had this been done? What could it mean? I managed to calm my concern only by telling myself that there must be reasons I did not know about or understand.

At the same time, I found myself questioning the Church for a much more personal reason, a deep hurt suffered by my wife, Mary Louise. She had only one female cousin and they were quite close. When her cousin decided to marry, she asked Mary Louise to be her matron of honor at a Protestant wedding, a role and honor my wife was delighted to accept, until she spoke to our local Catholic priest. Despite her tearful pleas, the priest denied her the right to take part in a ceremony of another religion. Like myself, Mary Louise had always been a staunch Catholic. The priest's words were law.

Her cousin, Mary Jane Schermerhorn, now Mrs. Reynolds, known to her friends as Skippy, must have had difficulty in understanding this. I am sure that she felt that Mary Louise should refuse to obey this arbitrary rule. As a result, not only was my wife denied the opportunity to be matron of honor, but a very important relationship was jeopardized. She and her cousin obviously must have had a strained friendship after this. Fortunately, their innate intelligence and their admiration and affection for each other prevailed, and now they are dear and close to each other.

Doubts of a much more troubling sort occurred during my internship at Lenox Hill Hospital. I vividly recall one young patient who arrived dying of sepsis as a result of an abortion performed by some back-alley butcher. The memory of that girl's face remains with me to this day. She was so very young and as I talked with her I realized that she did not even fully understand the sex act that had brought her to this critical condition. In truth, it seemed she would have been more comfortable playing with dolls than entertaining a lover.

I worked day and night to save that child, missing meals and sleep, but to no avail. I was devastated by her death. Then when I met her family and saw their grief—even the agony of the childlike partner who had caused the pregnancy—doubts about Church laws, particularly those against sex education and contraception, assailed me.

I also found myself questioning the Church and clergy when, in 1970, after speaking out so often against the proposed New York law to liberalize abortion, I stood virtually alone facing pro-abortion pickets at my home and at Lenox Hill Hospital. My wife brought the concern to the surface when she said, "It's funny you haven't received any support for your stand—nothing from the Catholic hospitals and nothing from the Archdiocese of New York. I wonder why? It's such an important issue."

It was a good question. With the Church seemingly so adamantly opposed to abortion and with the State of New York considering passage of a bill that would virtually legalize abortion on demand, why had there been no opposition from the Archdiocese of New York? Why had mine been almost the only Catholic voice raised against the bill?

I would not learn the answer for almost a year. Then, at dinner with a friend, a man who had close contacts with the inner circle of New York State's Republican party, I mentioned my puzzlement.

"You got caught in the middle," he told me flatly. "I thought you knew that."

"The middle of what?"

"A deal between church and state, [Nelson] Rockefeller and the Archdiocese of New York."

"What kind of deal?" I asked skeptically.

"Rocky was worried about his reelection. It was his fourth time to run for governor and he was facing his toughest competition, former Supreme Court Justice [Arthur] Goldberg." My friend nodded knowingly. "Rockefeller wanted the endorsement of the *New York Times*, but everybody expected the paper to endorse Goldberg. To change that, Rocky was determined to out-liberal Goldberg, so he was desperate to have that liberalized abortion bill passed and signed into law. He figured the only way that would happen was for the Catholic Church to sit on its hands."

I shook my head. "They wouldn't do that."

He smiled patronizingly. "Don't be naive. You know how much the archdiocese wants state aid for church schools. The way I understand it, and it came like a bolt of lightning to me, was and still remains my opinion that Rockefeller promised to help with aid if the cardinal did nothing to defeat the abortion bill."

I could hardly believe my ears. "The archdiocese let it happen? No, no. That would mean he *allowed* all those women to come to this state and get aborted."

"Only temporarily," my friend explained. "Now that Rocky has won the election, future cardinals can do anything they like about that bill. It is the law of the State of New York."

Then it all came back to me. Francis Cardinal Spellman had a jungle cunning and would go to any extreme to achieve his goal. He wanted aid for parochial schools, particularly Catholic schools. He saw a chance to put a powerful political leader in his debt so he endorsed Rockefeller despite the fact that he had been condemned by many people, including religious leaders, for divorcing his wife of thirty years. Spellman died before the liberal abortion bill of New York State was passed. Although abortion was a hot issue during the last years of his life, he did not mount an aggressive campaign against it.

Deals and counterdeals were the methods chosen by my Church, which substituted irresponsibility for obligation and self-interest for brotherhood. While my faith was shaken, a great religion helped me overcome the machinations of the Catholic Church's male hierarchy.

But with Nelson Rockefeller safely settled in for his fourth term as governor with the surprise endorsement of the *New York Times*, the governor gave no help to Catholic schools. The archdiocese then put the full force of its power behind the elimination of New York's liberal abortion law. However, it still remains as the law of New York State.

During the year after Terence Cooke was named cardinal, a tremendous battle raged in the New York State Legislature over abortion. To his credit, Cardinal Cooke did not try to directly influence legislators. My fears about a deal between the archdiocese and Rockefeller surfaced again. A rumor was circulated in the legislature on the morning of April 10, 1970, that a deal had been worked out between Governor Nelson Rockefeller and Cardinal Cooke. According to the rumor, the cardinal had agreed to soft-pedal opposition to the abortion issue in return for the Mandated Services Law for Private and Parochial Schools. The law spread through the legislature, and the legislature, who saw the bill as a political hot potato, went along with it. The bill passed, 31 to 26.

After a great deal of controversy, the New York State Legislature passed a repeal of the abortion law of 1970. Governor Rockefeller opposed a compromise bill that would have reduced the number of weeks during which an abortion could be legally performed. Of course, the Catholic bishops had no choice but to reject Rockefeller's compromise. Their opposition was sent to the governor in a document of May 5, 1972. On May 13, Governor Rockefeller vetoed the repeal of the abortion law of 1970. At this point, I had mixed feelings about the veto. Because of my personal position on the issue, I was sad, but having been a pawn in behind-the-scene dealings, I was also resentful.

It is well known that Francis Cardinal Spellman had made one of his main missions as cardinal to obtain public funds for parochial schools. There was great debate at that time over whether taxpayers' funds should be used to support parochial schools or not. Cardinal Spellman had come out strongly in support of the use of federal funds for schools operated by the Catholic Church. Mrs. Roosevelt, in reasoned and dignified language, strongly disagreed with the cardinal in her column, which was syndicated throughout the United States.

Her statement stimulated the most astounding blast from the cardinal, who was recognized as the most influential Catholic official in America. He stated angrily that she had been influenced by "misinformation, ignorance or prejudice" and went on to say, addressing himself directly to Mrs. Roosevelt, "Even if you cannot find it within your heart to defend the rights of innocent little children and heroic helpless men like Cardinal Mindszenty, can you not have the ordinary charity not to cast another stone? . . . I shall not again publicly acknowledge you . . . your record of anti-Catholicism stands for all to see . . . documents of discrimination unworthy of an American mother."

This, of course, led to a great deal of controversy and Cardinal Spellman was reprimanded by many prominent Catholics and non-Catholics alike. Ex-governor Herbert Lehman of New York expressed his shocked surprise at the cardinal's attack and the long statement in the *New York Times*. "The real issue," he said, "is not whether one agrees or disagrees with Mrs. Roosevelt on this or any other public question; the issue is whether Americans are entitled freely to express their views without being vilified or accused of religious bias." The cardinal, realizing that sentiment was completely against him, made a courtesy call on Mrs. Roosevelt at Hyde Park in a rather obvious attempt to soften the public animus stimulated by his attack on her. Mrs. Roosevelt had restated her position with dignity and clarity, said that she had no anti-Catholic bias, and added, "I am firm in my belief that there shall be no pressure to bear by any church against the proper operations of the government, and that there shall be recognition of the fact that all citizens may express their views freely on questions of public interest." Later, Cardinal Spellman backed a bill at the State Assembly for appropriations for Catholic schools. The Speaker of the House had added some riders to the bill, and it is my understanding that Governor Rockefeller tried to get the speaker to delete these riders, but the cardinal had counted votes and felt that he had the support needed to obtain public funding for Catholic education. His stubbornness resulted in the defeat of the bill. I bring this up to show the depth of feeling that the Archdiocese of New York had toward obtaining public funding for Catholic education, and, in my judgment, they would go to any lengths to get this. I strongly believe that this is why the Archdiocese of New York was silent in the months before the abortion bill was passed. Once it was passed and there were no funds forthcoming for public funding of Catholic schools, the campaign for Right-to-Life was launched. Granted that the bill to support Catholic education came before the passage of the abortion bill, the hope was that once again it would be resurrected and passed and that funds would be available for Catholic education.

Once again, I tried to come to terms with my doubts about the Church through prayer and inner insistence that there must be facts unknown to me, or spiritual reasoning I could not comprehend. But this time, doing so proved far more difficult. For the Church to turn its back on abortion, even temporarily, meant thousands upon thousands of unnecessary abortions. That fact was beyond my comprehension. And, as if to add insult to injury, the reason behind the Church's silence was a desire to obtain state aid for Church education, an effort that could only further obscure the line between church and state in this nation. Strangely enough, it would be this issue—the Church's blurring of separation of church and state—that would finally bring me face-to-face with doubts that could no longer be silenced.

It began in 1979 when Lenox Hill Hospital decided to form an affiliation with New York Medical College. In the past, several departments at Lenox Hill had enjoyed excellent working arrangements with various elite medical schools, such as Cornell, Columbia, and New York University. But now, as these arrangements began to go into eclipse, it was decided that an overall affiliation with a single medical school should be sought for Lenox Hill Hospital. The school eventually chosen was New York Medical College.

No sooner had this affiliation reached the handshake stage than I was approached to be the professor and chairman of obstetrics and gynecology at New York Medical College, which is controlled by the Archdiocese of New York. Currently their stationery has a statement, "A Medical University in the Catholic Tradition." I refused. In fact, I had refused this position earlier—prior to the Lenox Hill affiliation—when a search committee had contacted me. I had no desire or time to travel to Valhalla, where New York Medical College is located. In addition, something about the position did not sit well with me, perhaps a premonition of things to come. To compound my concern, my wife reminded me of my distrust and hers of the male hierarchy of the Catholic Church.

But once the overall affiliation had been worked out, I found it difficult to refuse the offer. For one thing, I was assured that the offices for my department and for my students would be located at Lenox Hill Hospital in Manhattan and all of my lectures would be given there. No regular travel to Valhalla would be required. In addition, I was strongly encouraged to accept the chairmanship by Dr. Samuel Rubin, the dean of New York Medical College. A wonderful man, Dr. Rubin related well to other physicians. He possessed a great deal of professional and personal integrity. Dr. Rubin had played a major role in persuading Lenox Hill to affiliate with New York Medical College and now he did the same with me.

In particular, when I mentioned disturbing rumors that the Archdiocese of New York, having agreed to underwrite the debts of New York Medical College, might be taking more than the allowed interest in the school's faculty and curriculum, Dean Rubin assured me this was untrue and gave me his word that my department would suffer no interference whatsoever from the Church. This assurance was of vital importance. A fine medical college must keep its students fully abreast of all the latest developments in medical science, no matter whether these developments are connected with procedures fully approved by the Catholic Church or whether they are connected with contraception, in vitro fertilization, or abortion. Finally, with Dean Rubin's many assurances and personal persuasion, I accepted.

Although there were some difficulties from the beginning, I tried to write off these problems as simply the natural result of any relationship of such magnitude. Moreover, I had little time to worry beyond the needs of my own department at New York Medical

College. Despite the best efforts of my predecessor, who was well qualified to be the chairman but who was held down to the level of acting chairman, the department was in a shambles—not too surprising in view of the fact that the school had been searching for a new chairman for more than two years.

I began building a new department, restructuring the teaching program and making a strong effort to recruit good candidates into the specialty of obstetrics and gynecology. I found that the students of New York Medical College had a great inferiority complex when it came time to apply for a residency position at the hospital of their choice. I worked with them to bolster their self-esteem and I personally called the directors or chairmen of various programs in the students' preferred hospitals. As a result, many of the students received excellent appointments. I have since followed their careers and they have done well.

Despite this success with my own department, there were signs around me that things were not going as they should. The reason emerged only when Dean Rubin, having stayed beyond his retirement, insisted that a replacement must be found. This meant that the man who had persuaded me to come to New York Medical College was leaving.

A search committee was chosen, of which I was a member along with others on the faculty, doctors from affiliated hospitals, and the president of New York Medical College, John Connolly. There was one final member, the man who proved to be the key to the school's current and future problems. He was James Cassidy, monsignor of the Archdiocese of New York, a man who had absolutely no academic credentials whatsoever in terms of medicine. He had been placed on the committee at the cardinal's request and it soon became apparent that he, Cassidy, would be the final arbiter in choosing the new dean.

The work of the search committee proved to be little more than a charade, the choice for dean having already been made. When, for example, members of the committee suggested that the dean should be chosen from within and suggested possible candidates on the faculty, Monsignor Cassidy became visibly agitated and blurted angrily that no one on the school staff would be considered for the position. At this stage, several of the committee members, myself included, pointed out that the monsignor's decision meant a condemnation of the medical school, announcing in effect that New York Medical College was such an inferior school that it could not produce anyone worthy of the position of dean.

Our protests fell on deaf ears. To us it became very clear—embarrassingly so—that President Connolly, despite his credentials, was simply a front man and that the real power lay with Monsignor Cassidy. Without Dean Rubin to fight for our causes, New York Medical College would be run by this man, a person without medical credentials, whose first thought would always be to please the cardinal by stating that the manner of teaching and running the medical school was through Church rules rather than medical science.

If I had thought that he really had any in-depth knowledge of Church rules, I could have had more respect for him. My contempt is softened, however, when I recall a passage from Father George Barry Ford's book, *A Degree of Difference*: "As for the honorary title 'Monsignor,' it was handed out by the head of a Roman Catholic diocese with the casualness that might accompany the giving of a piece of candy to a child. I once heard Archbishop Spellman, who was a far from eloquent speaker, say that, when he was visiting a church and could think of nothing else to say, he simply made the pastor a Monsignor."

I sometimes wonder if James Cassidy knows that the title has been discontinued. Since I feel sorry for him, I ask his forgiveness for a statement that I made about him and which is often repeated, that "as an academician, he belongs to the mentally disinherited."

As I look back upon my nine years as professor and chairman and associate dean of New York Medical College, I realize that the establishment of a high-risk pregnancy and neonatology center at the Westchester Medical Center was achieved almost entirely through the efforts of the personnel of the Westchester Medical Center and not the New York Medical College. As a matter of fact, during the time that I worked very hard with my colleagues to get approval for the center, the Archdiocese of New York was totally silent and gave no public approval of our efforts.

I was shocked and disillusioned when I was told that Terence Cardinal Cooke had assured one of the trustees of the Cornell University Medical College and the New York Hospital Medical Center that he would not enter into this struggle to help establish the center. Although I personally asked the Archdiocese for help, none was forthcoming. Fortunately, the majority of the faculty joined with the administration of Westchester County Medical Center to achieve our goal for approval to open the High Risk and Tertiary Center. Dr. Gerson Lesser, a member of the State Committee, made an excellent speech to the committee saying he was speaking for those (fetuses and newborns) who could not speak for themselves. He objectively reviewed the data and clearly showed the need for this center in the mid-Hudson Valley of New York State. The committee voted unanimously for the center and Dr. Gerson Lesser's and the committee's reward will always be the mothers and babies saved by their decision. I know that a yet unborn number of babies will call them blessed. They have answered the pleas and prayers of the mothers and babies of the mid-Hudson Valley.

The indifference of the Archdiocese in establishing a much needed center reinforced my belief that the male hierarchy of the Catholic Church are only interested in deals, power, and money. This insensitivity and almost hysterical disdain by the male hierarchy of the Catholic Church for the grass roots was forever etched into my mind.

Through it all I continued to work hard with Bernie Weinstein, who was the county commissioner of hospitals, and Dr. Harry Dweck, who was to head the neonatology program at the Westchester Medical Center. We spent long hours traveling throughout the Health Systems Agency 6, which includes the mid-Hudson area of New York State. and rallied support for the center. Ours was a work of love on the part of Bernie Weinstein, Harry Dweck, and the numerous faculty members who helped us. Dr. George Reed had established a program for open heart procedures and he was so well respected throughout the area that his prestige and integrity provided priceless help to us as we struggled for this tertiary care center.

The Perinatology and Newborn High-Risk Center became a pivotal point and keystone for the New York Medical College. It was the administrative staff of Westchester County Medical Center who helped Dr. Harry Dweck and me to receive state approval for the center. The Medical Center is associated with but not controlled by New York Medical College. It served as the watershed in opening up tertiary care for many other units. For economy of space and time it is impossible for me to publicly thank all of those wonderful faculty members from the New York Medical College who worked so closely with us and who unselfishly took time from their practices and families to establish this center. We all knew in our hearts that this much-needed program would provide optimal care for patients throughout the mid-Hudson area.

I had already managed to convince some remarkable young talent to join the faculty of New York Medical College, but my proudest moment came when I had accomplished that goal with Dr. Frank Chervenak, without doubt one of the brightest lights in the field of obstetrical sonography and ethics. At the age of thirty-two, he had accomplished more than most of us achieve in a lifetime of medicine. He was productive, wrote many articles, and was recognized as a leader. As you might imagine, he was sought after by some of the finest schools in the United States and it was a real coup that I had been able to capture him for New York Medical College.

Frank Chervenak had received much advice against accepting the position. He was warned that because the college did not have a top academic reputation, his chance of going on to higher plateaus might be damaged if he accepted an appointment to the faculty. I countered by talking about the potential of the school, about the quality of the department I was building, and about how much the department had improved. I talked about what Frank Chervenak could do for the college and what it could do for him once, with his help, it had reached the standards we both sought. I finally won him over.

And then the roof fell in. I was advised that Dr. Chervenak's appointment to the faculty had been rejected by Monsignor Cassidy. At first I thought this must be someone's idea of a cruel joke. When my initial response proved not to be the case, I sought out the school president, hoping he would tell me that Cassidy did not have that kind of authority. The president told me no such thing. He simply looked embarrassed and admitted that Dr. Chervenak's rejection was a reality and could not be overruled.

What was wrong with Frank Chervenak in the eyes of the monsignor? Why would a school like New York Medical College, with its very mediocre academic standing, turn down a faculty member of this caliber? It seems that Monsignor Cassidy had read one of Dr. Chervenak's articles, which I had proudly passed on to the archdiocese, mind you. This particular article was devoted to the ethics of an option for aborting an anencephalic fetus, one with no brain.

Apparently all Monsignor Cassidy needed to see was the word *abortion* and that was sufficient to make him decide that Dr. Chervenak should not be a member of the faculty of New York Medical College. Never mind that Dr. Chervenak is a staunch Catholic, never mind that he wrote this particular article in cooperation with the Ethics Department of the Kennedy Division at Georgetown University Medical School, never mind that there is no known way to save the life of an anencephalic fetus, which lives only a few hours after birth.

Although all of this is true, what matters most is that Dr. Chervenak, one of the finest in his field of medical science, was being rejected because *his views might not coincide with Church law* as interpreted by a second-rate clergyman—an outrageous violation of academic freedom and, because of state and federal funding for this college, a violation of this nation's constitutional insistence on the separation of church and state.

Of course, Frank Chervenak was quickly hired by another, far better, medical school as soon as it was learned he was available. He was brought on board as the director of sonography and ethics within the Department of Obstetrics and Gynecology at Cornell University. The announcement of his appointment paid tribute to his remarkable reputation and great talent and to the wisdom of Dr. Bill Ledger, the chairman of that department. Meanwhile, New York Medical College was reduced to looking for someone whose background and ability would match that of Monsignor Cassidy.

I think I was more upset by all this than I have ever been in my life. You must understand that this was not simply a matter of the Church violating government rules or even the Constitution. In a very real sense, it was a matter of life and death. Where is it that the physicians of tomorrow learn to save lives but in the medical college where they get their training? If they are given less than the best in preparation, then those patients who seek them out for aid will almost certainly be given less than the best in treatment.

For a doctor to practice medicine, he must be certified by the state where he practices and, in order for that to happen, he must have completed his medical education at a university which has also been certified by that state. Such universities are sworn to teach their students the very latest in all areas of medical science. Only through this procedure can a patient who enters a hospital or a doctor's waiting room feel secure. To violate this code is to openly endanger the health and lives of thousands of human beings. Yet here was the monsignor of the Archdiocese of New York rejecting for the faculty of a medical college one of the finest doctors and professors in his field. Under Cassidy's arrogant use of power the school began to be an offshore school with a New York address, but without its good weather.

When my pleas to the president of the college proved fruitless, I appealed to New York's John Cardinal O'Connor. When the rejection of Frank Chervenak was again upheld, I took the only course left open to me: I resigned from New York Medical College.

Dr. Karl Adler was the current dean of New York Medical College and the hand-picked choice of Monsignor Cassidy. He came to my office at Lenox Hill Hospital and pleaded with me to withdraw my letter of resignation. I told him I would consider doing so only if two demands were met: first, the appointment of Frank Chervenak to the faculty and, second, proof that Monsignor Cassidy would have nothing more to do with the faculty or curriculum of the college.

Dr. Adler insisted the argument over Frank Chervenak had gone so far that intervention was impossible, but that he could personally assure me there would be no further interference by Cassidy, that the monsignor would be out of the picture entirely. I knew that was an absurdity. People I trusted had informed me that Dean Adler and Monsignor Cassidy were meeting almost daily and that all of Adler's instructions came directly from the monsignor. It is interesting to note that shortly after my resignation became effective, Monsignor Cassidy was officially appointed chancellor of New York Medical College. I always felt that James Cassidy wound up Dean Adler each morning and pointed him in the direction the monsignor wanted to send him—on a mission of search and destroy and less often of search and build.

It is difficult to express how deeply this experience affected me. I had accepted with misgivings the chairmanship at New York Medical College. I had said yes because men I respected had persuaded me that it was an opportunity to help develop fine doctors for the future. It was a labor of love. No salary was involved, only the opportunity to help build a strong medical college with a fine faculty—or so I hoped and prayed. It proved to be an intellectual exercise in futility. Power will win out over reason, and rhetoric will sustain an idea no matter how false it is.

This episode, like some sort of emotional percussion cap, caused a blue-white explosion in my brain, suddenly illuminating a truth I had been told but never understood: There is a vast difference between religion and church. I saw that this terrible experience with Monsignor Cassidy, which had done nothing to discredit the Catholic religion, had done a great deal to discredit the Catholic Church. And I realized that throughout my life, the doubts I had encountered— about inequality of women in the Church, the silencing of great religious thinkers and doers like Father Ford, the refusal to teach or approve developments in birth control, and many others—these doubts had never been about my religion, but only doubts about Church rules and members of the male hierarchy.

The Church had been wrong in rejecting Dr. Frank Chervenak. There was no question of factors I might not be aware of. If the monsignor continued at New York Medical College, there would be more such mistakes affecting life and death. It was not enough for me to understand finally that whereas my religion might always be right, the Church might well be wrong. I had to *do* something about it.

THREE

Letters to Learn By

O n April 22, 1987, the *New York Times* published an article about me written by Dena Kleiman and entitled, "For a Catholic Doctor, a Crisis of Conscience." It presented a summary of what had happened at New York Medical College—the outrageous rejection of Dr. Frank Chervenak by the Archdiocese of New York—and explained how this act had brought me to a crisis of conscience in terms of the Church. Following the appearance of this article, my life changed dramatically. I received hundreds of letters and phone calls. People even stopped me on the street (the article had included my picture) to tell me that they agreed totally with everything in the interview.

Most of the letters and phone calls came from other Catholics and, in addition to agreeing with what I had to say, many quarreled with other Church rules or positions and raised some very important questions.

"There's nothing surprising in what happened at New York Medical College," wrote one man. "This is precisely what we should expect from a Church which gags the greatest thinkers—men like Hans Küng and Charles Curran—and promotes the yes-men over the best-men for Bishop and Cardinal. In today's Church, priests with an eye on promotion know their job is not to help their parishioners. Their job is to please the Pope." It is my opinion that John Cardinal O'Connor, by constantly mimicking the Pope, epitomizes this philosophy. Unfortunately, he does it badly and often without the dignity befitting a Cardinal appointed to represent the Archdiocese of New York.

A Catholic doctor whom I had never met, but whose name is

[28]

recognized, wrote, "What you saw with the lack of academic freedom, many of us have had to face over and over again with other
issues. That's why we're all becoming a bunch of Cafeteria Catholics."

This was a term I had never heard before: "Cafeteria Catholics." At
first it made me smile, but then, as the letter continued, I realized the
term was symptomatic of deep divisiveness within the Church.

"Just like in a cafeteria," the doctor went on, "the people accept
the rules they believe in and reject the ones they don't. They all go
up for Communion just the same. They don't figure they're doing
anything bad because they honestly believe the Church is wrong. But
I ask you, is this healthy for the Church? Is it healthy for the parishioners?" My answer is no, it is destructive.

A woman wrote, "You've only touched the tip of the iceberg. What
do you think it feels like belonging to the Church and attending Mass
if you're a woman? How do you think it feels to stand up and profess
your faith—'We believe in one God . . .'—when it gets to the part,
'For us *men* and for our salvation he came down from heaven.' If you
were a woman, how would you like saying 'For us *men*'? Did you
ever notice how the group-sound in church fades at that point?
Plenty of us can't bring ourselves to say the word. So why hasn't it
been changed? After all these years, after all the changes in women's
status throughout the world and especially in this country, why hasn't
that been changed?

"Why should something as important as the Nicene Creed, the
words we use to profess our faith, why should they include 'For us
men'? What's wrong with leaving out the word 'men' completely or,
if it has to be said, what's wrong with adding the words 'and women'
so it would read, 'For us men and women and for our salvation he
came down from heaven.' Is that too much to ask? We already know
the Church doesn't think women are good enough to become
priests, but do they have to rub it in every week by making us repeat
the words that prove it?"

"You're worrying about academic freedom? Well what about overpopulation of the world?" asked another woman. "How can the
Church be so out of step that it goes on condemning birth control?
Even if I weren't educated enough to know that we will soon kill this
planet through overpopulation, I'd know that my husband and I can't
support more than our three children. So here I am having to feel
guilty because I'm practicing birth control.

"And what's so ridiculous is that almost every couple in our church is doing the same thing unless they're too old. You're a doctor. I often wondered what our local doctors (two are Catholic) think when they see us walking up to take Communion—the wives, I mean. These doctors know we're practicing birth control. They gave us the pills or fitted the diaphragms. What do they think when they watch us accepting Communion? . . . The whole thing is absurd and I am sick to death of feeling guilty."

Another letter on birth control, this one from a man, asked, "Why is the Church so hung up on sex? Where does it say in the Bible that the sex act is a sin unless you're doing it to make a baby? Does the Church really think men and women are going to keep away from each other except to have kids? Would that make a happy marriage? Of course not. So what's the point of all the mumbo-jumbo? . . . Now you know why they don't see me at Mass anymore."

"The Church is like a bad parent," suggested a mother. "If you tell your teenager not to have sex and not to take dope, and you make one sound as bad as the other, look at what you've done. Your teenager is almost sure to have sex, so he will decide your rules are meaningless and take dope as well. And when that happens, it's the parent's fault . . . But don't try to tell that to my priest. It seems like in the eyes of the Church we're all rotten, unless we keep our mouths shut about the truth."

"What bothers me more than anything," wrote a young man, "is that you don't have anybody in the Church to talk about this. If I try and talk to the priest, all he does is tell me to pray or offer penance. He never acts like there's any possibility I might be right. And our lay people, well, they're nice enough. In fact, one of them is a grand woman. But I'd never dare to open up to her about my real feelings. I think I'd scare her to death."

One correspondent suggested I learn to laugh about the matter. "Haven't you heard the old joke about Big John?" the letter asked. "He was always having his way with the ladies, getting drunk and generally sinning in every way he liked. Then, just in time for Sunday Mass, he'd nip into the confessional so he'd be ready to enjoy Holy Communion on Sunday. He did this over and over again until finally Father Murphy said to him, 'Now see here, Big John, you can't go on doing whatever you please, sinning in the eyes of the Church, and then making it right by confessing your sins and asking forgiveness every week.' Big John thought about that, then nodded and said, 'All right, Father. How about every *other* week?' "

"Lots of us are experiencing the kind of crisis mentioned in that article," another man wrote me. "That's why church collections are down in this country and have been for a long time. Watch the collection baskets. The fives and tens are gone. It's the *ones* you see now. And it won't get better unless the Church gets better, especially not when we read all the scandal about the Vatican losing money due to crooked bankers. Why does the church hold on to all that money and real estate anyway? They ought to deal in religion, not real estate. If they want us to give until it hurts, why don't *they* give until it hurts? Is it anything to be proud of that we have the richest Church in the world?

"I think the Church got along just fine in the United States while most members were uneducated immigrants. But when we came along—the children and grandchildren of those immigrants—and got some education, the Church didn't know what to do. We aren't going to sit back and let them tell us we're a bunch of worthless sinners just because they insist on rules that are out of step with the world. Isn't it about time for an *American* Catholic Church?"

A woman wrote, "At Mass a few Sundays ago, the scripture reading was about the need to be ready for the Kingdom of Heaven. Father K said to us, 'You think you live in a nation of Christians, don't you? Well, you don't. You live in a nation of *pagans*. Just watch your television set every night, or even during the daytime. Watch the men and women engaging in illicit sex.' He was saying that all people who engage in sex out of wedlock are *pagans*. What a choice of words. I could feel people all around me squirming. *Pagans*? Tell me something, Dr. Barber, how many married people do you think you could find today who didn't have pre-marital sex? Especially if they're under 40. I'm talking about women as well as men. If you did find a woman who was a virgin when she married, by statistics she may be a minority. Is she less of a good person? She is if she is judged by the double standards established by men.

"Most women don't jump into marriage in their teens anymore. Not unless they have to. They wait and have a life before marriage. Doesn't the Church realize that? And is it really logical that these women will never have an affair with a man during all that time? And does that make them *pagans*? I find that word disgusting. The Church is living back in the Dark Ages."

A man wrote, "I read about you in the *Times* and I was very glad to find someone finally speaking out about the Church. But I noticed that, although the article mentioned in vitro fertilization, you never came out and said what your feelings are about it. This is a marvelous advance that any sane person should applaud. What in God's name can the Church find wrong with helping childless parents conceive, whether in the womb or in a dish? Is something automatically wrong because it's new? Is it wrong because it came from science rather than the Church? I wonder how we'd have done with our Space Program if we'd been guided by the Church—still believing the sun revolves around the earth!"

A young woman wrote, "I can't respect the Church when it bars me from Communion because I'm divorced, but allows the rich and connected to find a way out through Paul or Peter or by buying an annulment. This isn't God's way."

A teacher who had studied to be a priest, but left before taking his vows, told me, "As you probably know, the Church is having great difficulty finding qualified young men to study for the priesthood, yet they will not relinquish their ban on marriage for priests. Where is it written that there is anything sinful about marriage for members of the clergy? In view of the scandal concerning some priests and young boys, the Church would be doubly wise to reconsider. Incidentally, in case you are not aware of it, Saint Peter, the disciple who became the founder of the Church and the first Pope, was *married*. Could marriage really be so bad for priests?"

There were many other letters, some very long, some very angry, some very hurt, and some a bit lost. There were statements and questions on many other subjects—abortion, euthanasia, ecumenism—but the letter that affected me most strongly was the one I received from a woman who introduced herself as a "senior citizen."

She wrote, "I read about your crisis in the New York Times and it troubled me deeply. I am sorry for you and want you to understand that you are not alone. The Church is full of Catholics who feel just as you do. They too are suffering from a crisis of conscience. I know, for I am one of them. What I ask is that you not let it end there. Something must be done. I fear for my Church. I fear for its future.

"What has happened to all the promise Vatican II seemed to hold? I was overjoyed by the great steps Pope John XXIII took. Then came his untimely death and now it seems we are walking backward instead of forward. Why? Who is causing this? It breaks my heart.

"I am not one of those silly people who think the Church should change its laws the way women change their fashions. I don't want a

Church that tells people it's all right to steal or hurt your neighbor even if the majority in the Church want it that way. We are meant to try to live as Christ lived. I will always believe that. I will always try. But many of the rules laid down by the Church have nothing to do with Christ and nothing to do with bettering the hearts and souls of Catholics.

"You're in a far better position to help them than most of us, Dr. Barber. Find the answers. And tell us what we can do to help our Church return to the vision of Pope John XXIII."

This letter and the others started me on an intellectual and emotional odyssey that would last more than three years. It included many interviews, much reading, and endless soul-searching. I found answers to the letters and I became convinced that in the modern world of educated parishioners, the Church cannot and should not expect blind obedience to controversial rules not of Christ's making; that the Church is like a family and when the parents can speak to the children, but the children cannot speak to the parents—openly and honestly and without guilt—the family is in grave danger. I learned what has happened to distort and delay the picture and the promise of Vatican II and what I believe each of us must do to return the Church to this picture and promise by way of Vatican III.

Let me begin by offering a program to you in just the way I received it myself—by finding answers to the questions and issues raised by the letters touched on here.

FOUR

Birth Control

How can the Church be so out of step that it goes on condemning birth control? Even if I weren't educated enough to know
that we will soon kill this planet through overpopulation, I'd
know that my husband and I can't support more than our three
children. So here I am having to feel guilty because I'm practicing birth control.

I f there was ever any truth to the old expression, also used as a title
for the book *Cheaper by the Dozen*, it is truth no longer. Children
are costly and the more there are, the greater the expense, especially
if the children are to be given the kind of home environment, care,
and education they need and deserve. Only on the farm are there
economic reasons for the larger family, and even here the evolution
of method and machine is rapidly making this notion passé. Limiting
the size of the family is a must for most couples if they are to keep
their heads above financial hot water.

Even if money were not a problem, many husbands and wives
have another reason for practicing family planning: the need to delay
the first pregnancy. Where both parties are at work, either building
careers or helping to feather the family nest, there is reluctance to
bring offspring into the world. Children not only need what money
can buy, they need parental time and attention. The emotionally
starved child of today is often the emotionally troubled adult of
tomorrow. Many caring partners prefer to postpone pregnancy until
one of them is in a position to stay home full-time.

Money and time. Both factors are major reasons for family planning. But today, even if parents have all they need of both these

commodities—vast wealth and ample time—there is still a compelling reason for limiting the size of the family: overpopulation of the world. It is a danger of which some social scientists have been conscious for more than a century, but which the man in the street has acknowledged only recently.

In 1959 presidential contender John F. Kennedy told his friends somewhat proudly, "I chose Bobby to be my campaign manager because I wanted to be sure all of his children work for me." In those days, Robert Kennedy's rapidly growing family was still proudly mentioned by all members of the Kennedy clan.

But only eight years later, in 1967, public awareness of overpopulation dangers had increased to such a degree that it was used against the popular Robert Kennedy. A right-wing critic, James F. Reilly, said of Kennedy, "It's only the uneducated Catholics who vote for Bobby. They think he's great because he doesn't practice birth control. He ought to run for Pope."

Social pressure to limit the size of the family increased in the late sixties by way of dire warnings issued by the second United Nations World Conference on Population held in New Delhi in 1965. There had been strident voices warning about the problem for a long, long time.

The man who first foresaw the problem was Thomas Malthus in 1798. A well-to-do British economist, he wrote his "Essay on the Principles of Population" to refute the unbridled optimism of the most influential men of the time, who believed that mankind, simply by applying mind over matter, could achieve a never-ending utopia of peace and prosperity for an unlimited world population. Malthus's essay predicted that without some effective form of population control, increases in food production would not keep pace with increases in population and the result would mean misery for millions.

According to Malthus, any improvement in living standards, instead of helping to alleviate the situation, only allowed more children to be born, and this meant more mouths to feed and less rapidly increasing supplies of food. In the first edition of his essay, Malthus could see "hope" only in the negatives—war, pestilence, vice—insofar as they restrained the growth of population, but in his second edition he looked for less horrific preventive checks: late marriages, sexual abstinence in marriage, and, especially, abolition of the generous poor law that gave monetary relief to poor people with large families and unwed mothers, thus, according to Malthus, encouraging them to continue in their reckless child-breeding way. Malthus also stressed the hope that education of the masses would give them a desire for higher living standards, so that when they acquired property, they would use their money to buy luxuries rather than having more children.

Unfortunately, most of mankind has not seen fit to follow Malthus's suggestions. However, his dire predictions are proving to be all too accurate. Having already passed the 5 billion mark, world population, if it continues at the present rate of growth, will reach the shocking figure of 10 billion human beings before the year 2025. Long before we have reached that number and date, unless we have embarked on a worldwide program of birth control, life on this planet will be unbearable for not millions, but billions.

Anyone with even a semblance of an education is aware of the international concern over the world's rapidly increasing population and, thus, the social stigma that attaches to those who ignore the problem and let nature take its course in terms of family size. Yet the Church continues to oppose any form of birth control, unless one includes the all-too-fallible "rhythm method," thus forcing Catholics to choose between social guilt or Church guilt. Ninety percent of Catholics have responded by choosing the latter, using artificial birth control in precisely the same numbers as non-Catholics. This has made birth control the largest symbol of dissent within the Church and has seriously eroded Church authority and leadership in many other areas, including premarital sex and even abortion. This danger was suggested by the letter-writer who compared the Church to a bad parent:

> If you tell your teenager not to have sex and not to take dope, and you make one sound as bad as the other, look at what you've done. Your teenager is almost sure to have sex, so he will decide your rules are meaningless and take dope as well.

That is precisely what has happened with adult Catholics. Having decided that the Church is wrong about birth control, members are now beginning to question the Church's infallibility in other areas. Why, then, does the Church insist on continuing its ban against the use of artificial birth control? Or as another letter-writer put it:

> Why is the Church so hung up on sex? Where does it say in the

Bible that the sex act is a sin unless you're doing it to make a baby?

Contraception is quite old. In his *Medical History of Contraception*, Norman Himes cites evidence of the existence of contraception among the Romans and Greeks and the ancient Egyptians and Asians. The Bible's Book of Genesis documents Onan's use of a well-known method in early biblical times. He used the withdrawal method and spilled his seed on the ground. Yet there is nothing in the Bible, Old Testament or New, that forbids the use of contraception, artificial or otherwise. The ban is based solely on Church dogma growing out of two beliefs:

1. The body is bad.
2. The way to win the world to Catholicism is to increase the percentage of Catholics.

THE BODY IS BAD

The concept of dualism was widely accepted in the early days of the Church when Clement of Rome, the first-century Church father, wrote *Epistle to the Corinthians* and Justin Martyr, the second-century author, wrote *Apology for Christianity*. Having its basis neither in Judaism nor the teachings of Christ, dualism was an outgrowth of Eastern philosophy, which saw the earth as a place of exile from heaven and the flesh as a prison of the soul. The innumerable mystery religions of the time were usually dualistic, and the concept crept into Christianity. Thus, for many Christians and pagans alike the body became the chief locus of all the evil and frustrating powers of the world. The body was bad. The soul, trapped in the body, was good. To "know" the body was bad. To "know" the soul was good.

Both Clement and Justin reflected this dualistic teaching in their view that marriage and sex—"knowing the body"—was justified only by the intention to procreate; that is, sexual intercourse was not a sin only when the purpose was a good one—to create the repository for a new soul. Thus, most Church fathers approved of intercourse *only* if procreation was directly intended.

Still, there was no legislation against the use of contraception. The Church father most influential in this regard was Aurelius Augustine (A.D. 354–430), whose writings greatly accentuated the Church's negative attitude toward sex by his strong association of original sin and sexuality.

Augustine's mother was a Christian, but his father was a pagan Roman official. The boy was raised a Christian until the age of eleven when he was sent to Madauros, a center of paganism. The environment adversely affected his moral and religious development, and when, at age seventeen, he went to live in Carthage, he led a licentious life that eventually led to his taking a mistress, a woman of low birth, by whom he bore a son.

Later, Augustine was converted from paganism to Manichaeism, which attempted to graft the teachings of Christ onto the Zoroastrian doctrine of dualism. According to the Manichaeians, God was the cause of all good, matter was the cause of all evil. Spirit was good; flesh was bad.

Although Augustine originally embraced the teachings of the Manichees, by the time he arrived at Milan in 384 he had become disillusioned with them and their doctrine of absolute certainty. He believed truth might be attainable, but not in their simplistic fashion.

In Milan he was introduced to the Neo-Platonic movement, where he found a remarkable affinity with his faith. Augustine was able to shake off the lingering materialism of the Manichees and to achieve the concept of a purely spiritual reality. He felt in this system of thought he could reach absolute truth and rely on this inner vision for the direction of his moral life.

At the age of thirty-three and under the influence of his mother, Monica, he refused to marry his concubine of many years. He considered marriage a sinful state. He turned toward Christianity and, with his son, was baptized on April 25, 387. He was finally ordained a priest in 391. One of his most remarkable writings is his *Confessions*, which is a masterpiece of introspection in which he analyzed his spiritual evolution. *The City of God* was written to pass judgment on the history, culture, and religion of pagan Rome. He relates it to the ultimate meaning of history itself.

Although a brilliant religious thinker and writer who would become the major Christian theologian of the early Western Church, Augustine was clearly biased. Like many reformed people, he had a very aggressive attitude toward the "sins" in which he had indulged as a young man. This can be seen in his *Confessions*, especially as they reflect his monodimensional attitude toward sex. Feeling guilt for his many brief liaisons in Carthage, as well as the sexuality he displayed with his mistress, he sought to slam the door on others. Later, these writings became the basis for Church dogma when, at the Council of Braga in 572, the first Church legislation banning contraception was enacted.

Put simply, the Church's ban on contraception is a legacy of Eastern dualism's teaching that the body is bad, coupled with St. Augustine's guilt over his own sexuality.

Rosemary Radford Reuther in *Contemporary Roman Catholicism: Crisis and Challenge* on page 38 offers an explanation on the sexual ethics bequeathed to Catholic Christianity by St. Augustine. An introduction to some of St. Augustine's statements about sexual intercourse states that if it was separated from procreation, even within marriage, then it became pure lust or mere fornication, no better than the brothel. On page 38 there was a continuation in the last paragraph about St. Augustine where it also allowed a second purpose of sexuality as the "remedy of concupiscence." Needless to say, it was male concupiscence he had in mind. The male sexual impulse was seen as a tempestuous demand that would run amuck and corrupt the other good wives of the society unless it was confined to one's own legitimate wife.

Augustine also defended the necessity of prostitutes on the same ground, as better than the corruption of married women by men other than their husbands. Prostitutes are compared by Augustine to sewers, filthy but necessary for the good order of the city. It is not farfetched to see that, in such a view of sexuality, each man's wife is his private sewer into which he dumps his lust so that it won't flow outside into the streets. What is left completely undeveloped in this view is any understanding of sexuality as love and expression of relationship. This, more than anything else, shows that so many of the teachings on sexuality in the Catholic Church are arbitrary and self-perpetuating.

INCREASING THE PERCENTAGE OF CATHOLICS

Although it is heard less often and less openly these days than it was in the past, the Catholic hierarchy clearly harbors the hope that by having a Catholic "population explosion," it will achieve world dominion. How many young women have been told it is their duty to bring many new Catholics into this world? The shortsightedness of this attitude is obvious. What good will it do for the Church to "save" mankind through Catholicism if, in the meantime, it helps to cause the crumbling of the planet?

There have been four United Nations World Conferences on Population: Rome in 1954, New Delhi in 1965, Bucharest in 1974, and Mexico City in 1984. Obviously, these conferences were a result of intense international concern about the issue of overpopulation. Yet at each of these conferences, the Vatican voted *against* the plan proposed by the conference, the only participant to do so. In 1984 at Mexico City, instead of supporting the final statement on overall control of population, the Vatican once again reaffirmed its belief in the immorality of artificial contraception and sterilization and insisted that the emphasis should be placed on more development rather than on population control. As one critic pointed out, that is tantamount to letting the children keep playing with matches while trying to build extra houses for them to burn down.

Although the desire to increase the percentage of Catholics worldwide has strongly influenced the Church's attitude toward family planning and population control, the major stumbling block to a change in this attitude is the ban on artificial contraception. The origin of this ban—dualism and Augustine—has already been explained, but the Church's more modern rationalization for the ban is based on two quite different themes:

1. Natural law is violated when some artificial impediment is used to prevent each and every act of marital intercourse from being open to the possibility of conception.
2. The sacramental symbolism of married life is violated when an impediment of an artificial nature is permitted to interfere with fertility.

The key word in each of these themes is "artificial," especially since the Church long ago approved its own method of contraception, the so-called rhythm method whereby marital sexual intercourse is limited to the dates when conception is least likely (based on the wife's menstrual cycle). This system was sanctioned in 1930 by Pope Pius XI. In his encyclical on marriage (*Casti Connubi*), the Pope stated:

> [N]or are those considered as acting against nature who in the married state use their right in the proper manner, although on

account of natural reasons either of time or of certain defects, new life cannot be brought forth.

Many theologians believe the Church's approval of the rhythm method was the first step in undermining member adherence to the ban on contraception. After all, if the Church's prohibition grew out of the belief that sexual intercourse is justified only when it has as its immediate purpose the creation of new life, how could it be justified if limited to dates when conception is least likely? It has the same intent as artificial contraception, but is less reliable.

There were, however, other theologians who supported the Church's distinction between the rhythm method and "artificial" contraception. It was not unrealistic, said these voices, to expect that mechanical devices, such as condoms, might cause marital partners, especially wives, to experience emotional discomfort. This could diminish the "sacramental symbolism" of marriage, a danger pointed out in one of the two Church themes.

No wonder, then, that these people, along with millions of others, rejoiced at the synthesis of the oral contraceptive pill, which would eliminate a married couple's need for condoms or diaphragms or sponges. This was the process for isolating progesterone from a Mexican yam, a process that allowed Dr. John Rock and his associates to produce the miracle contraceptive pill that has changed the world.

Since the use of Dr. Rock's pill allowed husbands and wives to practice birth control *without* the use of artificial contrivances such as condoms or diaphragms, there were high hopes that the Church, although originally negative, would be converted to its use. Toward this end, Dr. Rock, a staunch Catholic, crisscrossed the nation explaining the safety and advantages of the pill. He also wrote a book, *The Time Has Come*.

Women by the million, Catholics and non-Catholics alike, responded positively to Dr. Rock's message. So favorable was this response that the Church was forced to make a move. Pope Paul VI appointed a special commission to study and make a recommendation on the possibility of change in the Church's position on birth control. The commission included theologians, legal experts, historians, sociologists, and family members. After a long period of study and discussion, the commission produced by an astounding 64-to-4 vote a majority report suggesting to the Pope that a change in the Church's position was both possible and advisable.

The commission suggested that the Church's ban on birth control should relate to a marriage as a whole rather than to any single act of sexual intercourse; that while it should be forbidden for husbands and wives to practice artificial contraception with no intention of *ever* having children, it should not be forbidden to practice artificial contraception for purposes of limiting the number of children or postponing their arrival.

With the world waiting anxiously, especially in view of the growing need for population control, Pope Paul VI issued his encyclical (*Humanae Vitae*) on July 24, 1968. Shockingly, he ignored completely the advice given by the commission he himself had appointed. Instead of supporting the commission's recommendations, the Pope condemned birth control in general and the pill in particular, reaffirming the principle that each and every marriage act must remain open to the transmission of life.

World hopes were dashed.

The decision of Pope Paul VI to condemn the use of artificial methods of contraception, including the pill, against the overwhelming majority of his birth control commission was not just a mistake, but a blunder. The Pope's decision precipitated the most serious crisis for papal authority since Luther. Leading theologians, priests, a good section of the Catholic press, and even various episcopates took stands somewhat at variance with the papal declaration. He did not act collegially with the bishops in issuing his encyclical. This independent action by the Pope galvanized the clergy to demand, as Leon Cardinal Suenens of Belgium has so many times before, that the Pope no longer act as though he were outside but above the Church. The galelike winds of discontent and a demand for change in papal authority continue to blow across the Church. *Humanae Vitae* has marked the end of the totalitarian rule by the Pope.

It is obvious that most lay people simply chose to disregard the encyclical and to continue to practice contraception. The conflict began to make clear that papal authority could no longer count on passive acquiescence to its teachings, that this failed to respect the informed conscience of the Catholic people. It also suggests that one of the major barriers to rethinking traditional teaching on sexuality, or any other subject, lies in the notion of irreformable authority. Hans Küng, a leading German conciliar theologian, took this as the impetus to write a major book challenging the doctrine of infallibility. Father Charles Curran, a moderately dissenting Catholic ethicist, had been under fire in the 1960s and this was again revived. Despite careful efforts to qualify his position, Father Curran was declared by the sacred congregation as unfit to teach Catholic moral theology in August of 1986. Thus, the Pope seems to turn back the clock and restore the consensus against birth control that had disappeared in the late 1960s.

It is interesting that the Vatican denied a German television report that its bank once held shares in a drug company producing birth control pills. Serono Pharmaceutical Company admitted that the Vatican did have shares in its Rome subsidiary in the 1960s and possibly the early 1970s. The German television report on private station RTL Plus alleged that the Church received financial gain from the sale of birth control pills while the Vatican bank held a majority of shares in Serono. The report further alleged that Serono began producing birth control pills in 1968, the year the Roman Catholic Church staunchly laid out its opposition to artificial contraceptive methods in Pope Paul VI's encyclical *Humanae Vita*. The report stated that the Vatican bank, formally called the Institute for Religious Work (IOR), sold its shares in Serono in 1970 to a Milan-based bank in which it held a 20 percent stake. This was reported in the *Newark Star Ledger* in November 1990.

THE FUTURE

As the situation exists today, the Church continues its ban on artificial contraception, yet, as previously noted, 90 percent of Catholics ignore the ban, most convinced that the Church is in error. In practice, many priests resolve this destructive stalemate by insisting in theory on the official position while in practice tolerating contraceptive intercourse as a concession to "human weakness." Although such a pastoral solution may be acceptable to the curia, it offends millions of Catholics who do not want to be told that there is something evil or weak about their marital love.

Many brilliant theologians here and abroad disagree with the Church's position and believe it may be changed. From Father Bernard Haring, professor of moral theology at the Redemptorist Seminary in Rome, to Charles E. Curran, widely recognized author of *Issues in Sexual and Medical Ethics*, important Catholic voices have asked the Church to eliminate the ban on contraception and, once and for all, dissociate Catholicism from the sexual legacy of dualism and Augustine.

The body is not evil, women are not unclean, and procreation is not the only valid reason for sex in marriage. For the Church to continue a ban based on such degrading dogma is to place Catholics in a totally untenable position. Consider the effect on only one group the Church seems to ignore completely—those wives who have passed the childbearing age. While psychiatrists and psychologists, as well as magazines, TV, and movies, are telling these women not to feel they have lost their femininity or that they are less desirable or threatened by younger women, the Church has failed to acknowledge that sexual intercourse without limitation would compensate them for their years of guilt and abstinence. What else can be meant if procreation is the only justification for intercourse?

What the Church must acknowledge is what students of the biological sciences and human nature—and sociologists like Andrew Greeley—have long understood: that sex is a very important pair-bonding mechanism, even more important to humans than to the rest of the primate species, and that relatively frequent marital sex is an essential part of human nature and of a happy marriage. Thus, so long as the act of sexual intercourse facilitates the possibility of pair-bonding, it does not violate the essence of human nature.

The Church should welcome Dr. John Rock's birth control pill. Progress in learning and technology show that both in living things and in the forces of nature, an astounding order reigns. It also bears witness to the greatness of mankind, made in God's image, who can understand this order and who creates suitable instruments to harness these natural forces and use them to the benefit of all human beings. If the broad concepts of the Catholic religion are based on natural law and common sense, as the Church has long insisted, there must be *uniform* acceptance of the ability to control the forces of nature.

Man has split the atom, explored space, landed on the moon, and made dramatic progress in conquering disease—and all of these developments have been applauded by the Church. Why, then, when human beings, with their God-given intellect, manage to control the awesome power of reproduction, should the Church make an exception? This is especially shocking in view of the great bonus offered by the pill. Over and above its near-perfection in family planning, the pill actually protects many thousands of women from illnesses (and possibly death) they would otherwise encounter. These include iron deficiency anemia, endometrial cancer, ovarian cancer, functional ovarian cysts, ectopic pregnancy, pelvic-inflammatory disease (PID), and rheumatoid arthritis—more than 100,000 hospitalizations are avoided every year in the United States alone, thanks to the use of the pill.

No matter how loud the Church preaches, it will not be able to convince Catholic women that the pill is bad. The Church must change its attitudes, must revise its position. Married couples will not listen to a Church that tells them not to practice birth control, but they will listen to a Church that emphasizes responsible parenthood and the importance of living, faithful relationships.

What is needed is a new Church encyclical that not only accepts the use of artificial contraception in Catholic marriages, but also recognizes the dire threat of overpopulation in almost every land and promises support of strong measures to meet this challenge. Such a position paper would be a landmark development in the history of the Church and would be applauded throughout the world. There is an urgency for an encyclical that will address the disaster that population growth will bring to humankind.

Women

What do you think it feels like belonging to the Church and attending Mass if you're a woman? How do you think it feels to stand up and profess your faith—"We believe in one God . . ."—when it gets to the part, "For us *men* and for our salvation he came down from heaven." If you were a woman, how would you like saying "For us *men*"?

One of my women correspondents expressed her feeling succinctly with the above statement, and I took the opportunity to paraphrase the statements of many others for this chapter. Nothing is more degrading than to ignore people when they are in your presence. It is a particularly hurtful insult, calculated to make the individual feel beneath contempt, unworthy of any form of recognition.

Even as children, we learn how easily we can disturb our friends if we ignore them, refusing to acknowledge their existence. Some parents use this technique as punishment for their children, but psychiatrists tell us it is a very dangerous tool. If employed for any length of time, it can induce permanent emotional injury. And yet the Church chooses to practice this technique with more than half its membership. The male hierarchy may say that men and women are equal, but are they? There may be differences anatomically, but spiritually, there is and must be equality. Yet all tests and decisions are the product of an androcentric patriarchal culture and history. It is best said by Yogi Berra, "like deja vu all over again."

More accurately called the Nicene-Constantinople Creed, following the second Council of Nicaea, the Nicene Creed is the one now

[46]

used in the liturgy. It starts by saying, "We believe in one God, the Father almighty, creator of heaven and earth, of all things both visible and invisible." Later the creed continues, "For the sake of us men and our salvation he came down from heaven, was made flesh by the Holy Spirit from the Virgin Mary, and became man," and so on. In numerous hymns and prayers and codicils, women are referred to as "him" or "he" or "man" or "brother" or not referred to at all. But the Nicene Creed stands out, not only because it is repeated with such regularity, but also because it has become a sacred symbol—a member's pledge of allegiance to the Church—and because it seems to say by implication that Jesus came down from heaven only for men, not for women. Why are women so clearly ignored in this creed?

No part of the creed came to us from Christ. Kenneth Scott Latourette writes in his *History of Christianity*:

> So far as records enable us to determine, Jesus gave little thought to a continuing organization and did not put the heart of his teaching in any single verbal formula which was to be binding upon his followers . . . The one set of words which he gave to his disciples is what has traditionally been called the Lord's Prayer. That is a prayer (the voluntary response to God's presence) and not a creed and even it was not phrased as something which was to be held to with slavish accuracy, but as a suggested outline—"after this manner . . . pray."

The Nicene Creed grew out of the first general council of the Catholic Church. Held at Nicaea in Asia Minor in the year 325, the council was the result of an argument raised by Arius, a presbyter in the Alexandrian Church. Arius and his followers claimed that Jesus was not as great as God, that "the Son of God has a beginning but that God is without a beginning," and that "the Son is not part of God." The majority of the Alexandrian Church vehemently disagreed, insisting that "God is always, the Son is always and the Son is the unbegotten begotten."

The emperor Constantine told the two factions he found the cause of their differences "to be of a truly insignificant character" and that it should be regarded "merely as an intellectual exercise"; nevertheless, they would not be silenced. When the argument threatened to split the Church, Constantine called the council. Three hundred bishops attended from throughout the Roman Empire, as well as representatives from Persia and the Goths.

Beginning with a creed that had been used by Christians of Caesarea in Palestine, additions and changes were made in an effort to find words that would satisfy both factions in the Arius dispute. It was toward this end that the bishops included the words "he came down from heaven," preceded by "for . . . us men and our salvation."

As to why the words "us men" were chosen, the Church insists that the answer is simple and innocent: The Creed was designed as an oath; that is, all of the bishops were to repeat it as proof of their allegiance to a single Catholic Church, and since all of the bishops were men, there was no mention of women or concern about the mention of men only.

This is to be considered the history behind the Creed, and since the reason for the use of the words "us men" indicates no disrespect for women, the Church asks, why bother to change it? The answer is quite clear. It is not the words alone that are an insult to women, it is the *attitude* they represent on the part of the male hierarchy. Women are not only *spoken* about ignominiously, they are treated this way. I find it highly unlikely that the young woman who wrote to me about the Nicene Creed would feel as she does if women were treated as equals in the Catholic Church. But they are not. Although women account for more than 50 percent of Church membership and perform an estimated 70 percent of all Church work, they cannot become priests, permanent deaconesses, or even altar girls.

"Under canon law women were classed with children and idiots," a young nun remarked bitterly some years ago. "The Church and women is a most depressing subject. I hate to think what Freudians would say about a patriarchal Church which refers to itself as 'Holy Mother Church.' I feel intensely hurt for what women have been forced to endure in the name of Christ." In my opinion, preventing women from performing a sacramental role makes them lead a half-life. The arrogant or frightened male hierarchy, by keeping women from ordination to the priesthood, is saying that they cannot be trusted to bring Christ to people. To Catholic women, I say it is not a question of will equality happen. It has to happen, and soon.

For what reason has the Church insisted upon making women second-class citizens? How could this occur in view of the wonderful example Jesus set in his contact with women? It is a shame and a disgrace that a relationship which began with such promise should have reached the sorry state it is in today. How did it happen?

Women had an inferior role in the Jewish world into which Christ was born. Writings from that time are scornful of women, who as nearly as possible lived a life withdrawn from public view, never to be seen in the company of men. Although Judaism is a patriarchal religion, it does provide laws that protect and sanctify women. Nevertheless, men were instructed by tradition to "talk very little with their wives, still less with other women." In the temple, women were allowed only in one portion of the forecourt and, for their prayers, were separated from men during religious services. Even today in the preliminary morning service men say: "Blessed are thou, Lord our God, King of the Universe, who has not made me a woman." It is my understanding that this permits men to say their prayers and tend to their work without the responsibilities of doing the daily household chores performed by women. In addition, women were allowed only in the forecourt so that men would not be distracted during their prayers. Never to be forgotten was the fact that woman was made from man, not man from woman, and that it was Eve, not Adam, who first hungered for the apple. Women were, according to Flavius Josephus (ca. A.D. 37–100), a Jewish historian, in every respect inferior to men.

In light of all this, Jesus' conduct is truly astonishing. No wonder Hans Küng, in *On Being a Christian*, says that Jesus "brought suspicion on himself by the company he kept"—women. Not only did Jesus have public contact with women, not only did he show no contempt for them, he displayed precisely the opposite attitude. He was caring and affectionate and "surprisingly at ease with women," treating them always as equals with men. Jesus was often supported by women followers who had money, women attended Christ as he was dying on the cross, and women saw to his burial.

Mark's gospel describes the response of Mary Magdalene, Mary, the mother of James, and Salome, who had come to the tomb to anoint Jesus. Arriving and finding the stone rolled back, they are told by a man in white that Jesus, who was crucified, has been raised. The women are then sent to share the good news: "Go and tell the disciples and Peter that he is going ahead of you to Galilee" (16:7). According to Matthew's gospel, in the midst of their mission they experienced Jesus' word of "peace" and his own commission: "Go and carry the news to my brothers" (28:10). Historically, there is evidence that Jesus not only wanted but almost commissioned or demanded that women preach and carry out his own commission. In John's version, when Jesus commissions Mary to tell his brothers, she goes immediately and announces what she has experienced: "I have seen the Lord" (20:18). The history of most women as disciples and as preachers is some combination of each of these responses.

It should also be noted that although Christ offered his followers very little in the way of a civil code, he made a point of changing one law, which would have a profound effect on women's status. Before Jesus, a husband could be rid of his wife simply by issuing a writ of divorce, without her agreement or even notice to her. According to Hans Küng, Jesus' strict prohibition of divorce except for the breaking of marital bonds "considerably upgraded the legally and humanly weak position of woman." He declared, "Christ would not have women abandoned in marriage at the whims of men."

There is little doubt that Jesus' attitude toward women astonished his disciples. It was a dramatic lesson in humanity and one not soon forgotten. The early Christian Church remained well ahead of its time in its estimation and treatment of women. Kenneth Scott Latourette writes, "While Paul would not allow them to speak in the meetings of the Church, he declared that in Christ Jesus there could be neither male nor female and, in the churches of the first generation, women were honored as prophetesses." They seem also to have served as deaconesses, and virgins and widows were held in especially high respect.

It was only as time and space distanced the Church from Christ that its attitudes toward women began to resemble those of society. As death overtook the apostles and the other followers of Jesus who had actually witnessed his respect and affection for women, the central church in Jerusalem drifted toward more usual non-Christian attitudes. As Christianity spread into the non-Jewish world, it was affected by the Hellenistic background of many of its converts. Here again the doctrine of dualism, previously mentioned in chapter 4, remained in sharp contrast with Jesus' own beliefs. Dualism held that the flesh was considered evil. Since sex was of the flesh, it must be evil, and since women produced lust—the desire for sex—they too were evil. By the end of the first century, women were portrayed as a threat to the virtue of celibates and to the manliness of married men.

In the third century, Tertullian, the earliest Church father whose writings have not been lost, told women, "Do you not know that you are Eve? You are the devil's doorway. It was you who profaned the tree of life. It was you who disfigured the image of God which is man."

A hundred years later, St. Ambrose agreed. "Adam was led to sin by Eve, not Eve by Adam." Also in the fourth century, St. Athanasius thought women were "a clothed serpent." In the fifth century, St. Jerome called woman "the doer of the devil." No less a great figure, John Chrysostom wrote, "Among all savage beasts none is found so harmful as woman."

In Andrew Greeley's autobiographical *Confessions of a Parish Priest*, he quotes from Umberto Eco's historical novel *The Name of the Rose*, which contains repeated references to women as "swamps and tramps designed to swallow up the souls of men." John Broomyard, an English Dominican, warned that woman was "a graveyard, well-kept on the outside but filled with death and corruption," and one medieval saint called woman "vomit and ordure; a sack of rottenness."

In the twelfth century, Bernard of Clairvaux heard in women's voices "the hissing of serpents," and a hundred years later, even the great scholar and theologian Thomas Aquinas was convinced of the inferior and subordinate status of woman. Moreover, he found a confirming explanation in Aristotle, who defined woman as "a misbegotten male." According to this theory, the male seed carried the total genetic structure of the offspring and therefore should reproduce only the image of its origins—a male—unless some accident happened to the male sperm, in which case the inferior female was "misbegotten." Woman was a deformed man.

The devil's doorway, a clothed serpent, the doer of the devil, swamps to swallow up the souls of men, a graveyard filled with death and corruption, vomit and ordure, a deformed male. Even as I write these words, it is difficult for me to believe that men, especially scholarly men of supposed intelligence, could believe such insulting claptrap. It is even harder to accept the fact that these men were purported Christians. How could the example set by Jesus Christ have led to such concepts?

Thankfully, improvement had begun even before Thomas Aquinas's death in 1274. A number of women of the thirteenth and fourteenth centuries were eventually canonized. Thus the Church recognized they were worthy of emulation by all Christians. The cult of the Virgin Mary took on new strength and popularity as chivalry extolled loyalty to the lady who had won the devotion of a conquering knight. "There may be more than coincidence," Kenneth Scott Latourette notes, "in the fact that the accentuation of the cult of the Virgin and the development of chivalry were features of the same century."

The years 1300 to 1500 were the most glorious for women since the passing of the Apostles. Latourette continues, "Now women appeared as leaders and exemplars of the faith. It was still a man's world. The clergy was exclusively male. The great theologians and the founders of the monastic orders were men. But women were coming to the fore as mystics and saints."

In growing numbers, women also presided over monasteries, assigned parish priests, gave confessional jurisdiction, and soon had more power in general than in any period before or since. In England, abbesses were among those to whom the king looked when he needed help in defending the country. They provided leadership and even fought in armies. Heads of major religious houses, bishops, and the archbishops of York and Canterbury were all summoned when Parliament sat, and this extended to abbesses; in 1306, for example, fifteen abbots and four abbesses were called to Westminster.

Glamour magazine in 1991 carried an article by Lucretia Marmon entitled, "Why Can't Women Be Priests Again?" The article states that Leta, Martin, Flavia, Vitalia, and Nepos were Catholic priests over fifteen centuries ago. This information was uncovered by Mary Ann Rossi, Ph.D., an honorary fellow at the Women's Studies Research Center at the University of Wisconsin, in Madison. Over the years, many American Catholics have fought women's exclusion from the priesthood (I am one of these Catholics). Dr. Rossi's work helps to disprove one of the Church's (the male hierarchy) defenses of the status quo—that there is no precedent for the ordination of women.

The article reports that letters and tombstones mentioning early women priests, even bishops, were reported nearly a decade ago by an Italian scholar, Giorgio Otranto. His work went virtually unnoticed by the English-speaking world until Dr. Rossi came across it in the Vatican Library. Her translation of Otranto's work appeared in the summer of 1991 in the Harvard Divinity School's *Journal of Feminist Studies in Religion*.

To this date, Rome (Vatican) has been silent. This is to be expected, for emotion on the part of the male hierarchy outweighs facts and precedence.

Father Eugene Lauer, director of the Center for Continuing Formation of Ministry at Notre Dame University, says the findings are persuasive, but the Church's case against women's ordination is complex. The example given in defense for refusing women's ordination is that Jesus' choice of male disciples is considered divine precedent. It is obvious that they are ignoring the women around Jesus, their faithfulness during the journey to Calvary, their desire to bury him, and the command by Jesus to go and announce the good news to his followers that Christ was risen. It is the single most important event in the Catholic Church and it was entrusted to women. In John 20 there is the story of the woman who would in later tradition be called "the apostle to apostles." This woman was Mary Magdalene. Today many women disciples are seeking God but meeting confusion, even empty tombs. However, women are discovering the power of the resurrection and are experiencing a real call and empowerment to preach the good news.

Lucretia Marmon reported that some scholars claim that there actually were female disciples and apostles; later, church leaders just renamed them and painted beards on their pictures. She accepts that this is politics. The article reports that one of the Pope's top priorities is the unification of the Roman and Orthodox churches. "And the Orthodox Church," says one conservative theologian, "is even more resistant to women priests." My message is: Women, do not despair. We need you, your counsel, your wisdom, and your advice. The greatness of the Catholic Church will be enhanced by your leadership. I pray it will happen in my time.

"The power of these women was well-founded in goods and lands," writes Marcelle Bernstein in *The Nuns*. "Nor was their spiritual power confined to the women beneath them. In the double monasteries, when men and women inhabited the same religious houses, it was always under the rule of an abbess." There were priests who ministered to the nuns spiritually and lay brothers who did the manual work, but it was the abbesses who were in charge. Within their own boundaries, these women held the powers of a bishop.

And then, even more abruptly than it began, this brief recognition of female talent and ability, this long overdue progress toward equality, abruptly ended. The chief cause for this regression was the Council of Trent, called by Pope Paul III in December 1545. The council's primary purpose was to effect reforms that would halt the shocking flow of Catholics into the Protestant fold, but it did so with such vengeance that, according to Latourette, "it scrapped much of the machinery that had mushroomed from the measures of the reforming Popes of the Middle Ages." This revived and augmented the authority of the bishops in the diocese and severely reduced the newly won power of abbesses.

Bishops who formerly had no right to enter the houses of abbesses with episcopal jurisdiction were now able to do so as delegates of the Holy See. Marcelle Bernstein writes, "Even more damaging was the curtailing of movements. Nuns were forbidden to leave their enclosures." This restriction prevented the abbesses from answering summons to Parliament and kept those who ruled the German foundations from attending the Imperial Diet. The episcopal role of the abbess was on its way to extinction and all the progress of women in the Church had effectively been halted.

While history moved forward, women moved backward in the Church, and by the seventeenth century, Spanish Jesuit Gracia could write, "It is clear that woman is under man's dominion and has no authority." Although the power and privilege held during the brief period from 1300 to 1500 had been sufficient to lift woman's image, it had provided no lasting improvement in her position in the Church, and this regression to second-class citizenship remained unchanged for another four hundred years.

MODERN HISTORY

It was like removing the shutter and opening the window in a dark, dank room. In 1962, twenty-six hundred cardinals, archbishops, and bishops assembled under Pope John XXIII for Vatican II. Their purpose, according to the Pope: "We are going to shake off the dust that has collected on the throne of St. Peter and let in some fresh air." And indeed they did. Vatican II brought about a great improvement in women's rights, as evidenced by the encyclical Pope John issued on feminism. Tragically, this Pope would not last out the council, and the promise Vatican II had offered for women was never realized

Even so, remarkable strides were made in some areas and, more important, the stage was set for still greater improvements by future Popes.

There is no doubt in my mind that John Paul II had a singularly remarkable opportunity when he was elected Pope. Thanks to Vatican II, women in the Church were riding a tide of optimism. Many nuns were shedding or modifying their habit. Well-educated, they took their place in the world and contributed to advances in world affairs. Many were feminists, not in the sense of destruction, but in a more enlightened approach dedicated to construction. They were leading the way in what Hans Küng called the "New Reformation."

Much of the world was engulfed in a socially dynamic climate fostered by the ethos of women's liberation. A new solidarity emerged among women across continents and cultures. In its women, the Church had the largest single group of educated, articulate bonded human beings. They were prepared for leadership in society and in the Church. All the new Pope needed to do was reach out his hands to begin the process that would set these women free. How did Pope John Paul II respond to this opportunity?

He did nothing. Rather than act in this most important area, he chose, as Hans Küng suggests in *On Being a Christian*, "to find relief from the burden of the uncongenial and often fruitless 'internal policy' by seeking success in an apparently 'foreign policy.' " In other words, rather than face the challenge of granting women's rights, the Pope chose the pleasure of traveling around the world and responding to the cheers of foreign idolaters. However, many agree with Eugene Kennedy that these "papal visits belong to a bygone era of spectacles, of world fairs and centenary exhibitions, of nineteenth-century circuses, Teddy Roosevelt's great white fleet sailing majestically into the great harbors of the world to show the flag."

When the Pope finally decided to speak on the cause of female rights (1976), he agreed that women have a role to play as fully equal with men, but said that this role should be in the area encompassed by the family. What a tragic mistake.

As Marcelle Bernstein quotes one Jesuit on this subject, the Pope has "refused to understand the aspirations of women in the modern world and has preferred to keep to the old way of doing things, even at the expense of sacrificing these intelligent women."

That is precisely what is happening. Those women are being sacrificed on the altar of male chauvinism. In growing numbers, laywomen are looking to other churches and Catholic sisters are seeking or being forced to seek ministerial-service positions in organizations unrelated to the officially sponsored ministries of the Catholic Church. In one notorious confrontation (1970), some 350 Sisters of the Immaculate Heart in Los Angeles departed en masse during a dispute with James Francis Cardinal McIntyre over the type of lifestyle and dress they wished to adopt. The Vatican (the Sacred Congregation for Religious and Secular Institutes) backed McIntyre and even refused to acknowledge correspondence from the sisters. They were ignored, just as the Church ignores all women in the hymns and codicils and the creed.

"How can some men in Rome say what I as an American woman can or cannot wear or do?" asked Sister Patricia McKeough. "They're still laboring under their own culture lag."

Many other religious communities supported the Immaculate Heart Sisters, but the Vatican was not moved. The sisters were forced to give in or sign dispensations and become laywomen again. Of the four hundred sisters, only fifty remained. The others signed away their sisterhood and the first to do so was Sister Anna, who had made her vows in 1905. At ninety-nine, she signed the document in a firm hand and then announced, "I am now going to the chapel to make my vows to *Jesus*." Until her death two years later, she continued to wear the full habit of the order.

Sister Madonna Kolbenschlag, a member of the Sisters of Humility of Mary of Villa Mona, Pennsylvania, put it into its proper perspective. She said, "The Church cannot put toothpaste back in the tube" or "make us caterpillars after we have become butterflies."

"If you are a woman," says Sister Joan Chittister in her book, *Women, Ministry and the Church*, "there is very little in the Catholic world that is new. Except talk, of course. There is a great deal of new talk. For instance, everyone is talking about women being 'different but equal' and everyone is surely sincere. Most women and probably all men in the Church accept women as different. It is simply difficult to find proof of equality. Government is male. Business is male. The Church is certainly male. These areas accepted as female—service positions and volunteer projects—are underpaid and undervalued. There is indeed a lot of talk, but, unfortunately, very little is actually done."

What is it that makes the male hierarchy of the Church so consistently antifemale despite all the progress women have made in society, especially in the United States and in most of Europe? Is it possible that the ancient image—"doers of the devil"—still prevails? A lecturer in psychiatry at the University of London thinks so. He suggests that the passionate reaction on the part of the male hierarchy to the idea of female equality in the Church—some priests have called it "disgusting," "repugnant," "shameful"—indicates that powerful unconscious forces may still be at work, relating back to the association of women with the body and lust and the devil.

But a more likely explanation has to do with power and privilege. The male hierarchy of the Church fears that allowing equality for women in almost any area might one day mean loss of male power. "The hierarchical Church," says Madonna Kolbenschlag, "seems to be affected by a kind of 'Saturnian complex'— reminiscent of the Greek deity who swallowed the children of his own loins, fearing they might one day displace him." This statement summarizes my feeling about the fear and terror that the male hierarchy of the Church has toward women.

What was, or at least appeared to be, a matter of image for almost two thousand years has now become a matter of power. Women want and deserve equality in the Church and the male hierarchy is afraid to give it to them. The results, since the dimming of the promise of Vatican II, have been explosive. Women have refused to accept the situation in silence. Protest has shown itself in a variety of ways—from the reduction of dollars in collection baskets to the formation of the National Coalition of American Nuns, the National Assembly of Women Religious, and networks of feminist theology schools and workshops in Europe, England, and the United States.

In England, the Women in Theology Group and the Catholic Women's Network gather Christian feminist women together for lectures, reflection, and worship. In the United States, the feminist worship gatherings have greatly proliferated in major urban areas, networked through a group of Catholic feminist organizations called the Women of the Church Convergence. The name "Women-Church" has been taken as their way of claiming power for Catholic women.

And there has been confrontation—from the 23 nuns who dared challenge the Church on abortion (see chapter 6) to Mercy Sister M.

Teresa Kane, the president of the United States Leadership Conference of Women's Religious, who had the courage and audacity to confront Pope John Paul II in Washington, D.C., on the equal role that should be women's "in all ministries of our Church."

Agnes Mary Mansour listened intently as the Vatican's ultimatum was read to her at the Sisters of Mercy provincial house in Detroit: resign her position as director of social services for the state of Michigan or become subject to a canonical process that would lead to an imposed dismissal from the religious order she had been a member of for thirty years. At issue was her position on abortion. Although she had personally condemned the practice before her appointment, she had indicated that she would tolerate the use of federal funds for abortion in the performance of her secular duties. She said that such an action would be a vote for the poor rather than a vote for abortion.

This is another expression of Catholic feminism that is less concerned with the subtleties of canon law than with the dynamics of social interaction; these women are less preoccupied with dogmatic definitions than with humans. Their philosophy has evolved from their dedicated work among the poor, the homeless, children of broken homes, alcoholics, and the underprivileged who plead for a better life. Ex-sister Mansour continues her work helping people of all races and creeds.

Women no longer accept their second-class status without protest, but protest alone is not enough. How are women to engineer changes when the line of command continues through men from the Pope to cardinals to bishops to priests? In 1971, when the International Synod of Bishops met to talk about justice, not a single woman representative was present. "Imagine!" exclaimed Sister Margaret Ellen Trafler, who formed the National Coalition of American Nuns. "They're talking about justice and more than half their membership is denied a presence, much less a vote."

The women of the Catholic Church have a vision. Someday that vision will be a reality, but the celibate, male hierarchy lapses into almost hysterical disdain for everything feminine. The time has come and women will not only survive in the Church, but they will prevail.

Recently, Chicago Catholic women developed an alternative fund to the "Peter's Pence Fund" called "Mary's Pence." The annual Peter's Pence Fund supports the Vatican. Mary's Pence will be used to support the ministries by and for women. Women, with their own power to pray, to pay, and to obey, can confront the male hierarchy of the Catholic Church with a challenge it cannot ignore, stifle, or control. If it continues to ignore women determined to seek equality, the Church will lose its capacity to govern unilaterally.

Daniel C. Maguire, a theologian at Marquette University, has perhaps stated all of this in slightly different terms when he said, "In the time of Galileo, it was physics and astronomy. Today, it's pelvic theology. But the issue is the same. The issue is power, and the issue is control."

Says Father Andrew Greeley, "The Second Vatican Council released tremendous social and intellectual forces. If these forces had been properly understood and properly channeled, there could have been tremendous growth."

But these forces were not understood, especially in the case of women's rights. Pope John XXIII showed the way to the boldest change of course in modern Church history when he endorsed feminism in one of his social encyclicals, but the vision is dying due to, says Hans Küng, "a vacuum of intellectual leadership in Rome and in the episcopate as a whole."

The result is that the institutional Church today is no less antifeminist than it was four hundred years ago when Teresa of Avila wrote, "The very thought that I am a woman makes my wings droop."

THE FUTURE

We already know the Church doesn't think women are good enough to become priests, but do they have to rub it in every week by making us repeat the words that prove it?

This has been expressed by many religious women. *Not good enough?* Nuns deal with more of life's harsh realities than most priests ever see: alcoholism, homicides, drug addicts, deserted wives, delinquent children, prostitutes. Consider, for example, the work of the Daughters of Charity of Saint Vincent de Paul, who operate Marillac House in Chicago.

According to Marcelle Bernstein in *The Nuns*, "They go out day after day to serve an area with the highest crime rate, venereal disease, illegitimacy, illiteracy and poverty rates in the whole of the United States. In another Chicago slum, Woodlawn, a community of

Loretto Sisters works in a shabby building set among the gaping shells of houses filled with rats. Here Sister Therese Rooney heads a team deeply involved in putting the mainly black population on their feet both emotionally and financially. The community runs educational courses for those who have dropped out of school and teaches office skills to women. It has also created a unique training session for people who want to set up their own small businesses."

Not good enough? Many women in the Church already handle more responsibility—spiritual and managerial—than almost any priest or bishop except, perhaps, the Pope himself. Let me quote again from *The Nuns*:

> Mothers generally shoulder immense responsibilities. Some of them govern the lives of thousands of women. Mother Mary Aquinas Lee is a perfect example. For many years she has been mother general of the Good Shepherd Sisters. She is a woman of wide culture who speaks several languages. She needs to—the congregation has 475 centers in five countries. She has responsibility for ten thousand sisters, as well as thousands of women—delinquent girls, unmarried mothers, state prisoners—in their care."

Not good enough? How could that possibly be true when the roll call of Catholic women today include such names as Madonna Kolbenschlag, Mary Collins, Mary Catherine Hilkert, Rita Burns, Fran Ferder, Camille D'Arienzo, Mary Milliagan, Joan Chittister, Rachel Conrad Wahlberg, Mary Jo Weaver, Rosemary Radford Ruether, Elisabeth Schüssler Fiorenza, Arlene Anderson, Dianne Bergant, Barbara Ferraro, Patricia Hussey, Claire Lindegren Lerman, Anne E. Patrick, Sandra M. Schneiders, Margaret A. Farley, Anne Brotherton, Lisa Sowle Cahill, Kay Ashe, Monika K. Hellwig, Sister M. Teresa Kane, and a whole army of other women from all walks of life? I would pit the Catholic skills of these women against those of any priest or cardinal or bishop, foreign or domestic.

Oh yes, women are good enough. There is no biological reason for their exclusion from the priesthood. I have heard it said by some members of the clergy that women should not be priests because they do not have the "image of God." These men can only envision God as a man. This is not a problem for most of the Catholic Church. Certainly, it is not a problem for me. Perhaps because of the extraordinary impression made on me by the women in my family and the sisters of St. Joseph in Erie. Pennsylvania, my personal definition of God is a *brilliant, sensitive, inquisitive woman with a sense of humor*. But this choice of image is personal and so is the one selected by the male hierarchy of the Church. In truth, God is neither man nor woman, but rather an intangible spirituality existing beyond the twilight of infinity. Spirituality is synonymous with equality.

It is incomprehensible to me that a woman can be the mother of God and at the same time be denied ordination into the priesthood of the Church. The reason for this denial is not biological or theological. It is pathological. The male hierarchy is fearful of losing power. How is this fear to be overcome?

First, women in the Church, both lay and religious, must themselves be convinced of their equality with men. A young nun comments, "The Church has conditioned women to be subordinate to their husbands, and religious women are never allowed to forget they're living in a man's world. We are dutiful and follow. But we should be pathfinders; we should be prophetesses."

A French superior general admitted sadly, "If I tell my nuns that I share a certain view, this view carries some weight. But it carries ten times more if I say that it is shared by a *père jesuite*."

Catholic women must become convinced of their own equality and be ready to fight for it. "Until sisters get involved in their own liberation," says Sister Ethne Kennedy, former chairperson of the National Assembly of Women Religious, "there is not much hope of it happening. We've been locked into this monastical society in which men do the decision-making."

Some feminists suspect a kind of masochism in their own or other women's continued defense of a Church that continually marginalizes and insults them. As Mary Jo Weaver, author of a recent book on contemporary Catholic feminism, has put it, "We need to know that the Catholic hierarchy doesn't want us, has never wanted us and never will want us. What is it then that we want when we continue to hang around an institution that they govern?"

The only intelligent answer is that women hang around because they want to change the rules, they want to get the vote and win the equality they deserve. Only if Catholic women face this fact and decide they are ready and willing to fight—and to accept the possible consequences of a battle—is there hope they can force the changes needed. I can speak for more than half of Catholic men in saying that you will have our total support in bringing about this equality that is long overdue.

The organizations—the National Assembly of Women Religious, the National Coalition of American Nuns, the National Council of Catholic Women—are very important, but what is needed is the full thrust of the vast majority of *all* Catholic women, united in the demand for the end of second-class citizenship. Women must reject their usual pray-and-pay-and-obey role. They must make their opinions known, by conversation in their churches and by their power at the collection basket. In the same way that they once donated wooden nickels to protest the collections for diocesan seminaries, which train only men to be priests, women must show by paucity at the plate that it is time for an end to more than nineteen hundred years of discrimination and degradation.

THE BISHOPS' LETTER ON WOMEN

On Thursday, November 19, 1992, the *New York Times* reported that the Catholic bishops in the U.S. rejected the policy letter on the role of women.

Over the past nine years the nation's Roman Catholic bishops have been trying to draft and approve the pastoral letter about the role of women in the Church and in American society. Four drafts of the letter were prepared, as a committee of bishops struggled to reach closer compliance with Vatican teachings.

Although the issue of ordaining women to the priesthood played a central role in the letter, changes in the draft also reflected the way the committee handled the question of opening other ministerial offices to women, ranging from the ordained office of deacon to that of acolyte or altar server.

As a practicing Catholic, my evaluation is that starting in 1988 the bishops decided that the critical mass of brilliant women should be allowed to participate in all the clerical ministries that do not require ordination. Obviously the long arm reaching from the Vatican in 1990, early in 1992, and now in the fall of 1992 has had its effect. The bishops have felt the power of Rome and have chosen to stay as bishops with the hope that they will someday be eligible to become a pope rather than to vote their conscience on the importance of women in the Church and run the risk of being forced into early retirement.

They are not unmindful that a number of dissenting theologians have felt the sting of the papal whip. These theologians have been accused of sowing confusion among the faithful and of using the media to set up a countermagisterium. The Vatican showed its power in December 1979 when it censored Hans Küng after a lengthy but very secretive investigation. The widely read and popular Swiss theologian was disqualified from teaching theology in the name of the Church. If this can happen to a great theologian with one of the best minds since the time of Thomas Aquinas, imagine what could be done to a poor bishop who has never written a document and is not known outside of his small area.

When I read the articles in the *New York Times*, I thought of Joan Chittister, who stated, "If you are a woman, there is very little in the Catholic world that is new for women. Except talk, of course. There is a great deal of new talk. For instance, everyone is talking about women being 'different but equal' and everyone is surely sincere. Most women and probably all men in the Catholic Church accept women as different. It is simply difficult to find much proof of equality."

She also states that the Church is certainly male. Those areas accepted as female—service positions and volunteer projects—are underpaid and undervalued. There is indeed a lot of talk, and unfortunately very little is actually done.

The male hierarchy and particularly in this instance the bishops should be made aware that women are probably the most important catalyst in the change that is taking place, because they have discovered the "Great Lie" about the spirituality that has shaped our world. They are in the process of revealing an authentic, life-giving spirituality brought forth from their own experience. Women are creating a "new wisdom" literature.

In the 1975 Vatican declaration against women's ordination, there was an effort to abandon the historic connection between a patriarchal social order and the denial of ordination to women. The declaration is filled with sweet sounding words that says the gospel promotes equality between sexes and implies that the Church has always promoted women's equality in society.

It is filled with half truths and there is a flat denial of the actual historical tradition of the Catholic Church toward women. They are trying to justify exclusion of women from priesthood because it is related to a Christological mystery. It is said that there must be a physical resemblance between the priest and Christ. Needless to say, this physical resemblance is not extended to Semitic facial features. It is maleness that is regarded as the sacramental matter that makes the priestlike Christ.

As a practicing male Catholic I am ashamed when I realize that working behind the sacramentalizing of maleness lies the Thomistic-Aristotelian anthropology which held the belief that women were imperfect humans and hence could not represent perfect or normative human nature. In order for Christ to represent the fully human he must be male. The male hierarchy that can accept this are either totally misinformed, stupid, or have a pathologic bias and hatred of women. They could prove me wrong by accepting the inevitable and in our lifetime welcome the ordination of women.

The tally, taken by secret written ballot, fell fifty-three votes short of the two-thirds majority of the active hierarchy necessary to approve a pastoral letter. However, voting against the rejection were 110 bishops. This gives all thinking Catholics hope that right will someday overcome might. It is obvious that there is not a unanimous opinion among bishops to prohibit ordination of women.

Archbishop Rembert G. Weakland, of Milwaukee, challenged the reference in the pastoral letter to traditional teachings, noting that the traditional reasons given for nonordination of women, the ones that were consistently taught in our history, centered on the inferiority of women. He indicated that the contemporary reasons given in the letter—that to symbolically represent Christ and his spousal relationship with the Church, priests must be males—are more recent and not yet tested and also not convincing to our population. Although Archbishop Weakland has experienced the sting and retaliation of the Church, he is gaining in stature as a man of principle.

I was saddened but amused when I read that Auxiliary Bishop Austin B. Vaughn, of New York City, argued that the Church's bar against ordaining women was "infallible" and "unchangeable."

He declared, "In the year 2000, 20,000, or 2 million, there will still be a Catholic Church and it will still have an all-male clergy. A woman priest is as impossible as for me to have a baby."

Fortunately, he can't have a baby, but if he had, retribution and justice would be done and he would probably have a misbegotten male, which is the designation that earlier theologians gave to women and he obviously supports. I, like so many of the women and men in the Church, can forgive the auxiliary bishop for the statement he made. He undoubtedly hopes to become a bishop and therefore it was his voice but the ideas were those of John Cardinal O'Connor.

The rejection of the policy letter on the role of women merely represents the patriarchal domination and a sexual repression that is pathologic in Catholic Christianity. Some think it is incurable but I have faith in the power of Catholic women, both in religious life as well as lay women, in meeting this challenge.

John Paul II by his personal misogyny has created a loss of ethical credibility of the Church for women as well as men supporting the proposed new role for women in the Church. Women in their rebellion have expressed the feeling that they have to reject God because they cannot differentiate God from the institutional Church and the patriarchal culture imagery for God. It is all directed to the male and it is obvious that it makes women subordinate to male dominance. Women must know that someday they will not only survive but also prevail in the Catholic Church. I draw to their attention that the Vatican as well as American bishops opposed women's suffrage in the early decades of the Church and now women's votes control elections.

By the Catholic bishops' rejection of the policy letter on the role of women, they have rekindled what some feminists suspect is a kind of masochism on their own and other women's continued defense of remaining in a Church which continually marginalizes and insults them. However, other churches have ordained women and have changed and I am sure that the Catholic Church, like the Anglican Church, will soon ordain women. The Catholic and Anglican churches have been working toward a reconciliation in an ecumenical spirit after 458 years of separation. It is obvious that the acceptance of women by the Anglican Church and the rejection of women for ordination by the Catholic Church will adversely affect these efforts.

The Vatican has vowed that Catholicism will never accept women for ordination. The decision by the Anglican Church sealed the fate of a twenty-two-year effort to undo King Henry VIII's legacy and reunite the Anglican and Catholic churches.

"The problem of the admission of women to the ministerial priesthood," declared a Vatican spokesman, in a November 1992 issue of *Time* magazine, "touches the very nature of the sacrament of priestly orders. The decision by the Anglican Communion constitutes a new and grave obstacle to the entire process of reconciliation."

I hope that the opinions expressed by Mary Jo Weaver will change as the Church changes. However, Mary Jo Weaver, author of a recent book on contemporary Catholic feminism, has stated, "We need to know that the Catholic hierarchy doesn't want us, has never wanted us, and never will want us. What is it then that we want when we continue to hang around an institution that they govern?"

She has justification for her statement; however, I would like to quote that there is some hope for change. The hope is expressed in the aforementioned tally that fell short of the two-thirds majority needed to approve a pastoral letter. The message rings loud and clear that we Catholics need and want women not only as members of the Church but also as leaders of the Church and as ordained women.

Not only must the language of the Church be changed, so must the attitudes this language represents. Not only must the male terminology be eliminated in favor of universalism or equivalence of address, so must the male chauvinism that makes all seven sacraments possible for men, but only six for women, who are barred from Holy Orders.

"Women," says Hans Küng, "should have at least that dignity, freedom and responsibility in the Church which they are guaranteed in modern society: equal rights in canon law, in the Church's decision-making bodies, and also practical opportunities of studying theology and being ordained."

Pope John Paul II has not listened to the hopes, later the entreaties, of the critical mass of the Catholic Church which is its women. Hopefully, he will listen to the prayers and warnings of a grass roots Catholic layman such as me. Holy Father, you must know that the Thomastic-Aristotelian anthropology which believed that women were imperfect humans and hence could not represent perfect or normative human nature has been disproved. Do not let this masculinist theology which threatens to exclude women from ordination, and possibly redemption, happen. Your guidance to change this will place you on a pedestal as one of the great, if not the greatest, popes. You must know that, if women cannot represent Christ, then it is debatable whether Christ represents them.

Unless there is a change, the Church cannot represent a new humanity in Christ, in which there is neither male nor female, but all are one in Christ. Unless there is a change, the patriarchal clericalism will result in the final denial in the universal claims of the gospel. The exclusion of women from the priesthood is related to a Christological mystery. Since the 1975 Vatican Declaration against women's ordination is an arbitrary decision, change it so that it is not compounded by the sin of "self-perpetuating." It would be a tragedy if women formed a Women's Church. Forming a new church will not reform the church.

It has been said that to be born a woman is not destiny but fate. What women make of it is destiny. Pope John XXIII in *pacem in terris* states clearly, "Those that discover that they have rights have the responsibility to claim them." Women united around the world stand ready to accept this challenge.

It is not only women's rights that are at stake here. It is the soul of the Church itself. With better than 50 percent of its membership ignored and deprived, the Church is in deep spiritual difficulty. If it is going to be saved, the truth must be acknowledged. She who cleans the altar is worthy to serve upon it.

S I X

Abortion

I t is the Church's stand on birth control that makes its position on abortion so untenable. This is not the case with Protestants. In asking the world to stop abortion, they accept the use of the pill as a far better method of birth control than abortion. But not Catholics. Pope John Paul II flies around the world, visiting places like Africa and Mexico where the population explosion threatens the lives of millions with starvation or pestilence. At the same time, the Pope's denunciation of abortion is matched by an equally forceful denunciation of birth control—like someone inveighing against the number of deaths caused by automobiles while simultaneously insisting that people drive without brakes.

Consider the number of unwanted pregnancies that could be avoided by the increased use of birth control. An estimated 90 percent of U.S. women of childbearing age use some form of birth control. Only 10 percent do not, but they account for half of the 1.6 million abortions performed in this nation each year. So the 10 percent of women *not* using some form of birth control account for 50 percent of abortions. Yet the Pope continues to denounce *birth control* as loudly as *abortion*.

The problem of abortion is difficult enough without the Pope making it more so. Consider some of the major questions: What are the rights of a pregnant woman? What are the rights of the unborn? When does life begin? When does the fetus have a soul? Are two "natural deaths" better than one "murder"? These are age-old questions and there are no easy answers—except for the extremists on either side.

If you are certain that a woman deserves total control over her

[68]

body and that no one should be able to tell her what she can or cannot do with that body, then the answers are all easy. Or if you are certain that life and soul are infused from the moment there is conception and no one must ever do anything to negatively affect that conception, no matter what the extenuating circumstances might be, then the answers are easy. But for many millions, the proper legal and moral position lies somewhere in between these two outer poles, and that makes the subject extraordinarily complex.

Although I take a much more liberal view of the subject than I did ten or fifteen years ago, I still have great reservations about the indiscriminate use of abortion. I have never performed an abortion and hope never to do so, but moments of deep consideration of this problem have led me to an understanding of both sides—of pro-choice and pro-life activists. Both sides are sincere in their beliefs but remain totally divided because there is no common definition or common language for starting a dialogue.

Look where this has led us. No other nation in the world is as divided as the United States over abortion. Here, organizations, including the Catholic Church, spend more funds to affect the legal status of abortion than they contribute to saving starving children around the world. Here, voters often select or reject a potential legislator strictly by the candidate's position on abortion, without regard to whether or not he or she is the best candidate for the job. It is a triumph of emotion over reason.

What is it that has caused us to place so much emphasis on the abortion issue in this nation? What can be done to calm the troubled waters; to bring voters back to choosing a candidate based on job qualifications rather than a single issue, more religious than political; to divert funds now spent on this issue to more meaningful needs here and around the world?

HISTORY—B.C.

Induced abortion has been one of the principal means of population control used by the human race throughout known history. First recorded in the Royal Archives of China, "prescriptions" for abortion date back some five thousand years, including such dangerous suggestions as having the pregnant woman belly flop into the sea from a high cliff. (On a small Caribbean island, yanking out a back tooth was supposed to induce an abortion. As a result, a man checking up on a prospective wife would look into her mouth to see how many abortions she had had.)

Records indicate that abortions were induced in Egypt as far back as 1900 B.C., and in the Roman Empire abortion was frequent and widespread. The poets Ovid and Juvenal, as well as the dramatist Seneca, all recorded the use of abortion and Rome's natural historian Pliny the Elder listed prescriptions for drugs that would accomplish it. Roman law not only allowed abortion, it posed no criminal penalty for the abandonment of a child and even permitted infanticide. Many years earlier, the citizens of Sparta had taken deformed infants or those who appeared unusually puny and left them on the mountainside to die of the elements.

Despite the frequency with which abortion was practiced in ancient times, there were many who gave consideration to the rights of the unborn. For example, the Stoics (300 B.C.) believed the embryo had some of the rights of an already born child, but they held these rights to be of a different moral order and believed that to end their existence by abortion was not tantamount to murder. The Pythagoreans (500 B.C.) went further. Feeling that abortion was wrong because the embryo was the "moral equivalent" of the child it would one day become, they condemned abortion at any stage.

HISTORY—A.D.

So far as we know, abortion was not mentioned by Christ. It was ignored in the most central Judeo-Christian writings. It was not mentioned in the Jewish Mishnah or Talmud or in the Old and New Testaments. It is a matter of record, however, that abortion was denounced by the Apostles and by early Christian writers such as Tertullian (second century), Clement of Alexandra (third century), and St. Basil (fourth century). Abortion was placed on the same level of malice as infanticide. The Church has denounced abortion since early times and has stated, "You shall not procure an abortion. You shall not destroy a child." Thus, abortion was classified as a violation of the Sixth Commandment, "Thou shall not kill."

It should be recognized, however, that in the early days of the Church, the legal and moral treatment of those who committed or procured abortion was never consistent with the rhetoric, and the attention given to abortion in those early years was minuscule compared to the attention it is receiving today. For example, early Church councils, such as those of Elvira about 306, which was called to specify the legal groundwork for Christian communities, outlined penalties only for those women who committed abortion *after* a sexual crime, such as adultery or prostitution.

More important, from the third century onward, Christian thought was divided as to whether early abortion—abortion of the unformed embryo—was in fact murder. Different sources of Church teachings and law simply could not agree on whether early abortion was wrong and, if so, what the penalties should be. As the Christian era began in the Roman Empire, the legal regulation of abortion existed not to protect the rights of the embryos but to protect the rights of the fathers.

At the beginning of the twelfth century, Ivo of Chartres, a prominent Church scholar, condemned the practice of abortion, but held that abortion of the "unformed embryo" was not homicide. Ivo believed that only when the fetus was "formed" did it acquire a soul, a process called hominization, and he believed that the journey of the soul to the fetus did not occur until forty days after conception for a male fetus and eighty days for a female fetus. Ivo's work became the beginning of a consensus.

Fifty years later, Gratian, the Benedictine who compiled and distilled canon law of the Middle Ages, agreed with Ivo's stand on abortion, and Gratian's work became the basis of canon law for the next seven hundred years. This meant that until the nineteenth century, Catholic moral theology and canon law—which were, in effect, the moral and legal standards for the Western world until the coming of the Reformation and secular courts—did *not* treat what we now call first-trimester abortions as murder.

Lasting change in this position did not occur in the Church until 1864, when the theologian Jean Gury suggested that hominization was an irrelevant basis for abortion. Gury went back in time to the belief held by the Pythagoreans and decided that all abortions, regardless of stage, involved a potential human being and hence were immoral. Gury's belief quickly gained support, and in 1869 Pope Pius IX published *Apostolicae Sedis* in which he abandoned the distinction between the animate and inanimate embryo and stipulated excommunication as the penalty for anyone who successfully procured an abortion, even a therapeutic one, at any stage of development.

Between 1884 and 1902, the Church's Congregation of the Inquisition (now the Congregation for the Doctrine of the Faith) specifically addressed a number of issues surrounding therapeutic abortion. In 1884 it held that a craniotomy (crushing the fetus's skull to end a very difficult labor) was not permissible. In 1889 any operation that directly killed the embryo or fetus was outlawed, and in 1902 the congregation forbade even surgery for the removal of an ectopic pregnancy, where the fertilized egg implants in a fallopian tube instead of the uterus and, without sufficient room for expansion, the fetus almost always causes the woman's death.

Today, of course, the Church does allow abortion for ectopic pregnancies. I have often wondered why, during those years it was forbidden, Catholic women did not rise up en masse against the Church. It was probably due partly to fear and a deep reverence for the teachings of the Catholic Church that they did not react more aggressively and violently.

The Church's tightening of the laws concerning abortion continued from the late nineteenth century until the present day, but this action by the Church had little effect on life or death for the unborn. Abortion "doctors" flourished and abortion "remedies" proliferated. Tens of thousands of newborns were destroyed every year by exposure, by drowning, or otherwise. The waters of the Thames, the Seine, and the Yangtze River carried them off by the scores every night of the year, and there are reports that infanticide continues even now in some Third World countries.

Today, abortion is legal in almost all the nations of the world. In the Scandinavian countries, in Japan, in the former Soviet Union and its satellites, abortion performed by qualified doctors is substantially unrestricted except that it usually must be performed within the first three months of pregnancy, the safest period. In Britain, abortion is legal if two doctors agree that there is risk to the mother's life or injury to her physical and mental health or that of her children or that the fetus has serious abnormalities.

In the United States, abortion is legally allowed almost everywhere, either by specific legislation or by judicial construction. In the 1973 decision in *Roe* v. *Wade*, the Supreme Court ruled that abortion cannot be denied during the first six months of pregnancy. Even so, the controversy continues in this country, advocates and opponents operating at a fever pitch unmatched anywhere else in the world. Why? Unfortunately, there are no easy answers. The hysterical approach by each side has made it almost impossible to have an intelligent and productive discussion.

U.S. History

The view that abortion is murder is a relatively recent belief in this nation. It may surprise those not well acquainted with American history to learn that abortion was as prevalent at certain times in the nineteenth century as it is today. Early laws in America followed the Anglo-Saxon tradition of English common law. There, based on cases in 1327 and 1348, courts established the right of a woman to terminate a pregnancy at any time. This right was confirmed in 1670 when an English judge ruled that if a woman died as a result of an abortion, the abortionist was guilty of murder, but if she did not die, the abortion was legal.

It was not until 1803 that the first restrictive abortion statute was passed in England. This was the Lord Ellenborough Act, which made it a crime to have an abortion after "quickening," about mid-term of pregnancy when the fetus's feet move in the womb. In 1812 the first abortion case was heard by the Massachusetts Supreme Court, which followed the Lord Ellenborough Act in ruling that abortion with the woman's consent was legal before quickening.

1850–1950

Between 1850 and the turn of the century, several elements converged to produce a marked change in the abortion laws. First, there was this nation's shift from agriculture to industry. As the population moved from rural areas to cities, the commercial value of the large family disappeared. Children became a heavy financial burden, and more and more women turned to abortion as a method of birth control. The number of abortions increased dramatically.

Vast numbers of these abortions, even though they were legal, were performed by untrained men and women whose methods were often deadly for the pregnant women. In those days, prior to the advent of antibiotics and decent anesthetics, even in the best hands abortions were extremely dangerous, one of the leading causes of death among women of childbearing age. When death was not the result, many of the women suffered crippling disabilities for the rest of their lives.

Doctors believed that women seeking abortions should be treated by the best-trained professionals available, that lay abortions should be eliminated. To accomplish this objective, they decided to try to make induced abortion illegal except when the woman's life was in danger, a decision only a licensed physician could make.

The American Medical Association had just been formed (1847) and now members of the AMA began to lobby their state legislatures to make abortion illegal. In response, the states began passing anti-abortion laws that would eventually close down the enormously successful "abortion factories" like that of New York's infamous Madame Restell. She was born Caroline Trow and called herself a female physician. She performed abortions without interference from her mansion at Fifth Avenue and Fifty-second Street from 1838 until Anthony Comstock had her arrested and closed her practice in 1878. By 1900 every state in the union had a law forbidding the use of drugs or instruments to induce abortion at any stage of pregnancy unless the procedure was necessary to save the woman's life.

Another factor during this period was the "Catholic influence." This was not the influence of the Catholic Church on lawmakers, but rather the influence that resulted from Protestant feelings *against* Catholics. The great number of abortions sought by Protestant women plus their increasing use of birth control (*Moral Philosophy* by Robert Dale Owen, describing existing methods of birth control, was published in New York in 1831) led many Protestant leaders to worry that Catholics would, as suggested by Bernard Sinclair in *Crowning Sin of the Age*, soon "overrun the country." It was in response to this fear that Congress in 1873 passed the Federal Comstock Law (signed by President Ulysses S. Grant on March 6, 1873), designed to make it more difficult for Protestant women to obtain information on abortion and birth control. Anthony Comstock was a special agent for the New York Society for the Suppression of Vice. He and his allies waged open war on everything from pornography to abortion.

Prior to the Comstock Law, family newspapers carried discreet advertisements about where women could get private treatment for "menstrual blockage," which was a euphemism for an induced abortion. But the Comstock Law prohibited sending through the mail information or equipment for either abortion or contraception. This federal law prevented lay abortionists from advertising, and most state laws made induced abortions performed by a nonphysician a criminal act.

1950 to the Present

By 1950 physicians in the United States were once again beginning to change their position on abortion. Despite the federal and state laws, thousands of women still managed to obtain illegal abortions in "back alleys," and with the practice having gone further underground, the "quality" was even worse. Abortions remained one of the leading causes of maternal death and shocking numbers of women who did not die suffered lifelong complications.

Meanwhile, legal abortions became safer than ever due to the advent of antiseptic surgery, antibiotics, and new abortion techniques. In addition, many doctors were disturbed by the number of therapeutic abortions they were not allowed to perform. Although life-saving abortions had remained legal in most states, hospitals continued to restrict the number that could be performed each month. There were also doctors willing to do abortions for reasons they considered valid, but which were not allowed by law—reasons such as ending a pregnancy that was a result of rape or incest or pregnancies that were not a threat to a woman's life but were nonetheless a threat to her physical or emotional health. The laws also did not allow a physician to abort a woman carrying a deformed fetus.

For all these reasons, there was a growing campaign within the American Medical Association to convince state legislatures that abortion laws should be liberalized. In 1957 the American Law Institute joined the battle, recommending that the criteria for legal abortion be extended to include the mental health of the mother, pregnancy due to rape or incest, and fetal deformity.

By 1967, three new abortion laws were passed in Colorado, North Carolina, and California. They were modest steps that broadened the indications for abortion from saving life to preserving health, with approval required by hospital committees. Interestingly, in California, Governor Ronald Reagan signed the bill into law.

Despite such pressures from both doctors and lawyers, the first significant change did not occur until 1964, when the Supreme Court ruling in *Griswold v. Connecticut* virtually repealed the 1873 Comstock Law, stating that a married couple was entitled to the right of privacy and should be guaranteed protection from government intrusion in matters as personal as contraception. In 1972 this right of privacy regarding contraception was extended to single people in the Supreme Court ruling in *Eisenstadt v. Bond*.

Neither of these decisions produced a great stir, but one year later, when the Supreme Court legalized abortion in *Roe v. Wade*, there was a great outcry. Despite the fact that abortion and contraception were combined in the Comstock Law, people do not tend to view them in the same way. Long before 1964, the use of birth control methods, such as condoms or pills, was an accepted fact for the American public. Thus, the *Griswold v. Connecticut* decision or that in *Eisenstadt v. Bond* did little more than help to legalize an already accepted practice. *Griswold v. Connecticut* neatly addressed privacy rather than birth control directly.

This was not true for *Roe v. Wade*. At the time of this 1973 decision, few states had legalized abortion on demand. For the most part, people had never been forced to take sides on this subject. Until 1973 it had been a legal and medical issue, controlled by the courts and doctors. Now suddenly it was a matter that could be controlled by *people*; by the pregnant woman herself.

For the first time in this nation's history, the highest court had ruled in effect that any embryo during at least the first six months of pregnancy was *not* a person. Groups of people who had never been involved with the pro-life cause saw this as a decision with far-reaching consequences, and they joined the battle. Members and resources for pro-life causes mushroomed. For example, before *Roe v. Wade*, most major cities in California had only one pro-life organization or political group and one service-and-education group, but today most major cities have several and most suburban areas have their own.

In the 1960s the antiabortion movement was largely elite, male, and Catholic, unable to present demonstrations of any massive support for its cause—the kind that characterized the pro-choice movement. But after the 1973 Supreme Court decision, millions of new pro-life advocates joined the cause and soon began to phase out the old activists. The new groups were far more vocal and aggressive.

As the ranks of the pro-life organizations increased, so did those of the pro-choice. Eventually not one but *two* issues emerged: the status of the fetus and the status of women in American society. The duality of this argument has made it personal and emotionally charged for women in America. The argument includes not only attitudes about sanctity of life, but also about the place women should occupy in society and the proper structure of the family.

In effect, the right-to-life movement is an attempt to form a moral cartel to use state power to define the social role of women. It seeks not only to protect the fetus, but also to ensure that the family, as opposed to careers for women, has the highest priority. It is also an attempt to give to women whose work involves the home the same prestige and status as career women. The right-to-life movement, then, may be interpreted as a subtle means to put the power of the state behind moral positions.

No wonder that the rhetoric in the pro-life–pro-choice battle is often so loud and feverish, often generating far more heat than light, more confusion that direction. The reason is profoundly significant. While the two groups appear to be arguing over the future rights of unborn children, they are actually arguing over the future rights of women.

ANOTHER OPINION

My own opposition to abortion stems not only from the Church, but also from a source that predates Christianity by some four hundred years. Hippocrates (460–377 B.C.), the "father of medicine" and the most famous of the Greek physicians, taught the sanctity of human life at whatever stage and in the Hippocratic Collection of writings attributed to him specifically admonished physicians not to induce abortions, requiring them to bind themselves by oath not to give women drinks fatal to life in the womb.

It seems to me that a doctor should encourage not discourage life, and while I am more willing to accept legitimate reasons for abortion now, especially when the woman's life is threatened, I continue to oppose the tendency of some physicians who too readily find therapeutic value in abortion. My most serious reservations concern abortion on demand because women are encouraged to treat the procedure as simply a form of birth control. Education and the acceptance of contraception would eliminate to a great extent the number of abortions.

It may be desirable to pass legislation that could improve the acceptance of abortion clinics. Perhaps "a waiting period" would permit the woman to carefully explore the pros and cons of abortion before exercising her right for pro-choice. Women seeking repeated abortions should be counseled and offered an option for a birth control method that would be safer than future abortions. Guarding the physical and psychological health of the woman is the height of professional integrity.

The abortion issue will remain a divisive and emotional issue for years to come. However, I do not believe we will ever return to the days when abortion was illegal in this nation.

First of all, it is highly unlikely that the state abortion laws and the Federal Comstock Law could have been enacted without the support of the medical profession. That support arose primarily because of the life-threatening nature of the abortion procedures. In the last century, all methods of terminating a pregnancy posed a serious threat to the woman's life. Any surgery, including abortion, brought with it three chances in eight that the patient would die.

Today, the situation is markedly different. An early abortion offers less risk than a tonsillectomy. In fact, there is less risk in aborting a pregnancy in the early months than there is in bearing children. Thus, it is highly unlikely that the AMA would ever again support the antiabortion forces.

Second, despite all the arguments mounted by the pro-life forces, it will never be possible to prove "scientifically" that the aborting of a fetus is equivalent to the killing of a human being outside the womb. Is there "life" at the moment of conception? Is the fetus a "person"? A human being? While discussion of such questions might help to change the mind of those considering abortion, such arguments cannot make abortion the equivalent of murder.

For example, due to the proliferation of life support systems in our hospitals, it is the state of the brain, not the heart, that most often decides the legal questions. "Brain dead" has become the legal rationale for removing a human being from life support systems. If this ruling were to be applied to the unborn, abortion before eight weeks would certainly be legal because measurement of brain waves indicates no life in the fetus before eight weeks.

Even for the Church, allowing abortion prior to the eighth week would be more in keeping with the Church's great theologians, such as Thomas Aquinas. He did not believe, as does the Church now, that a single fertilized ovum was the moral equivalent of a human being. Following the traditions of Aristotle, Aquinas maintained that the soul was not infused into the fetus until some forty to eighty days after conception.

He based this concept on his biological beliefs, which are now outmoded, as well as on philosophical views. Aquinas accepted the theory of hylomorphism where a reciprocal causality occurs between matter and form, so that form cannot be received into matter that is not capable of receiving it.

For example, a tabletop cannot receive the form of a human soul because the matter is not disposed to receive it. The argument continues that in the very beginning, the conceptus is not capable of receiving a human form that is the soul. Only after some time is the matter disposed to receive the soul.

Obviously, this argument is no more susceptible to proof than any of the more familiar beliefs. But the position of Thomas Aquinas and other great theologians of the Middle Ages is far more in keeping with Church history than the views held now. Therapeutic abortion in the first trimester had been allowed or accepted for nearly all of the nineteen hundred years after Christ until Jean Gury suggested the change in 1864. In America, early abortion was accepted, as it was in England, throughout history except for the hundred-year period (1850 to 1950) when the medical profession and religious fundamentalists combined to outlaw the process.

We cannot realistically expect any lasting change in the legal status of abortion in this country. Perhaps more important, even if the law could be changed, it would have no significant effect on the number of abortions performed except among the very poor. Unfortunately, such legislation would greatly increase the loss of life among pregnant women who would be forced to seek illegal means of abortion. Having taken medical histories of many thousands of women over the past thirty-five years, I have an appreciation of the number of abortions performed prior to and since *Roe v. Wade*. While there is little difference in the number of abortions, there is less morbidity and mortality connected with this procedure since the Supreme Court declared abortions to be legal. Unless there is some cataclysmic disaster, safe abortions done by legitimate physicians will remain a way of life in the vast majority of states in this nation.

Should the Church change its position? In a recent study reported by George Gallup, Jr., and Jim Castelli in *The American People*, 47 percent of the Catholics participating rejected the statement, "The Catholic Church should relax its standards forbidding all abortions under any circumstances." However, among Catholics under thirty, 49 percent supported a change while 42 percent were opposed.

Catholic women look at abortion from two points of view—as a life issue and as a sex issue. Although in general they disapprove of abortion, they believe a woman should have the right to make her own decision.

It seems to me that this is the path the Church should follow. After all, there is no question of infallibility involved here, and the uncertainty of the issue is clearly demonstrated by the fact that early abortion was an option for Catholics until little more than a hundred years ago. Strong theological dissent still continues. Thus, although the Church has every right to continue its position of forbidding all direct abortions, the time has come to accept the rights of women, who should be guided by their conscience in making their decision. If the most brilliant theologians, philosophers, and statesmen cannot identify whether a soul is present or not, how is the average layperson expected to make a decision on this much-debated problem?

In Catholic morality, abortion is either direct (that is, induced) or indirect ("natural"). Direct abortion is any destruction of the product of human conception, whether before or after implantation in the womb. A direct abortion is intended as either an end in itself or as a means to an end. As a willful attack on an unborn human life, no matter what the motives, direct abortion is considered a grave evil in the eyes of the Church.

Indirect abortion is the foreseen, but permitted, evacuation of a fetus that cannot survive outside the womb. The evacuation is not the intended or directly willed result, but the side effect of some legitimate procedure such as the removal of a uterus (womb) complicated by a pregnancy, and as such is morally allowable. Therefore, the Catholic prohibition against terminating the life of a fetus is not absolute.

According to Catholic moral theory, under some circumstances ectopic pregnancies or removal of a severely diseased uterus are licit and de facto will lead to the death of the fetus. Such termination of pregnancy is justified in light of the moral "principle of double effect": an operation with two results, one good and one bad, with the bad result not flowing from the good one. Of course, once one has conceded the possibility that there are certain kinds of Catholic abortion, one has acknowledged that the issue is a great deal more complicated than simply a fetus's right to life.

There are few if any Catholic theologians who are ready to defend abortion, but some Catholic women activists, not excluding nuns, have campaigned for a woman's right to make her own decision about abortion on the grounds that every woman has a right to make a decision of her own.

The Church should teach Catholic women and have a dialogue with them about the sanctity of life and even admonish them against inducing abortion. However, the Church should recognize that ultimately the choice must rest with the pregnant woman and there should be no punishment or guilt attached to this decision.

The absurdity of demanding dismissal or excommunication for those who subscribe to abortion became clear in 1984. The issue centered around the candidacy and national election campaign of a Catholic woman, Geraldine Ferraro, seeking the office of Vice President of the United States. When pro-life advocates began to campaign against Ferraro because she supported the law of the land (*Roe v. Wade*) rather than the Catholic position, an ad appeared in the *New York Times* defending the right of Catholics to differ on public policy. The ad called attention to the diversity of opinion in the Catholic community on certain noninfallible moral teachings of the Church, such as abortion. Along with many other prominent Catholics, the ad was signed by four priests and brothers and twenty-six nuns.

The ad drew an unprecedented response from the Vatican. All members of the cloth who signed it were threatened with dismissal if they did not recant. Within a month after the announcement, the four priests and brothers had publicly retracted or "clarified" their positions.

But not the nuns. On the contrary, thousands of other nuns around the world closed ranks and supported these twenty-six signers. The Vatican then began a witch-hunt to ferret out any nuns or sisters in the United States who supported the twenty-six signers and thus "opposed the Vatican."

This entire episode served only to make the Church look foolish and to reinforce the feeling that the male hierarchy is sexist, seeking to keep women oppressed. This conclusion is obvious in view of the Church's continued stance on birth control. The Vatican's double denial—birth control and abortion—leaves women with no choices in the matter of sex and pregnancy. The question has been raised whether this position carries the connotation—and I accept it—that celibate males in the Catholic Church are punishing women for their sexuality.

Instead of recognizing that the majority of all Americans and the overwhelming majority of American women demand the right of choice concerning their own bodies, the Church insists on using more desperate measures to turn support against free choice by women. Throughout the United States, liberal Catholic bishops are constantly being replaced by conservative men who will actively join the legal struggle against abortion. Worse, the Church joins hands with fundamentalist organizations, many of which have such questionable credentials on other subjects that intelligent Americans, Catholic or otherwise, would be ashamed of the association. Working with such groups, Catholics are offering both time and money to help elect candidates who very often have little or no qualifications for the job except that they promise to support antiabortion legislation.

In the article "Virtue, Providence and the Endangered Self: Some Religious Dimensions of the Abortion Debate," from her book *Abortion and Catholicism: The American Debate*, Anne E. Patrick writes:

> My interest in this symbolism of the abortion debate stems from a general concern for the well-being of women and girls and from a specific concern about the way Catholic energies and resources have been used in the last twenty years to fight what seems to be the wrong battle. To be more precise, I am troubled by the Catholic voters who have been manipulated into voting on a single issue—the anti-abortion issue— manipulated into voting for candidates whose positions on many matters are quite opposed to Catholic principles of social justice. The question I want to explore is why so many Catholics are vulnerable to this sort of manipulation. My supposition is that certain religious symbols contribute to this vulnerability and that reinterpretation of some central beliefs is necessary if Catholics generally are to move to a stronger, more consistent position on public policy questions related to social justice.

Of course, the Catholic Church is not the only institution deeply involved in the abortion issue. So are the Southern Baptist church and the Mormon church. But what has set the Catholic Church apart is the amount of money and time it has devoted to this issue. While the institutional Church certainly has the right to try to persuade its own members that abortion is immoral, it does not have the right to use its tax-free status to force its views upon non-Catholics through political influence. This is clearly in violation of the constitutional guarantee of separation of church and state.

As the Vatican continues to pour millions into this nation's abortion battle, the Holy See jeopardizes the Church's very important tax-free status. Having lost the abortion fight in all the important Catholic countries of the world, including France, Italy, and Spain and possibly soon in the bastion of Catholicism, Ireland, the Church seems determined to "win" in one major country no matter what the cost.

Thus, the Church in the United States finds itself in the position of withdrawing support from responsible leaders like Mario Cuomo and Patrick Moynihan while supporting politicians like Jesse Helms. The Church also supports fundamentalist publications like *Christianity Today*, which absurdly calls for "the validity of virginity and the management of masturbation"; and spends millions upon millions of dollars on an effort that, even if the Church won, would not halt abortion and would kill millions of American women. Meanwhile, in this nation alone, 12 million children go to bed hungry every night of the year. Clearly, Catholics must demand of the institutional Church a shift in priorities or the right to vote on how contributions will be spent.

RU486

My personal antipathy to abortion is based not only on a respect for the potential human being the pregnant woman carries, but also on the fact that I do not believe doctors should be in the business of taking life, but rather of giving it or improving it. Further, I object to the necessarily impersonal atmosphere in which this procedure must be carried out and, in particular, to the cold commercial atmosphere of many abortion clinics. They give a woman a sense of guilt and may damage the psyche of pregnant women.

For all these reasons, I am greatly encouraged by the development of RU486 (after the maker, Roussel-Uclaf in Romainville, France). RU486 was not invented with the goal of pregnancy interruption. Nevertheless, by the time it was synthesized, social concerns and scientific events had already set the stage for that use. International agencies were calling for the introduction of a variety of new birth control technologies. Chemically it resembles the hormone progesterone, and like progesterone, it binds tightly to the progesterone receptors in cells. It proved not to evoke the hormone's usual effects.

Instead, this chemical blocked them. Because progesterone is crucial to the maintenance of pregnancy, the drug's action raised the possibility that it might prevent pregnancy, as well as serving to interrupt pregnancy.

RU486 has proved it can do both. Furthermore, it may also have a role as a noncontraceptive. This property is being explored by scientists working in the field of cancer, where it promises to make a contribution to cancer therapy. RU486 is currently being evaluated outside the United States as a treatment for breast cancer, endometriosis, and certain brain tumors.

RU486, which is not available in the United States, works as an abortifacient by blocking progesterone. It causes the embryo to be detached and expelled from the uterus. RU486 is administered as a tablet in conjunction with a small dose of prostaglandin, which increases the frequency and strength of the uterine contractions needed to expel an embryo. In France, it is approved for ending pregnancies of up to forty-nine days' duration, counting from the first day of the last menstrual period. RU486 causes a process resembling a miscarriage, the uterus or womb shedding the early embryonic development during a period of heavy bleeding. At this early stage after taking RU486, Dr. David Grimes, professor in the departments of obstetrics and gynecology and preventive medicine, University of Southern California School of Medicine in Los Angeles, states flatly, "You can't even find a trace of the embryo." It is interesting to note that there is a 20 percent spontaneous abortion (miscarriage) rate even for the most wanted pregnancies. Obviously, a certain number of women having an abortion would have had a miscarriage if the pregnancy had not been removed by an abortion.

The Catholic Church preaches that God has given us free will. In its broad sense, free will may be synonymous with free choice or pro-choice. The decision by a woman to be guided by her conscience and choose RU486 without consulting anyone may represent the ultimate in pro-choice.

Although I had my doubts about this product in its original form, I now see the revised pill as a remarkable answer to the needs of the world. (1) It makes the doctor a minimal part of the abortion procedure, and (2) it can allow the woman to eventually avoid the clinic entirely and to carry out the inducement at home in a guilt-free atmosphere.

Let me make my position very clear. I am against abortion except for the most essential reasons. But, if history has taught us anything, it has taught us that when women wish to end a pregnancy, *they will do so no matter what*. Any attempt to deny women a safe way to obtain abortions will only lead to *unsafe* abortions—more death and disablement. Therefore, what we must hope for is the safest, most guilt-free method of abortion possible. Using RU486 seems to be that method. Thus, it is with great sadness that I must take note of the institutional Church's efforts to put pressure on our government to prevent the women of this nation from obtaining the product.

If a biased pressure group can have the drug RU486 banned in the United States, the First Amendment is being flaunted and violated. The First Amendment allows every moral and religious belief to have full sway, but the banning of RU486 from the United States could erode, if not crush, the First Amendment.

In summary, it can be said that all dimensions of the abortion debate are controversial, some more than others. Whether abortion can be debated at all by Catholics is perhaps the most controversial of all issues. Many Catholics, within and without the magisterium, consider abortion a closed topic. *Roma locuto, causa finita* ("Rome has spoken, the issue is finished"). However, many Catholics have raised questions about both the method used to resolve the problem and the quality of arguments which support the teaching. While the antiabortion tradition among Catholics is a long one, many believe that its dimensions need reformulation. More radically, some Catholics, and the number is increasing, simply reject the traditional teaching altogether. The fact is there is a debate on abortion within the Catholic Church.

The following statistics on United States Catholics were published by CBS News/*New York Times*:

15 percent opposed legalized abortion
55 percent approve abortion after rape or incest
26 percent approve the current abortion laws

However, among young Catholics, abortion on demand is receiving increasing support.

As a Catholic I am grateful that the Church continues to preach the protection of innocent and defenseless life. However, I am disturbed that some of the Catholic hierarchy continue to harass conscientious men and women who support pro-choice public policies.

Madonna Kolbenschlag has written, "It is too bad that so much of the energy of one of the greatest engines of conscientization that the world has ever known, the Catholic Church, should be spent on regulating women's anatomy instead of promoting their autonomy and empowerment as moral persons." She also states that women's experience will be the hermeneutic of the future. She sums up my feeling by writing that Solomon's wisdom is worth remembering: Let those who are more intimately affected by the consequences of a decision make that decision.

Infallibility

M any of the letters I received in response to the *New York Times* article had a tone of futility. They agreed that change in the Church is needed desperately, but they did not believe it could be accomplished.

Asked one writer, "How can the Church ever be proven wrong, since it is right even if it's wrong? What's the point of arguing if the Pope is infallible?"

Indeed, there would be no point at all. And I understand this feeling very well. As a young boy, I was taught that all the supposed "failures" of the Church were somehow transformed into *triumphs* because the Pope could never be in error. But the fact of the matter is that the Pope has been in error many, many times. Remember that the Church once tolerated slavery and taught that usury was intrinsically evil—meaning that people could be kept in chains, but you must not charge them interest! As for the Pope's infallibility, it is a matter of record that Popes such as Liberius, Vigilius, and Honorius proposed teachings that were highly erroneous and that were subsequently rejected through theological dissent.

It is important to remember that in the beginning of the Christian Church there was no single voice to tell followers the "final truth" about faith and morals. People relied upon the communities founded by the Apostles and their close followers, and the teachings were not always the same from one community to the next. The move toward control from Rome could not be felt strongly until the fourth century, when "special reverence" began to be given to the Church of Rome, St. Peter's community. This slowly became the center of Christianity so that Catholics began to accept that the Bishop of Rome (the Pope) had the final word on matters of faith and morality.

Still, it was not until the 1300s that the term *infallibility* was coined. Having Latin roots, it translated as "unable to deceive." There was much vagueness about precisely what this term meant until 1870, when Vatican Council I declared that infallibility was a dogma and that whatever the Pope teaches ex cathedra must be held by the universal Church. This position was reaffirmed in 1964 by Vatican II, but again it refers only to ex cathedra teaching; that is, the Pope (and the whole college of bishops with the Pope) speaks infallibly only when it is explicit that the teaching is binding on the Church as an absolute decision.

How often does this occur? Papal infallibility has been formally exercised only *twice* in the last 140 years: first by Pius IX in 1854 about the Immaculate Conception, and second by Pius XII in 1950 about Mary's assumption into heaven.

The Church would be in absolute chaos today if the dogma of infallibility had applied to all announcements by the Popes down through history. Consider only two of the more blatant examples.

Past Errors

Aristotle, who died some 332 years before Christ was born, believed the universe was a great sphere with the earth at the center. The philosophy of Aristotle, known as the Peripatetic School, would eventually become the basis for the Catholic Church's ideological and theological substructure, which placed man at the center of the universe. The Greek astronomer and geographer Claudius Ptolemy (A.D. 139–161) supported the Aristotelian position, and science accepted his theories of astronomy for well over a thousand years. Ptolemy worked out an elaborate system of movements in which the sun, moon, and planets all moved around the earth in the following order: nearest to earth was the moon, then came Mercury and Venus, then the sun, then Mars, Jupiter, Saturn, and the stars.

It comes as no surprise to us that the Ptolemaic system, based as it was on an erroneous model of the universe, contained great complexities and contradictions requiring a plethora of epicycles to account for the observed movements of the heavenly bodies. As a result, astronomers faced an increasingly laborious task of computing the future positions of the planets. Yet when the world was offered a much simpler explanation for the movements of the planets, the Church rejected it out of hand because the new theory dared to place the sun rather than the earth (and man) at the center of our universe (our planetary system).

This new theory came from the Polish mathematician and astronomer Nicolaus Copernicus (1473–1543). He did not believe that the observable motions of the heavenly bodies could be so confused and complex as the Ptolemaic system made them. Copernicus chose a simpler hypothesis that the sun was the center around which the earth and the other planets revolved. Copernicus was able to anticipate many other principal astronomical truths, such as the motion of the earth around its axis, the immense distances of the stars, which made their apparent position the same from any part of the earth's orbit, the variations of our seasons on earth, the precision of the equinoxes, and so on.

The great work in which Copernicus explained his theory, *On the Revolutions of the Celestial Orbs*, was completed in 1530, but it went unpublished for many years because of the expected response by the Church. Finally, in 1543, with Copernicus growing ill, close friends persuaded him to have the book published. Even then, the publisher, Andreas Osiander, was so fearful of Church criticism that he inserted a preface which emphasized that the heliocentric, or sun-centered, hypothesis was "only a convenient means for simplifying planetary computation."

Because of this preface, the book did not result in official censure and the author was not excommunicated as some had feared. But the Church forcefully condemned the Copernican theory, effectively halting much of the research that might have flowed from the publication of *On the Revolutions of the Celestial Orbs*. Other astronomers either divorced themselves from the Copernican theory or went underground.

One of the latter was Galileo (1564–1642), an Italian astronomer and physicist. Although he became convinced of the truth of the Copernican theory, Galileo was afraid to express his opinion. In 1609, having learned of the recently invented telescope, Galileo built a greatly improved model, the first that could be used for astronomical observation. With it, he quickly proved the correctness of the Copernican model of the universe as opposed to that of Ptolemy.

Galileo demonstrated his telescope in Rome and because of the flattering reception ventured to publish *Letter on Sunspots*, making known his certainty that Copernicus was right and Ptolemy was wrong. Very quickly he earned the enmity of the Church. Dominican preachers fulminated from the pulpit against the new impurity of "mathematicians" and denounced Galileo to the Inquisition for blasphemous utterances that had been "freely invented."

Alarmed, Galileo wrote the Roman authorities, reminding the Church of its long-standing practice of interpreting Scripture allegorically whenever it came into conflict with scientific truth. He went on:

> The authority of the Sacred Scriptures has as its sole aim to convince men of those truths which are necessary for their salvation . . . But that the same God who has endowed us with senses, reason and understanding should not wish us to use them and should desire to impart to us by another means knowledge which we have it in our power to acquire by their use—this is a thing which I do not think I am bound to believe . . . It would be a terrible detriment for the souls if people found themselves convinced by proof of something that was then made a sin to believe.

A number of the Church's ecclesiastical experts were on Galileo's side. However, Robert Cardinal Bellarmine, the chief theologian of the Church, clung to the belief that "mathematical hypotheses have nothing to do with physical reality." At his bidding, the Church decided to check the whole issue by officially declaring in 1616 that Copernicus's work had been false and erroneous. His book was banned by the Congregation of the Index.

This was a quite different matter from rejecting the ideas of Copernicus seventy-three years earlier. Then the findings had been almost totally theoretical. But now, in 1616, Galileo's telescope had *proved* these theories to be true. The Church stated its official doctrine that the Copernican model was false and heretical and that the earth be named the center of the universe. Galileo was found guilty of heresy for his support of the Copernican theory. He was released only after he agreed to give up this opinion and promised that if he again wrote about the Copernican System, he would do so only as a mere "mathematical supposition," not as reality. He must neither hold nor defend the doctrine for, according to the Church, we could not presume to know how the world was really made because God could have brought about the same effects in ways unimagined by us and we must not "restrict his omnipotence."

Some twenty years later, when Galileo published the book *Dia-*

logue of the Two Chief World Systems, it was determined by the Church that Galileo had violated its demand, and he was tried for "vehement suspicion of heresy." Because he had followed the specifics of the Church's directive—stating that his work was simply mathematical speculation—his book had won the Church censors' approval before publication. In order for the Pope to be able to try Galileo, a document was suddenly "discovered" in the Church files (historians now agree the document was a plant) in which the astronomer promised never to write about the Copernican theory again in *any* form. Using this document and his new book, *Dialogue of the Two Chief World Systems,* the Church found Galileo guilty of heresy. Forced to recant any real or apparent belief in the Copernican system, the aging Galileo, now sixty-nine, was sentenced to house arrest for the remainder of his life and his *Dialogue* was banned.

Galileo died without the truth and genius of his work acknowledged to the world, as had Copernicus before him. Whether one judges the "error" here in terms of ignorance, dogmatic blindness, or subterfuge, the fact of the matter is that the Church deliberately placed roadblocks in the way of progress and education. Instead of encouraging men and women to appreciate the vastness, the awesomeness of God's magnificent universe, the Church insisted on upholding its smaller, meaner version in order to ensure that the earth and man stood at the center of it all.

The new cosmology was terribly threatening to the Church. The ideological and theological substructure was based on Scholasticism. This was based on Aristotle's philosophy interpreted by Aquinas, who had this philosophy dovetail with the sacred Scriptures. The new cosmology rejected the entire philosophy of Aristotle and in turn the doctrinal framework of the Church. The Church lost a great opportunity to receive credit for leadership and vision. Instead it resorted to condemnations as a means of dealing with intellectual challenges. The roadblock for the Church lay with the rigid understanding of tradition as interpreted by the Council of Trent (1545–1563), which laid down the rules that Scripture must be interpreted according to tradition and must be defined as the way it was understood by the Fathers of the Church. This dictum prevented Catholic thought. This example illustrates that the Church is far from infallible. Recently, after more than four hundred years, the Church forgave Galileo and withdrew its condemnation of his theory.

Of course, the Church has been in error regarding other kinds of advances. Consider the glaring religious abuses that led to the Protestant revolt, abuses that if left unchallenged might still exist today as they did four hundred years ago. These abuses included simony (the selling of Church offices), amorality of the clergy, nepotism, and the selling of dispensations, indulgences, and false sacred relics. Few of the Church hierarchy seemed to appreciate the seriousness of these rampant abuses or if they did, they cared very little because they were enjoying its fruits.

One who did was a Saxon friar and transient priest named John Tetzel. Friar Tetzel was so carried away with his hope of profit that he did not even demand repentance from those to whom he sold indulgences, which was more than Martin Luther (1483–1546) could bear. Luther, a monk, had become an important official of the Augustinian order and a popular professor at the University of Wittenberg in Saxony. In 1517, troubled by many of the injustices condoned by the Church, he nailed ninety-five theses dealing with the sale of indulgences and matters of Catholic belief and practices to the door of the cathedral at Wittenberg.

John Tetzel fled from his parish, the selling of indulgences ceased, and a great commotion spread rapidly through Germany. There is every reason to believe that the unrest would have faded away had the Church hierarchy been willing to acknowledge the errors of Tetzel and others and institute the necessary reforms. No Protestant rebellion would have occurred. Instead, the Church elected to support profit-making from religion over a just and moral challenge.

Pope Leo X sent Johann Eck, an eminent theologian and articulate debater, to Germany in 1519. In his debate with Eck, Luther stated his beliefs clearly. He said that he believed every man could interpret the Bible for himself; that he could approach God without the assistance of a priest as an intermediary; that justification came through faith, not good works; that the early Apostles knew nothing of masses, purgatory, pilgrimages, indulgences, or the political leadership of the Pope. Eck got Luther to admit publicly that he no longer believed in the divine origins of the primacy or the infallibility of general councils. For Luther, "Scripture alone" was the supreme authority in religion. Henceforth this phrase became the rallying cry of all Protestants. At that time, it appeared that Eck had won the debate, but history proves otherwise.

Western Christianity rapidly chose sides between Luther and

Rome. Pope Leo X (served 1513–1521) condemned forty-one of Luther's theses and formally excommunicated him. The following December, when Luther publicly burned the "bull of excommunication," his break with Rome was complete. The stage had been set for the Protestant Reformation.

There is probably no point in history where the destructive power of Church error has shone through more clearly. Had the Catholic hierarchy been sensitive to changes in Europe and willing to acknowledge the amorality of much of the clergy, no reformation would have been needed. Instead, the hierarchy chose to cling to its mantle of primacy and infallibility, and the Church was torn asunder.

The Protestant split not only took members and influence from the Catholic Church, it forced change upon the Church in spite of itself. To check the tide of Protestantism, the Church strengthened its institutional structure and became more dedicated to the work of evangelization and more positively influential in world affairs.

Can the Church be forced to change? The Protestant Reformation makes it clear that the answer is yes, but change need not always be accomplished by revolution or counterrevolution. Desiderius Erasmus (1466–1536) was a brilliant classical scholar. In his book *Praise of Folly*, he ridiculed superstition, prejudice, upper-class privileges, *and* the abuses of the Church. He remained a faithful Catholic and his efforts to change the Church were always moderate and prudent. Although his pleas for internal reform went unheeded by the hierarchy, his satirizing of social evils did much to encourage Church members to think and talk about reform.

François-Marie Arouet, known to us as Voltaire, the celebrated French author and deist, proved much more successful at effecting change. In the name of enlightenment, he literally declared war on the Church—on its dogmas, its ethics, its tradition, and its clergy. His greatest work is the monumental satire *Candide*. This and other writings helped force many reforms in the Church. He attacked the Trinity, the chastity of the Virgin Mary, the presence of the body and blood of Christ in the Mass. The morality of the "Chosen People" he found abhorrent and the history of the Catholic Church a collection of idiotic arguments leading to war and mass murder. Voltaire was never dull. Voltaire could annihilate a man in a sentence: Jules Cardinal Mazarin, he said, was "guilty of all the good he did not do." It is part of Voltaire's immortality that this remark is just as applicable to certain politicians and the male hierarchy of the Church today.

Perhaps the most dramatic changes forced upon the Church concern its attitude toward evolution, changes brought about by Catholic scholars and scientists who pressed their views with the clergy.

Charles Darwin, the British naturalist, stated his theory of evolution in his book *On the Origin of Species by Means of Natural Selection*, published in 1859. Darwin held that over vast time, man and other complex forms of life evolved from simpler types by the process of natural selection or survival of the fittest. Darwin stated that only those best adapted to new conditions survive and in reproducing preserve those special attributes that have permitted them to thrive. A repetition of this process in all forms of life, through the ages, has generally produced progressively superior species.

Darwin's theories soon had far more than philosophical importance. Scientists such as August Weismann, Francis Galton, and Gregor Mendel developed a science of heredity founded on Darwinian concepts. This science is vital for major scientific investigation today. Predictably, the Church totally rejected Darwin's ideas. The First Vatican Council, meeting in 1870, condemned the theory of evolution and in terms of man's origin repeated what the Church had stated centuries earlier, namely, that after having made the angels and the material world, God "formed the creative man, who in a way belongs to both orders, as he is composed of spirit and body."

But after this initial reaction, Catholic scholars and scientists began making their case with the clergy. After all, it was pointed out, the Christians whose beliefs were threatened by the theory of evolution were those who had only biblical text as their guide and no extra-biblical tradition. The Catholic Church, as Galileo had pointed out in 1609, had a long history of interpreting Scripture allegorically whenever it came into conflict with scientific truth. But such was not the case for evangelical Protestants, and the rising tide of Darwin's theory struck them like a tornado with the publication of his most outstanding book, *The Origin of the Species*. Eventually, this controversy would result in the Scopes "monkey trial" in Dayton, Tennessee, and the famous legal battle between Clarence Darrow and William Jennings Bryan.

Meanwhile, Catholic biblical scholars became more subtle in their religious objections to evolution. Their concern was not with the necessity for reinterpreting most of the first three chapters of Genesis, but rather with the possible erosion in the value and dignity given to human beings if they were considered as originating from a subhuman life. Some Catholics believed Darwin's theory, while others felt that it undermined the accepted belief that the human soul was spiritual, individually created, and unconditionally precious to God.

In 1941 Pope Pius XII identified three elements that must be retained as certainly attested by the sacred author of Genesis, without any possibility of allegorical interpretation:

1. The essential superiority of man in relation to other animals by reason of his spiritual soul.
2. The derivation in some way of the first woman from the first man.
3. The impossibility that the immediate father or progenitor of man could have been other than a human being; that is, the impossibility that the first man could have been the son of an animal. In context, the statement reads, "Only from a man can another man descend, whom he can call father and progenitor."

Pope Pius XII said other questions still open for development include "the degree in which lower species may have cooperated in the formulation of the first man, the way in which Eve was formed from Adam, and the age of the human race." For these and other answers concerning the origin of man, "We must wait for more light from science, illumined and guided by revelation."

And in an encyclical letter, *Humani Generis*, dated August 12, 1950, Pope Pius XII added, "The Magisterium of the Church does not forbid that the theory of evolution concerning the origin of the human body as coming from pre-existing and living matter—for the Catholic faith obliges us to hold that human souls are immediately created by God—be investigated and discussed by experts as far as the present state of human science and sacred theology allow. However, this must be done in such a way that the arguments of both sides, those favorable and those unfavorable to evolution, he weighed and judged with necessary gravity, moderation and discretion."

A far cry from the Church's initial rejection of evolution. If scholars and scientists in the Church have been able to produce such a profound change in the Church's attitude on evolution, we have every right to believe that such changes can be forthcoming in other important areas.

The rebellion against primacy and infallibility continues today. Hans Küng is always fighting for a more liberal church. He has questioned the doctrine of infallibility. In fact, in his book *Infallible: An Inquiry*, he writes that the dogma of papal infallibility should be discarded, since it has been disproved by historical and biblical research. Among Catholics under thirty, scarcely 10 percent approve the official teaching of the Church on papal infallibility.

In a later section, I will discuss very specific measures by which each of us can contribute to the encouragement of change in the Church. Meanwhile, it is enough to demonstrate that the Church has been wrong—many, many times—and that it has been possible to force change upon the hierarchy. I recognize that Rome (Vatican) in the twentieth century has become a byword for intellectual sterility.

EIGHT

Priests in Peril

As you probably know, the Church is having great difficulty finding qualified young men to study for the priesthood, yet they will not relinquish their ban on marriage for priests. Where is it written that there is anything sinful about marriage for members of the clergy? In view of the scandal concerning some priests and young boys, the Church would be doubly wise to reconsider. Incidentally, Saint Peter, the disciple who became the founder of the Church and the first Pope, was *married*. Could marriage really be so bad for priests?

The above is representative of the many letters and conversations that I have had on this subject. Without a healthy, growing priesthood, it is unrealistic to expect a healthy, growing Church. Yet the future of the Catholic priesthood is in grave peril and the Church hierarchy is doing nothing to improve the situation. At a small New England church a few months ago, a Catholic priest celebrating fifty years as a member of the clergy talked about his early life. He told the Sunday audience:

"After I had completed the necessary training, I wrote to the Franciscan Order to apply for admission. They wrote me back that they were so crowded I would have to wait a year before I could enter." The priest laughed then and said, "What a difference fifty years makes. Today, if a young man applies anywhere for the priesthood, they go after him with a rope."

The audience laughed, but everyone present was well aware of the seriousness of the situation. According to Dean Hoge, a sociologist at Catholic University in Washington, D.C., for every 100 priests now leaving active ministry, only 59 others are replacing them. The key reason for this increasing shortage of applicants, says Hoge, is the Church's refusal to allow optional celibacy. But it is not the *only* reason. Due to life's increased complexity and pace, the duties of a priest today are considerably less appealing than they were fifty years ago.

The parish priest is responsible for "the care of souls" within his parish, which means all Roman Catholics residing within its limits. Ideally, the priest should know every member of his parish personally, and all dedicated pastors attempt to do this, a very time-consuming responsibility. Add to this responsibility a growing list of problems—recession, unemployment, homelessness, broken families, drugs, alcohol—and it is clear why the priests' burdens have become so heavy. The resulting stress is more than many young men are willing to bear.

Father David Brinkmoeller, director of priestly life and ministry at the National Conference of Catholic Bishops in Washington, D.C., said recently, "A priest is expected to be spiritually deep, theologically wise and fiscally clever, while being good at preaching and counseling with young and old. Each person in the congregation expects only a limited something, but today the conglomeration can be overwhelming."

In his book *The Roman Catholic Church*, Father John L. McKenzie, S. J., offers the following as a typical day in the life of a modern priest: "To summarize, from dawn to twilight the priest is flooded with calls, requests, invitations to speak, counseling sessions for the young and old alike. There are sick calls to make, funerals and weddings to be performed, but little time for spiritual or secular growth for the priest. The parish is often an unofficial center of Roman Catholic information for the press, for local merchants and businessmen, for ministers and members of other Christian churches, and for those who are simply curious. A priest is sometimes called to the phone to settle a bet at a cocktail party. He may be summoned to a hospital and, in any case, the wise pastor visits his sick daily."

The priest is left with virtually no time for self-fulfillment. "All too often," says McKenzie, "the priest cannot count on as much as an hour without interruption during the day to keep abreast of theological learning and cultural affairs. It should be added that most of his time is spent in personal encounters and these are even more fatiguing than work with things and papers."

To make matters worse, the problem is self-perpetuating. As fewer young men join the priesthood, more work is done by fewer priests, which means still more stressful responsibilities, which means still fewer young men will be attracted to the Church.

The additional responsibilities are also increasingly trivial. When business and domestic concerns begin to outweigh religious duties, the priest is troubled by the role he plays and his accomplishments in relation to his vows. The result: more stress.

Another reason fewer candidates come to the priesthood grows out of the fact that young people today are more worldly and knowledgeable than those novices who lived fifty years ago. For example, these young pastors will become assistant priests or curates in a parish that is too large for a single priest, but not big enough to justify the creation of a new parish. In most parishes, all the priests live in a rectory beside the church. Such close living arrangements can prove extraordinarily difficult even if the pastor and his assistants get along famously. Imagine the strain if personal relations are bad!

More important, the Church sets severe limits on intellectual, emotional, even physical freedom. The Church's power is absolute. Should a young priest's views differ from his superior's, he cannot find redress. During the era when absolute monarchs reigned, their subjects swore obedience to their feudal lord or king, which was not too different from that of the priest's relationship to bishop or Pope. But today, especially in democratic nations like the United States, the priest's total subservience seems unnatural. Yet the Church makes no effort to bring about improvement.

Moreover, a priest lives in the midst of a modern community, yet he is isolated from that community. That isolation begins with the clothing that separates the clergy from the laity. In addition, his loneliness is compounded by his need for someone close to offer help and share the burdens of ministering to a complex society. Camaraderie among priests lacks the freedom and companionship most young men desire and need.

"There is a long series of prohibitions of things which are regarded as innocent for the laity but unbecoming for the clergy," says John McKenzie. Depending on the diocese, the list could include "the theatre, the opera, the movies, sports events (especially racing), restaurants and bars, riding in an automobile with a woman of any age—even an infant or the priest's own mother—public beaches, going anywhere after sunset except for an urgent summons for priestly ministry—which means death, actual or impending."

All such prohibitions contribute to the isolation of the priest and make his life unattractive to many potential candidates. But surely the most isolating feature of all is celibacy. It is an undeniable fact that marriage is the normal state for men and women and that one who is celibate deviates from that norm. To preserve a balanced personality, the priest must somehow find compensation for a relationship that most men need for completeness. While some can accept celibacy, others simply cannot.

Father McKenzie writes, "Man achieves fulfillment by *doing* something, not by *not doing* something. The liability for a celibate person is that he risks becoming narrow and self-centered, less sensitive to the needs and wishes of others, less capable of genuine outgoing love."

To compensate for the absence of a wife, the priest seeks fulfillment through those to whom he ministers. For many priests, they find compensation and adjustment in a loving church. Cut off as he is from so much that is normal, the priest needs love and understanding from everyone in the Church, from Pope to bishop, and in today's Church, such love and understanding is often missing. So the priest must be celibate *without* adequate compensation. The results have been devastating.

In the United States alone, there are nineteen thousand former priests who left the ministry in order to marry. No figures are available on how many remaining priests have secretly forsaken celibacy. According to a recent television survey, 50 percent of those responding admitted breaking their vows. Reliable reports suggest that in some regions of the world concubinage is so common as to arouse no comment. There are also continuing reports of homosexuality. The debate continues whether this is abnormal, but in the eyes of the Catholic Church, it is a sin.

Child molestation by the clergy is shocking to Catholics and non-Catholics alike. It violates human decency. However, it is a mental illness and needs medical treatment just as cancer, heart disease, and other metabolic and medical conditions require. It is not the loneliness of the priesthood that results in child molestation; this has been present either in a latent or active form before entering the priesthood. Better screening methods of candidates for the priesthood must be established.

It is clear that forced celibacy, which started at the Second Lateran Council in 1139, has had a devastating effect on the clergy in our pluralistic and heterogeneous society. In my view, optional celibacy should be permitted.

In 1523, Martin Bucer, a German Dominican priest, publicly married, stating that celibacy might be a gift given to a few, and those who do not have it should marry rather than sin. Seven other priests in the fall of 1523 in the city of Strasbourg followed Father Bucer's example. They declared that most people are commanded by the rule of nature to marry. These priests noted that it was the original custom of the church to have married clergy. A celibate priesthood started with the Council of Elvira in 400 A.D., which mandated that all ordained priests and bishops withdraw from sexual congress with their wives. It was not until the eleventh century that mandatory celibacy was mandated based on an arbitrary assumption that the ascetic lifestyle is higher than the married state.

Catherine Zell was a new clergy bride. She was also a Scripture scholar. In March 1524 she preached a sermon in which she accused the bishop of enforcing celibacy in order to collect taxes on concubines and to prevent clergy children from inheriting property. Catherine Zell had great courage, for she defended the greater morality of marriage and denounced the irresponsible treatment of women and their children by priests. Rosemary Radford Reuther, in her book *Contemporary Roman Catholicism*, presents this very well in the chapter "Sexual Questions and the Challenge of Women."

HISTORY

It is absurd for the Catholic hierarchy to take the position that it cannot or should not change the rules that govern the lives of priests, for all of these rules were created by the Church itself. They are arbitrary and self-perpetuating. In the New Testament, neither the words of Christ nor those of his disciples call for the formation of a priesthood. In fact, during the early days of Christianity, no distinction was made between laity and clergy. According to Kenneth Scott Latourette's *History of Christianity*, every man and woman who had accepted Christ was held to be "a Priest unto God." All were considered equal.

This was true even for Paul. He wore no unique clothing nor lived in different housing. He did not even draw money from this new Church, but earned his living as a tent-maker. True, he was celibate, but he made it very clear that this was of his own choosing and that he could have married had he so desired. As for Church duties, all these were shared. Obviously, no one expected that Paul, who traveled so widely spreading the gospel, should also be burdened with clerical duties or the more personal needs of the growing number of Christians. These burdens were handled by others in the laity.

In those days, the Church shunned all forms of ostentation and ceremony with the exception of the Lord's Supper, especially altars and sacrifices, for the early Christians were anxious to avoid comparison with pagan religions. Even the distinctive word "priest" was avoided, and as late as the fifth century, the Pope expressly forbade any special ecclesiastical costume. Thus, there was no sense of isolation among the preachers in this new Church. They could do all the things allowed to Christians—live, dress, work, and play the same— and there was no danger of overwork comparable to the pressured world of the modern priest, for the work was shared by all members of the Church.

Over one hundred years later, the laity and the emerging clergy began to grow apart. This cleavage widened rapidly, and by the end of the second century, the clergy had become a separate "order." This particular designation derived from the Roman magistrates in the tightly organized society of the Roman Empire. In the same way, garments currently worn by today's clergy find their antecedents in the clothes worn by Roman civil officials of the fourth and fifth centuries: an undergarment—a tunic—with or without sleeves, bound around the waist by a girdle and an immense sleeveless cloak, closed in front, which was passed over the head. These special garments allowed the clergy to set themselves apart from other members of the Church. Though shaped by Roman custom, this religious order became a counterpart to the priesthood of the ancient Jews.

The increasingly separate and powerful clergy quickly became distrustful of the laity. In the early centuries of the Church, deacons performed most of the administrative work. But as Church business expanded, the hierarchy wanted the administration firmly in the hands of those it *controlled*—priests. So more and more priests became burdened with more and more work, which could have been better handled by laymen.

While this shift of responsibility occurred, the Church wrestled with the principle of celibacy for the clergy. Many people today are under the impression that the rule of celibacy for priests came from

Christ and the Apostles. This interpretation is simply not true. Peter, one of the original Apostles of Jesus, is honored as the "first Pope." His successors, the Bishops of Rome, have been the Church's Popes throughout the history of Christianity. Yet, as noted in the letter that began this section, St. Peter was married.

Paul chose a life of celibacy, but as mentioned earlier, he insisted that like all the other Apostles, he had the right to be married if he so desired. Nor was ecclesiastical celibacy drawn from Judaism. Although there were prescribed periods of sexual abstinence in connection with rituals and sacrifices and while engaging in holy wars, marriage was not only allowed but encouraged.

The concept of celibacy was first applied to the early church members during the first three centuries of the Christian Church, although marriages of the clergy were freely permitted. Early Christians believed that their present age was ending and the Kingdom of God was almost immediately at hand. Since all would be like angels in this new life, marriage was unnecessary. As a result, many gave up their family life to devote themselves to proclaiming and aiding the Kingdom.

Late in the first century and early in the second, there were many Christian groups or movements who viewed sex as evil. Such beliefs developed from dualistic faiths such as Orphism, with their view that the spirit is good but the flesh is evil. Sexuality of the opposite gender was regarded as a polluting factor, especially in sacred situations. As a result, Christian sects like the Marcionites of the second century forbade all sexual unions among members. Husbands and wives were required to separate and chastity and celibacy were demanded. In the Montanist movement of the third century, celibacy was strongly encouraged.

The power of these cults lasted a relatively brief time, but the pre-Christian idea that sexual activity was wrong for those who officiated at the altar was now being assimilated by the Christians. It became fairly common for ordained men to give up sexual relations with their wives, either temporarily or permanently. An important factor in this change to celibacy was the increasing stress laid on the basic abstinence from any sexuality of the ministry. At first the Christian presbyters or elders avoided any resemblance to the pagan clergy and saw the priest's primary function as the ministry of the Word of Christ. The ritualistic features of this ministry were kept in a low key. Even John Chrysostom, revered saint of both the Greek and Roman churches, as late as the fifth century still stressed preaching as the main task of the Christian minister. But the ministry of the Word (the most popular of the Christologies in the first several centuries of the Church proved to be the one known as the Logos Christology, from the Greek term *logos*, meaning "the word") diminished in importance when infant baptism became the rule rather than the exception, for infants could not be preached to and the image of the Christian presbyter gradually took on sacral characteristics.

The local synod of Elvira, Spain, in 306, decreed that all priests, as well as bishops, deacons, and other ministers, married or not, should abstain from sexual relations. However, in the year 325, just two decades later, the ecumenical Council of Nicaea declined to demand celibacy. In 692 the position of the Eastern churches was made clear by the decree of the Synod of Trullo (and it is still the same today): Bishops must be celibate, but priests can continue marriages established before ordination. Meanwhile, the breakup of the Roman Empire had the effect of extending the practice of celibacy in that part of the world even among the laity. Christians who fled the cities to live as hermits or to form monastic communities were seeking safety as much as purity.

But a new challenge to celibacy emerged in the tenth and eleventh centuries. The Viking invasions and the collapse of the Carolingian Empire produced the destruction of many churches. Priests then married or began living in concubinage. The Second Lateran Council, 1139, enacted what seems to be the first written universal law making Holy Orders a validating impediment to marriage. But the absence of a wife did not necessarily demand celibacy. In the diocese of Constance in the 1400s, for example, priests were permitted to have concubines as long as they paid a tax for each woman and each child. The revenue from this tax made up one-third of all the income of the diocese!

It was not until 1563 and the Council of Trent that the Church ruled definitely on the matter of celibacy and established the discipline. Marriage for Catholic priests has only been outlawed over the past four hundred years, and even today there are some exceptions to this demanding rule. Several married Protestant and Episcopalian (Anglican) clergymen who became converts and were subsequently ordained to the priesthood have been permitted to continue in marriage.

From all that I have read and researched, it is clear that the

Church's chief reason for demanding celibacy has an economic cause. It is easier and less expensive to support a single man than a family. Without the responsibility of raising a family, these men could spend more time attending to matters relating to the Church. Thus, the demand for celibacy allows the Church to pay less and get more.

Aware of all the harm caused by this insistence on celibacy, many members of the Church held out great hope for its abandonment by the Second Vatican Council. However, the change permitted only the permanent deacons to marry. Immediately following Vatican II, the number of priests abandoning the priesthood rose dramatically as their last hope seemed shattered. There was an outcry among European and American Catholics, urging that celibacy be made optional for priests. Sadly, the Pope responded with an encyclical, *Saderdetalis Caelibatus*, on June 23, 1967, reaffirming the traditional law of celibacy and insisting that priests must be totally free of domestic responsibilities to be ready for the coming of the Kingdom of Heaven.

THE ROAD TO CHANGE

All areas of the priesthood, from dress to duties to demands, can be changed if the need is there. They can be changed because none of them were part of the teachings of Jesus or his Apostles and none are suggested by the New Testament writings. The priesthood is primarily the product of *non*-Christian influences. We must remember that the spread of Christianity was nothing short of miraculous. In less than five hundred years, the faith of only a handful of men and women outstripped its many religious competitors—paganism, Platonism, Judaism, Gnosticism, Manichaeism, to mention only a few— to become the faith of the rulers of the vast Roman Empire and of the overwhelming majority of its population. It is not surprising that in the course of this miraculous rise, the structure of the new Church was shaped in large measure by the societies, philosophies, and religions it encountered: robes and rules from Rome, rituals from Judaism, celibacy from Orphism, and so on.

The fact that these rules and customs are not our own does not automatically mean they are bad and must be changed or discarded. Personally, I would be greatly saddened if it were necessary to abolish the robes worn and rituals performed by the priests at Sunday Mass. The paganistic ritual of the Catholic Church has a mystical quality. I am as much affected by the majesty of these moments today as I was in my childhood. I happen to find the usual Protestant service, even though it is closer to that of the early Christians, bleak and barren in comparison. But changes can and *must* be made in those areas that threaten the priesthood and thus the Church. More, not fewer, priests are needed to meet the demands of modern ministry, and we must find ways to reorganize the priesthood so that it attracts all those who are properly suited to its duties.

We must prevail upon the hierarchy to break down the barriers separating the clergy from the laity. Our bishops and priests are not emperors and lords "governing" their people. We are all basically the same. The difference lies only in the fact that the clergy has been provided with training to prepare them for their special duties, duties that should not be top-heavy with accounting and hiring and firing. There are laypeople far better qualified in these areas, and changes should be made to place the Church's clerical work back where it was originally—with the laity.

The hierarchy must be made to understand that priests are not children and must not be treated as such. Absolute power over their thoughts and emotions and actions is totally unacceptable in the modern world. Many priests are so inhibited that almost from the moment their priestly duties begin, their only happy thought is the day they can retire. Even after all their training, they are like schoolboys who spend their time looking forward to vacation or graduation.

There was hope that the senate of priests that came into being at the Second Vatican Council could ameliorate the stress produced by the Church's power over the priests. But results to date have been most disappointing. Far more meaningful steps are needed. Research should be undertaken to determine whether a portion of the priesthood might be made more productive and less stressed by reversing their collars, living among the people and perhaps working at another job for a portion of their income.

Shortly after World War II, such an experiment was tried in France. Concerned that the French nation had become virtually a non-Christian territory, the Church decided a new approach was needed to reach the people. The priests gave up their clerical clothing and dwelling and took employment in the factories. They sought to make friendships and to turn their apartments into centers for social gatherings and discussion groups.

Although Rome insisted the experiment was halted because some of the priests were marrying or turning communist, it is generally agreed that the real reason reflected the hierarchy's desire to continue the full separation between laity and clergy. Instead of wishing to help priests escape from their isolation, the Vatican is convinced value can be found in this approach despite the toll it takes on the priesthood. It will not willingly agree to anything that might break down barriers between clergy and laity. It must be made to see the error in such thinking.

Today's laity, as noted by John L. McKenzie S. J., in *The Roman Catholic Church*, are "the governed, the recipients of the sacraments and the listeners. Nothing more." A change will not only benefit priests by passing many of their duties to the laity, it will also benefit the laity, allowing us to become an integral part of our Church in a far more meaningful way than simply filling the collection basket.

But of all the changes that must be instituted to revitalize the priesthood, none is so important as making the vow of celibacy optional. The Catholic Church is the only Christian Church that has a universal law of celibacy, and while this law may offer economic benefits to the Church, these benefits are more than offset by the loss of talent produced by this vow.

The two changes the Church can make most quickly in order to swell the ranks of the dwindling priesthood are:

1. Opening the priesthood to women.
2. Allowing priests to marry.

Since both of these changes are strongly opposed by the male hierarchy and since both involve the introduction of women into the male-only environs of the priesthood, the Church's bias toward women is made all the more obvious.

There are strong arguments to ordain women as priests. Although the subject is covered in another chapter, it is important to reemphasize their importance. There is a critical mass of women who are brilliant, dedicated, and able to serve as priests. They are calling for greater declericalization, flexibility, realism, and credibility of the institutional Church. They are generally less concerned with the subtleties of canon law than with the dynamics of social interaction. And they are less preoccupied with dogmatic definitions than with human need. Women are as worthy a component as men in the human community. Women have full human dignity and human value, and their roles, their rights, and their voices merit recognition in all human affairs. New Catholic women clearly include the affairs of the Catholic Church as the institutional representation of their faith. They have made a firm commitment to the Church which they "call to conversion," even as they live out their new freedom in the faith that is their heritage. It is important to acknowledge that the women religious are rarely if ever involved in scandal.

NINE

Divorce

I can't respect the Church when it bars me from Communion because I'm divorced, but allows the rich and connected to find a way out through Paul or Peter or by buying an annulment. This isn't God's way.

I have had this question addressed to me many times. I have explored it and have arrived at my answer. I strongly believe, guided by my conscience, that the Church should and must change its teachings on indissolubility of marriage and acknowledge the possibility of divorce and remarriage.

According to George Gallup, Jr., and Jim Castelli, who surveyed American Catholics, the percentage of them who are currently separated or divorced has more than doubled since 1976. This statistic becomes more tragic since the Church receives its worst ratings regarding its treatment of separated, divorced, and remarried Catholics and its tribunal system for processing annulments. In these areas, Catholics who rated the Church poor to fair outnumbered those rating it good to excellent by a margin of two to one. And three Catholics out of ten rated the Church *poor*. How are these figures reflected in terms of Catholic opinion about the Church's stand on divorce? Recent polls show that almost 70 percent of Catholics surveyed believe that divorced Catholics should be allowed to remarry without religious penalty, and the percentage for younger Catholics is even higher.

The vast majority of Catholics want the Church to change its teachings and allow divorced Catholics to remarry within the Church. Yet the hierarchy remains adamant in its absolute prohibition of divorce. According to this ruling, no sacramental marriage between baptized men and women can be dissolved, even by the Pope. Where partners no longer can live peacefully together, they might be granted ecclesiastical permission to *separate*, but they will never be allowed to remarry as long as their partners remain alive. This edict has created tremendous hardship for those involved in broken marriages, as well as resentment toward the Church.

Because of the unity and indissolubility of marriage, the Church denies that civil divorce can undo the bond of a valid marriage. Many disenchanted Catholics say, "there is a way out through Peter and Paul," as mentioned in the young woman's letter at the beginning of this section. She is referring to the two dispensations known properly as the Pauline privilege and the Petrine privilege. The Pauline privilege is a dispensation granted in the instance of unbaptized persons in a legitimate, even consummated marriage, one of whom subsequently receives baptism in the Church. That person can seek dissolution of the marriage and remarry in the Catholic Church. The granting of this privilege is meant to protect the faith of converts to Christianity and is based on St. Paul (1 Cor. 7:12–16):

> If a brother has a wife who is a non-believer, and she is content to live with him, let him not put her away. And if a woman has a non-believer for a husband and he is content to live with her, let her not put him away. However, if the unbelieving partner does not consent, they may separate. In these circumstances, the brother or sister is not tied.

Petrine privilege is a dispensation granted in the instance of a legitimate, even consummated, marriage of a baptized and unbaptized person, freeing the baptized person to marry again. The name derives from the fact that the dispensation is granted by the Pope, the successor to St. Peter, in virtue of the privilege of faith. There are no formally prescribed conditions for receiving the Petrine privilege, as with the Pauline privilege, but the reasons are supposed to be grave and involve considerations of faith.

All too often, however, the granting of such a dispensation is allowed less for the gravity of the reason and more for the power of the party seeking relief. As every thinking Catholic knows, it is far easier for the wealthy and famous to obtain a dispensation or an annulment than it is for the poor and unknown. It was precisely this type of hypocrisy that led Martin Luther to revolt and split the Church. So why does the hierarchy continue the rigid stance on divorce?

The Church historically has some justification for its position on divorce. It goes back to the time of Christ, as mentioned in chapter 5. Jesus did not make a radical break with the morality of the Torah. He still recognized the sacred law as the authentic voice of God, but he did not hesitate to modify it, as in his prohibition of divorce. The main thing he insisted on, however, was complete submission to the will of God in all things. It was summed up in his command to love. At that time a wife could be discarded without any trouble by her husband. I am sure Jesus was influenced by the dedicated attention women gave him. They followed him, anointed his head with oil, and admired his gentleness. It is my opinion that he spoke out to protect them from the indignity of being discarded and thereby the violation of their human and spiritual rights. However, his pronouncement against divorce was not followed in the early years of the Church.

Many Catholics are under the impression that the Church's attitude toward divorce has been a fixed ruling throughout Church history, but this is far from correct. It is true that most first-century Christian leaders opposed divorce, but it is also clear that in some places in the early Church divorce and remarriage were allowed or tolerated. It was, at least in part, for this reason that Paul and others sought to enhance the importance of the marriage ceremony and make it a true *sacrament* of the Church, that is, a ritual like baptism or the Eucharist that could be said to have been instituted by Christ. Such an attempt is contained in Paul's letter to the Ephesians (5:22–33), but it is clearly too much of a stretch to be fully effective:

Wives should be submissive to their husbands as if to the Lord because the husband is head of his wife just as Christ is head of his body, the Church, as well as its Savior. As the Church submits to Christ, so wives should submit to their husbands in everything.

Husbands, love your wives, as Christ loved the Church. [He did not refer to it as the Church, but rather as the Kingdom of God.] He gave himself up for her to make her holy, purifying her in the bath of water by the power of the word, to present to himself a glorious Church, holy and immaculate, without stain or wrinkles or anything of that sort. Husbands should love their wives as they do their own bodies. He who loves his wife loves himself. Observe that no one ever hates his own flesh; no, nourishes it and takes care of it as Christ cares for the Church—for we are members of his body.

For this reason a man shall leave his father and mother, and shall cling to his wife, and the two shall be made into one.

This is the great foreshadowing; meaning that it refers to Christ and the Church. In any case, each man should love his wife as he loves himself, the wife for her part showing respect for her husband.

As sincere as this view may be, Paul's letter does not really establish the sacramental character of Christian marriage, and despite this and other Church efforts, it was never treated as such by the members nor even by some of the Church authorities during the early centuries. From the tenth century forward, a strong tradition existed in the Church in favor of the indissolubility of marriage. However, this tradition was violated again and again throughout feudal times.

During those years, as Kenneth Scott Latourette points out in his *History of Christianity*, "the demoralization caused by centuries-long series of invasions and constant fighting made sex relations notoriously lax. Kings and nobles divorced their wives almost with impunity and spawned illegitimate children. With such examples at the top, the masses could not be expected to be much better. At the end of the 11th century and beginning of the 12th century, synods and canon lawyers sought, so far as legislation could do it, to enforce continence and render divorce difficult."

It was the Church's stand against divorce that caused its second great schism. In 1530 Henry VIII, then king of England, sought the Church's approval of divorce from his wife Catherine, who had borne him no male heir and, moreover, had been the wife of his elder brother. It was the second point that served as Henry's grounds for divorce.

When the Pope in Rome refused to allow the divorce, the king put the question before England's Catholic universities. They offered their approval and in 1534, England's Parliament declared the king's marriage null and void so that he was free to marry again. The Act of Supremacy made the king of England the head of the church in

England (instead of the Pope). England broke with the Roman Church, setting up its own high religious office—Archbishop of Canterbury—and declared King Henry the protector of the English Church. At the same time, the English people continued to adhere to most of the theological tenets of Catholicism.

Today, of course, England is far from the only nation that allows divorce. In recent years, even the most predominantly Catholic countries, such as Portugal, Spain, and Italy, have introduced civil divorce. Only Ireland remains unchanged.

But civil divorce means nothing to the Catholic Church. It is regarded as simply a legal arrangement that does *not* affect the bond of a valid marriage. This bond is held to be indissoluble, whether it is the marriages of two Catholics, a Catholic and a non-Catholic, or two non-Catholics, so long as they have been baptized. The Church permits the aggrieved party in a bad marriage to obtain a civil divorce out of such considerations as family, health, or custody of children and property, but it does *not* concede that this civil divorce breaks the bond of a valid marriage. Thus, neither party to such a divorce is free to marry another or even to live separately unless the Church so agrees. So the suffering of those in broken marriages goes on.

There are voices in the Church which would have us believe that allowing divorce would immediately encourage Catholics to jump into more ill-considered marriages, resulting in a dramatically increased divorce rate. This is a minority view. It is my opinion that in a pluralistic society, the Catholic Church must change its ruling on divorce.

Father James Kavanaugh, in his very passionate book, *A Modern Priest Looks at His Outdated Church*, expresses my own thoughts precisely:

Catholics are not struggling to save their marriages simply because the Church threatens them with excommunication if they marry a second time. The divorce rate among Catholics is not lower than that among other men and women. Divorce is more often a reflection of an impossible marriage than a mirror of irreligion in the world. People stay together, with few exceptions, because they love each other or because a broken home costs too much in personal effort, confused children and social criticism. Only a minority are restrained by religious conviction when the chance for real love presents itself with reasonable convenience. A change in divorce would free this miserable minority and relieve the tortuous guilt of those who have remarried without the blessing of their Church.

Father Kavanaugh suggests that a major reason why so little has been done to bring the Church's stand into line with the wishes of the membership is that the Pope and the bishops are not in contact with the masses. "They do not see and feel the pain and heartache caused by the Church's adamant stand on divorce," says Father Kavanaugh, and he offers several tragic examples drawn from his own personal experience:

The wife whose husband was such a good Catholic during their courtship that he never got "carried away" with sex, but who, after marriage, proved to be a homosexual, having intercourse with his wife only twice, both times on their honeymoon. She became only a "token wife" who gave her husband respectability. She was married in name only, but the Church told her this "marriage" was indissoluble so she stayed with her husband in an empty, barren union, afraid to leave him only because she feared to lose God.

———

The husband who married at 18 and whose wife left him for another man after two years—left him and the baby as well. After four years alone, this man remarried and was cut off by his parents and excommunicated from the Church.

———

The wife who watched her home disintegrate around a hopeless alcoholic.

———

The husband who was married to a helpless and hopeless psychotic.

———

The couple who had not spoken a direct and personal word in twenty years.

———

The wife who was married to a brutalizing beast.

———

The nervous little woman who made novenas for her husband to abandon his latest barmaid.

"There are sadists and masochists, beaters and brawlers," says Father

Kavanaugh. "There are profane and rigid dictators who match Hitler at his worst. Yet the Church says these men and women are united in Christ and that no power on earth can loose the bond."

Father Kavanaugh is almost certainly right that the Church's rigidity on divorce endures in part because the Pope and the bishops are not in contact with those who suffer from this rigidity. But to give the Church its due, an equally important lesson has been the admonition against divorce contained in the Bible. Unlike any of the other controversial positions of the Church discussed thus far, such as abortion or birth control, the Church's position on divorce is based on what appears to be very clear words from the Scripture, words from Christ's own lips. Recall Mark 10:2–9:

> Then some Pharisees came up and as a test began to ask him whether it was permissible for a husband to divorce his wife. In reply he said, "What command did Moses give you?" They answered, "Moses permitted divorce and the writing of a decree of divorce." But Jesus told them, 'He wrote that commandment for you because of your stubbornness. At the beginning of creation, God made them male and female. For this reason a man shall leave his father and mother and the two shall become as one. They are no longer two, but one flesh. Therefore let no man separate what God has joined.' "

And in Matthew 5:31–32, as Christ is speaking on a mountaintop:

> "It was also said, 'Whenever a man divorces his wife, he must give her a decree of divorce.' What I say to you is: everyone who divorces his wife, except for porneia, forces her to commit adultery."

And Luke 16:18:

> "Everyone who divorces his wife and marries another commits adultery. The man who marries a woman divorced from her husband likewise commits adultery."

With words so seemingly clear and unequivocal, how could the Church suggest that divorce and remarriage were not sins? No matter that many, including some Church authorities, violated or accepted violation of the code for many centuries, how could the Church possibly subscribe to such conduct in view of the New Testament words?

It was Pope John XXIII who offered an answer to this question. He set the stage for a reevaluation of this subject in his opening address to the Vatican II Council when he called for study and exposition that would employ the literary forms of modern thought. He said, "The substance of the ancient doctrine is one thing and the way in which it is presented is another." With this statement, Pope John clearly endorsed the concept of historicity—the idea that Church doctrinal positions are not immutable in themselves, but historically condi-. tioned answers given by the Church at a particular moment to questions raised by the current thought of a particular time.

Encouraged by Pope John XXIII, a number of Catholic theologians began questioning the scriptural validity of the rigid divorce law. They wanted the Church to continue preaching the sacredness of marriage as a sacrament and as a divinely willed, lifelong commitment, but they sought a more flexible pastoral approach in dealing with couples like those described by Father Kavanaugh whose marriages have clearly failed.

These theologians saw three different ways in which historicity might bear upon the Scripture on which the Church's divorce position is based:

The Exceptions: The passage from Matthew previously quoted in this section contains one exception, "porneia," meaning immorality, fornication, or even incest, and Paul offered a second exception, his famous one concerning the nonbeliever. Since this is clear proof that exceptions were allowed in the early Church, the indissolubility of marriage cannot be said to have been absolute. Since these exceptions existed, others might have existed in other early Christian groups and there is no reason why new exceptions should not be allowed by the Church in view of changing times.

Aim: As explained in Chapter 5, Christ's time with his disciples came during a terrible period for women. A man could be rid of his wife simply by issuing a writ of divorce without her agreement or even her notice. Jesus' strict prohibition of divorce was an effort to counteract this deplorable situation. He did not offer his edict against divorce expecting it to be upheld universally by imperfect man, but rather as a goal to be worked toward. As Rudolph Schnackenburg suggests in *The Moral Teaching of the New Testament*, all Christ or early Christianity meant to do was to hold up permanent marriage as the ideal, as the fruit of Christian love. There was no intent to keep men and women chained together after the fruit soured.

Second Coming: Behind much of Christ's teaching and that of first-century Christian leaders, such as Paul, was the belief that the Second Coming was imminent. No one could be certain of the date, Christ told his disciples, but it would be soon. "Let me tell you this," said Jesus. "The present generation will not pass away until all this takes place" (Luke 21:32).

This belief had a great effect upon the early Christians' attitude toward marriage and divorce. If heaven was very near, why concern oneself with separation from one's mate? For this same reason, Paul told his fellow Christians that widows should stay unmarried, slaves should continue in slavery, and men should stay away from their wives: "I tell you, brothers," said Paul in his first letter to the Corinthians (7:29–35), "the time is short. From now on, those with wives should live as if they had none . . . Devote yourselves entirely to the Lord."

Firm in their belief that the Second Coming was almost upon them, early Christians like Paul would have found divorce illogical and unnecessary.

Although this reinterpretation of doctrine in terms of historicity did not result in immediate changes in the attitudes of the Church hierarchy, it did make the theologians who challenged the old tradition—such as Karl Rahner, Edward Schillebeeckx, Charles Curran, and Hans Küng—much in demand on the lecture circuit and their opinions were features in the world press. There is some evidence that the hierarchy was impressed. For instance, the excommunication formerly in force against Catholics who married before a non-Catholic minister was abrogated March 18, 1966, by the Congregation for the Doctrine of the Faith, and shortly thereafter, the Church broadened its pastoral ministry to include divorced and remarried Catholics. This is a beginning, but much more is needed.

The Church's rigid stance on divorce for almost two thousand years is understandable in view of the New Testament admonitions. But now that these admonitions have been reinterpreted thanks to the door opened by Pope John XXIII and Vatican II, it is time that the Church changed its position on divorce and relieved the heartache and/or guilt of so many Catholics while ending the hypocrisy that allows the rich and famous to buy their freedom. One marriage should continue to be the ideal set forth by the Church, but in recognition of the changing times and man's continued imperfection, divorce and remarriage within the Church must be approved.

Pope John XXIII said, "The substance of the ancient doctrine is one thing and the way in which it is presented is another." I interpret this to mean that there is a command to bring about changes that will give strength to the Church, and the acceptance of divorce and remarriage must be given top priority by the Church.

Polls conducted by the *National Catholic Reporter*, the *New York Times*, the *New York Times* Magazine and *Time* support the poll taken by Castelli and Gallup which reports that 69 percent of American Catholics favor a change in the Church's attitude toward divorce and remarriage.

Divorce has been consistently condemned by the Church, in keeping with its absolute prohibition by Jesus. However, Jesus did this to protect women who had no legal protection against divorce and if divorced had no property rights or means of making a living. In addition, he did not write this but rather it was written by his disciples. However, it showed his empathy and sensitivity to a situation which at that time and in that society was unjust. Today, women are not at the mercy of men to the extent they were in Christ's time. Jesus was protecting women from exploitation when he took a stronger stand against divorce than Moses. The doctrine in which Jesus proclaimed that a man committed adultery when he divorced his wife in favor of another woman obviously presumed a lifelong fidelity of the husband to one wife in contrast to the practices of some Old Testament figures (Mt. 19:3-12).

Currently there is a most significant change which has occurred in the question of divorce. Divorced and remarried Catholics are participating in the Eucharistic Celebration. The question is constantly raised about only changing the pastoral practice and allowing divorced and remarried Catholics to participate in the Eucharist. It is my belief that a change in the teaching on indissolubility is demanded by an in-depth and proper theological interpretation of scriptural evidence and contemporary experience.

TEN

Silencing Dissent

A great blessing for the Church has been its wealth of extraordinary theologians. Their value over the past three decades cannot
be overestimated. Without them, Vatican II and the changes it produced could never have taken place. True, the greatest single force
leading to Vatican II was John XXIII, surely one of the most important
Popes in history. But when he called for Vatican Council II, Pope
John was met with a massive wall of resistance. The curia fought the
council with every means available, fearful as its members were that
it would eventually mean loss of prestige and power for them. Only
the worldwide pressure produced by Catholic theologians through
their writings and public appearances enabled the Pope to go forward with his dream.

Even after the meeting of the council was assured, the curia did
not give up. If they could not *stop* the council, then it would make it a
sham; it would make its pronouncements paltry and its reforms
irrelevant. In this endeavor, the curia was aided by the worldwide
network of bishops, whose duty it was to agree upon an agenda for
the council. Trained as they had been in the anti-intellectual shadow
of the modernism heresy hunt triggered by Pope Pius X in 1907, the
bishops had no knowledge of theology in the modern world and
they were confused by the multiplicity of subjects listed as possible
for Vatican II. Not suprisingly, the agenda the bishops suggested was
mostly reactionary and conservative.

Again, the theologians came to the rescue. Brilliant and courageous in their leadership, they broke the curia's stranglehold on the
council agenda and with the help of cardinals like Lienart and Frinze
encouraged the bishops to go beyond their own limited training, to

begin meeting in small groups to discuss a real agenda for Vatican II. The bishops not only started to begin to read, study, and hold seminars, to their everlasting credit they actually invited many of these brilliant theologians to come to Rome and work *with them!*

All this determined activity and concern brought about the reforms of Vatican II, followed by fifteen years of progress until the election of Pope John Paul II. After Vatican II, theologians were asked to teach, lecture, and write about the reforms. All kinds of people, lay, religious, and clerical, Catholic and non-Catholic, sought them out. They were now in demand. At Temple University in conservative Philadelphia, for example, Bernard Häring, a priest and member of the Redemptorists and professor of moral theology at the Academia Alfonsian/Lateran University in Rome, considered the "father of modern Catholic moral theology," taught a course in Vatican II and ethical issues. Six hundred and fifty sisters, priests, and laypeople signed up for the course. At last, it seemed, the great Catholic theologians would have the impact they deserved. To mention only a few examples:

HANS KÜNG did not first begin speaking out as a result of Vatican II. In 1951 he wrote a thesis for his doctorate on the "Esthetic Humanism of Jean-Paul Sartre." Sartre, a French writer, was a leading exponent of twentieth-century existentialism, whereby man is free and totally responsible for what he makes of himself. In 1959 Küng wrote his thesis for his licentiate in theology on doctrines of justification and Karl Barth, one of the most influential *Protestant* theologians at the time. However, as the result of Vatican II, Küng began to travel much more extensively and his popularity soared. He made his first visit to the United States, speaking to huge crowds on the need for and lack of freedom in the Church. He quickly became the symbol of that freedom.

In 1967 he published *The Church.* It was, like all of his books, plausible and easy to read, even though it touched on many complex subjects. He discussed papal infallibility, the Virgin birth, the divinity of Christ. He urged that the hierarchy of the Church act on behalf of the youths who were so largely alienated from the Church. He defended women who, faced with the authoritarian and celibate male hierarchy, were leaving the Church and supported those theologians and nuns who had been unjustly reprimanded or browbeaten. He also wrote on behalf of Protestant churches as well as on behalf of Jews, Moslems, and members of other religions, asking the hierarchy to work for unprejudiced dialogue and understanding. He spoke out for the Church laity, asking the hierarchy to work for freedom of thought and conscience for all Catholics.

CHARLES CURRAN was a priest of the diocese of Rochester, New York, when the early announcement for initiating changes in the Church through Vatican II was made. Immediately, he began holding numerous conferences on moral theology that were enthusiastically received by most lay Catholics, both male and female, and the grass-roots clergy. Moving to the Catholic University in Washington, D.C., he became a popular teacher and lecturer. After the publication of Pope Paul VI's very disappointing *Humanae Vitae*, Curran joined a group of theologians who signed a statement questioning the encyclical's prescription of total or partial abstinence from sexual intercourse as the only morally permissible method for birth control. Due to his great popularity as a speaker and author, Curran had a great effect upon the laity in terms of their response to the Church's rejection of all reliable forms of birth control.

Curran also wrote and spoke about his differences with the Vatican concerning such matters as sterilization, abortion, masturbation, premarital intercourse, homosexual acts, the indissolubility of marriage, and euthanasia. His writings, especially *Tensions in Moral Theology*, challenged the distinction between the Church's infallible and non-infallible teaching.

EDWARD SCHILLEBEECKX occupied teaching posts at Lourvan and at Nizmegan in Holland, where he taught from 1958 until his retirement in 1983. A teacher, author, and lecturer, he began raising questions about the resurrection of Jesus and the evolution of Christology in New Testament times. He contended that Jesus did not rise physically from the grave and was not a divine being who "descended to the earth." Employing textual analysis, he argued the earliest Christians did not believe these claims either. Such conclusions were by no means new to theologians and biblical scholars, but what *was* new was to have them stated so publicly and with such evidence by a Roman Catholic theologian of such high repute. Schillebeeckx maintained that the synoptic gospels were closer to the truth about Jesus than the Gospel of John. In so doing, Schillebeeckx was suggesting a change in the ethical teaching of the Church—more freedom of conscience in religious matters and more sympathy with the ability of human history to instruct conscience.

JACQUES POHIER, professor of moral theology on the Dominican faculty of Saulchoir, France, challenged the curia when he published books that did not follow the official teaching of the Church in moral matters, especially *Quand je dis Dieu* (*When I Speak of God*).

Jesuit WILLIAM CALLAHAN disagreed with Pope John Paul II's statement in 1979, forbidding women to serve as ministers of the Eucharist at the celebration.

Father TERRY SWEENEY, a Jesuit theologian, developed a questionnaire on controversial positions in the Catholic Church, clearly proving a great difference of opinion existed among clergy at all levels, including bishops, about the established Vatican positions.

Archbishop RAYMOND HUNTHAUSEN of Seattle openly admitted his disagreement with the Vatican on a variety of matters—political, sexual, liturgical, and pastoral.

Thanks to men such as these, a window had been raised, just as Pope John XXIII had hoped. Light and air were being let in on a musty Church. The spirit of reform was greeted with joy and anticipation around the world, but Pope John XXIII had died, and without his moral strength and leadership, the situation began to change. Although Pope Paul VI (elected June 21, 1963 and died August 6, 1978) struggled to keep the spirit of reform alive and did so quite successfully in some areas, such has not been the case with the current Pope, John Paul II (elected on October 16, 1978). Almost as soon as this Pope was elected, the curia and its reactionary views became powerful enough to challenge the reforms Vatican II had wrought, reforms that members of the curia saw as an erosion of their own personal power. It was not long before they began taking steps to halt this erosion.

The Jesuits, recognized as the great teachers of the Church, were seen by the curia as major culprits in the continuing changes flowing out of Vatican II. As a result, Father Arrupe, the Jesuit General in Rome, was forced by the Pope to send out a letter telling the Jesuits to desist in their criticism of any position taken by the Vatican. When Father Arrupe was not successful in controlling the Jesuits, rumor had it that the Pope would replace him. At about that time Father

Arrupe became severely ill. Knowing the independent spirit of the Jesuits, I doubted the Pope could or would even try to replace him.

Soon, many of the theologians who had led the way to Vatican II were under pressure. On December 18, 1979, Hans Küng became the subject of a vicious attack by the Pope, so much so that theologians around the world were shocked and the attack backfired. In addition to *The Church*, Küng had written *Infallible? An Inquiry*, which challenged the infallibility of the Pope, *On Being a Christian*, and *Does God Exist?*

There were a number of basic reasons for the Vatican to silence Hans Küng: his effectiveness in communication; his absolute honesty; his dynamic, historical, critical understanding of truth statements; his placing of the historical person of Jesus as the center of Christian belief and practice; and his involvement with feminism and liberation theology. But, of course, the ultimate goal was to reduce Küng's popularity and influence. Organizations supporting Küng's views were formed in France, Germany, North America, and Australia.

The Vatican retreated while the Holy See consolidated and reorganized its forces. It was then that Joseph Cardinal Ratzinger was made head of the Vatican's Congregation for the Doctrine of the Faith, the better to enforce his and the Pope's archaic ideas.

Meanwhile, the Catholic sisters around the world had accelerated their campaign for reform. The curia struck back, sending warning letters with threats of dire consequences unless the activity ceased, but the sisters were not listening. Madonna Kolbenschlag in her book *Women in the Church* asked that all of the voices raised to challenge the Church call the Church to conversion, to evangelize itself by recognizing and empowering the full dignity of women, made also in the image of God. Kolbenschlag stated:

> The agenda for the *next* Council could easily be gleaned from these pages—theological, spiritual and canonical foundations; developing an ecclesiology that includes women; the scandal of sexism in the liturgy and ministry, as well as in marriage; the call to conversion from patriarchy and clerical culture; the legitimate self-determination of individual women and women's communities; the empowerment of laity; spirituality and strategy for a change.

The curia roared in protest, as it had when Sister Teresa Kane—on television—requested in the Pope's presence during his visit to

Washington, D.C., that women be ordained in the priesthood. The curia's roar reached a crescendo in its 1984 attack on the pro-choice Democratic candidate for the United States Vice Presidency, Geraldine Ferraro. The attack was engineered by John Cardinal O'Connor of New York, who sent some of his prelates to chastise Ferraro. But the attack resulted in a response different from what the curia had expected. Catholics, both lay and clerical, showed their rebellious spirit by signing a statement in the *New York Times* stating that there were different positions among Catholic theologians and with reflective Catholic laity on questions surrounding abortions. Twenty-six sisters signed this statement, so the Vatican began hounding them. Some called it "nun bashing."

Some rebelliousness was also shown by the U.S. bishops. During the early 1980s, they became increasingly vocal, opposing the Vatican more than once. Through their collaborative efforts on pastorals concerning nuclear war and the economy, the bishops enhanced their image, clearly indicating that left to their own devices and in close contact with their flocks, they could make significant contributions to the great problems facing the Church.

Such progress could not be taken lightly by the conservative Vatican. In 1985 Pope John Paul II announced that he was calling an extraordinary synod of bishops to *consider* Vatican II. It was obvious this synod would attempt to roll back reforms. The Pope appointed Joseph Ratzinger, head of the Congregation for the Doctrine of the Faith, to head this synod. The Pope and Ratzinger had the same bleak track record on reform, both lacking vision and any real contact with the laity. Reaction to the Pope's obvious intention became so negative that it could be felt by the bishops attending the synod. As a result, the bishops stood firmly behind the reforms of Vatican II.

Alarmed by this unexpected stand on the part of the bishops—as if they might dare to consider themselves partners of the Papacy in running the worldwide Church—the curia searched for a way to put the bishops in their place. First, letters of censure were sent. *U.S. News and World Report* for the week of November 17, 1986, carried a picture of Pope John Paul II on its cover. Inscribed on the first page were the words, "The Pope Cracks Down on American Bishops."

Later, it was "requested" that the bishops shelve their recently proposed system for resolving disputes with Catholic theologians because this system might increase the prestige and importance of the bishops. Behind-the-scenes pressure was brought by the cardinals to make certain the bishops accepted this "request." They did so, and since that date, as if properly chastised, the bishops have played only a small role in the continuing crises.

The curia had also been taking steps to silence the theologians. The Vatican's declaration concerning Hans Küng in 1979 had stated that he could no longer be considered a Catholic theologian and could not function as such in a teaching role. Following this statement, the bishop of Tübingen in Germany found legal grounds to request the state to replace Küng as professor of Catholic theology at the University of Tübingen. This was to be done on the basis of a concord between the Vatican and Hitler's Germany in 1933! It was all carefully planned and executed in a series of secret meetings involving key members of the Vatican and German goverment hierarchies that read like a James Bond novel.

Küng was summoned to Rome and was not allowed to have access to the documents in his Vatican dossier. However, Küng had become so popular that the Vatican was only able to remove him as a member of the Catholic theology faculty of the University of Tübingen and he was disqualified from teaching theology in the name of the Church. However, he remained professor of ecumenical theology and director of the Ecumenical Institute of the university. He published a scathing attack on the pontificate of Pope John Paul II comparing him unfavorably with the great reformer, Pope John XXIII. He accused the current Pope of halting Church reform, blocking ecumenical progress, and substituting unilateral preaching for serious dialogue with the modern world. Küng stated that this had been done without regard for the frustration and disappointment rampant among church members. Küng was especially intense in his criticism of the Pope's treatment of women, insisting that "the women's question will increasingly become the test case of this pontificate." He made a ringing call for the bishops to act courageously against the reactionary forces in the Vatican and to speak out forthrightly for those experiencing alienation and oppression in the Church.

In the *New York Times* on September 24, 1986, a leading archbishop challenged the Vatican on silencing dissent. One of the nation's most influential Roman Catholic bishops, Archbishop Rembert G. Weakland of Milwaukee, strongly questioned the Vatican's efforts to impose a stricter orthodoxy on the American church by disciplining leaders who dissent. It was the first time a leading

American bishop had criticized a series of Vatican actions such as those against Archbishop Raymond G. Hunthausen of Seattle, the Reverend E. Curran, and others. It represented an expression of the discontent among the clergy against the unilateral actions of the Vatican. His disagreement with Rome made him an even more popular lecturer, but the hierarchy continued to do all it could to prevent him from speaking or writing.

Charles Curran was also being dealt with. He was denied tenure at the Catholic University in Washington, but a spontaneous strike of almost all the professors and students demanded that Curran not only be granted tenure, but also promoted. The protestors won. However, Curran was soon summoned to Rome and interrogated by Cardinal Ratzinger. The so-called "official process" for Curran did not conclude until August 1986, when he was notified that in light of his dissent, Curran could no longer be considered a Catholic theologian. He was stripped of his teaching position at the Catholic University.

Other cases where the curia silenced dissent included:

EDWARD SCHILLEBEECKX, relentlessly harassed by the Vatican, was finally called to Rome for interrogation. Despite great support for this theologian led by Jan Cardinal Willebrands, Schillebeeckx has been effectively silenced.

French Dominican theologian JACQUES POHIER was attacked and told of the great displeasure held by the Congregation of the Doctrine of the Faith about his beliefs. He was given no fair opportunity to respond.

Father TERRY SWEENEY was told to destroy his questionnaire material proving disagreement among the clergy and when he failed to do so was dismissed by the Jesuits.

In September 1986, Archbishop RAYMOND HUNTHAUSEN was stripped of much of his authority by the Vatican. It was not only a startling but disturbing development for United States Catholics. A conservative bishop was appointed to share his ministry and to take charge of a number of critical areas of diocesan life.

Archbishop Hunthausen was charged with a lack of firmness because he permitted sterilizations in Catholic hospitals, with misuse of marriage annulments, and with affiliations with homosexual groups. In 1982 he withheld a portion of his income tax to protest the stockpiling of nuclear weapons. In April 1989, following a report of a commission that investigated Hunthausen, his authority was restored, but a coadjutor archbishop was to be appointed.

Pope John Paul II and his curia has set out to turn back the clock to the days prior to Vatican II in the fields of systemic theology, Christian morality, biblical studies, catechetics, and canon law. To achieve this goal, they have systematically attempted to demean, punish, and thereby silence the most important voices in the Catholic Church. Without the likes of Küng, Curran, Schillebeeckx, Rahner, and Yves Congar, there would have been no Vatican II, no educated bishops to provide an agenda, and no major reforms in the Church.

Since Karl Rahner and Yves Congar played a dominant role in shaping the agenda for Vatican II, it is important to briefly describe them.

Karl Rahner was ordained a priest in 1932. In 1939, he published a book, *Spirit in the World*, which was recognized by scholars as a contribution to philosophical understanding of human knowing. His lectures and writings often brought him into conflict with the Roman curia. Much of his time and energy was expended at the Second Vatican Council, where he served as a pexitus, giving lectures to the bishops and helping draft some of the major documents.

Yves Congar was a Dominican priest who devoted his life to an ecumenical vocation. He wrote and talked about it. His method was primarily historical, which helped him bring modern questions into perspective. He insisted that theology must be historical. Many of his insights were enshrined in the Vatican II Decree on Ecumenism. His labors helped bring humans to the point where all theological differences among the main Christian churches are now solvable in principle.

Why does the Vatican struggle so to silence its greatest theologians, thinkers, and talents? Are they dangerous? Does public questioning by a public theologian of the Church's position in a particular issue usurp the teaching authority of the magisterium? Does public questioning confuse and upset the laity? Does the academic responsibility of the theologian to examine and report conflict with the institutional role of the theologian as a teacher?

I do not think so. The curia seeks to silence these theologians only because the curia fears change, believes itself to be the sole custodian of divinely revealed mysteries, and sees loss of power if it must share this responsibility with others. Andrew Greeley states that the Vatican is not only corrupt, but, worse, incompetent.

After suffering endless abuses and harassment, Hans Küng was finally prompted to gather a group of brilliant scholars to write a book, *Church in Anguish—Has the Vatican Betrayed Vatican II?* In the introduction, Leonard Swidler stated that the book had grown out of the agony and concern engendered in the Catholic Church during the past decade through "what appears to many Catholics and non-Catholics as an attempt by the present leadership in the Vatican to reverse the momentous gains in maturity that were made at the Second Vatican Council."

The curia cannot totally silence men like Hans Küng and Charles Curran and Edward Schillebeeckx, but it can and has severely muted their voices. To the degree that each of us allows this to happen, we are guilty of helping the Vatican return to the era before Vatican II when to think was to sin.

We as Catholics must join with people of goodwill in an ecumenical movement that will bring the institutional Church into the twenty-first century. We must never betray the hopes and goals Pope John XXIII had for Vatican II. Anything less will almost certainly lead to death and decay for the institutional Church.

The male chauvinist wearing a Roman collar has lost his magic and power. Collegiality must replace the totalitarian power of the Pope and the curia. Lord Acton said that power corrupts and absolute power corrupts absolutely. With the papacy in mind, Andrew Greeley expanded on this on page 195. I add that unless clerical power is checked by lay power, there will be no justice in the Catholic Church.

Extraordinary
Childbirth

I read about you in the *Times* and I was very glad to find someone finally speaking out about the Church. But I noticed that, although the article mentioned in vitro fertilization, you never came out and said what your feelings are about it. This is a marvelous advance that any sane person should applaud. What in God's name can the Church find wrong with helping childless parents conceive, whether in the womb or in a dish? Is something automatically wrong because it's new? Is it wrong because it came from science rather than the Church? I wonder how we'd have done with our Space Program if we'd been guided by the Church—still believing the sun revolves around the earth!

These questions were put to me with almost the same wording by hospital personnel and by many of my colleagues. In 1978 a baby daughter was born to Lesley and Gilbert Brown of Oldham, Great Britain. Her birth was a landmark in infertility research because she was the first infant ever to develop from an egg fertilized *outside* the mother's body, the so-called "test-tube baby."

Because of a defect in Mrs. Brown's fallopian tubes, she had tried unsuccessfully for nine years to conceive a child. To bypass the defective tubes, eggs were removed from Mrs. Brown's ovary and placed in a glass dish, where they were exposed to sperm from her husband and then allowed to incubate. When the fertilized eggs began to divide, one was inserted in Mrs. Brown's uterus, where it implanted itself and developed. Delivered by caesarean section, the infant was normal in all respects.

Since then, in vitro (literally, "in glass") fertilization has become widely accepted. Many clinics now exist—in Great Britain, Australia, the United States, Canada, and other countries—to provide this science to infertile couples. Hundreds of test-tube babies have been born as a result.

Many technological and pharmacological advances made it possible to achieve success in creating life in a test tube. First, experiments were conducted to be certain the egg could be fertilized outside the body. When this had been proven, the use of a laparoscope (a fiberoptic instrument inserted below the belly button to visualize pelvic organs), ultrasound (a sound wave beamed into the pelvis giving an outline on a screen of the pelvic organs), and Clomiphine (a synthetic drug used to stimulate ovulation) or Menotropins (originally extracted, interestingly enough, from urine collected in nunneries) made it possible to predict accurately the optimal time to recover a freshly ovulated egg. Advances in neuroendocrinology (control of the endocrine system through nerve impulses) and research on gonadotropin-releasing hormones (hormones from the hypothalamus that control the release of hormones which directly affect the ovary) added still another dimension.

After much additional research, Dr. Patrick C. Steptoe, a gynecologist, and Dr. Robert G. Edwards, a physiologist, achieved the dream of generations of physicians, scientists, writers—and, most of all, infertile women—by transferring life from the test tube to a uterus or womb that had been carefully prepared to receive its precious visitor and carry life conceived in a test tube to a live pregnancy.

This miraculous technology led not only to in vitro, but also to other methods of fertilization: Gamete Intra-Fallopian Transfer, or GIFT, involves extraction of an ovum, placing it near sperm cells in a catheter, and then inserting both into a fallopian tube—there are now variations of this method but the basic idea is unchanged; embryo transfer (ET) is the transfer of an ovum fertilized outside of the body and transferred to the uterus, and other assisted reproductive technologies. Another method, surrogate motherhood, produced a remarkable result.

On October 12, 1991, in Aberdeen, South Dakota, twins were born to Arlette Schweitzer, the first American woman to bear her own grandchildren as a surrogate for her daughter. Mrs. Schweitzer, fifty-two, carried the babies for her daughter Christa and son-in-law Kevin. Christa, twenty-two, was born without a uterus, which made it impossible for her to have children. Eggs were taken from Christa's ovaries, fertilized with her husband's sperm, and implanted in Mrs. Schweitzer's womb.

Although born five weeks early, the twins, a boy and a girl, were both healthy with mature lungs. During delivery, Christa was at her mother's side, tears of joy running down her cheeks as she watched her children arrive. Said Mr. Schweitzer, grandfather of the twins, "They're just like two little miracles."

How incredible such occurrences would have seemed not too many years ago—an infertile mother giving birth to a test-tube baby and a woman able to act as surrogate mother for her own grandchildren. How did the Church respond to these miracles? The response was predictable, and it came from the Vatican transmitted by prefect Cardinal Ratzinger, speaking for the Congregation for the Doctrine of the Faith. The Vatican stated that test-tube fertilization reduces human beings to objects and degrades their being, value, and dignity. The Vatican held that the Church was morally opposed to virtually all forms of artificial fertilization that bypass sexual intercourse, require outside donors of sperm or egg, or involve the destruction of embryos.

The Vatican condemned the advances made possible by Dr. Steptoe and Dr. Edwards. The Pope attacked both in vitro fertilization and surrogate motherhood. These negative views were summarized by the Congregation for the Doctrine of the Faith in its "Instruction on Respect for Human Life and Its Origin and the Dignity of Procreation." The congregation termed the process of fertilization used for both in vitro and surrogate motherhood "illicit and indirect opposition to the dignity of procreation and of the conjugal union." The statement ignored completely the fact that these new technologies protect the human embryo, which the Church in other circumstances considers so sacred.

The Reverend James McCarthy, director of the Bioethics Institute at St. Francis Hospital, stated: "It is God's will that lovemaking and childbearing can never be separated." He does not say how he learned that this is God's will, and since there is nothing in Scripture that suggests such an idea, one can only suppose that the Reverend Mr. McCarthy is basing this on words from the Pope.

In a press conference, Joseph Cardinal Ratzinger stated that the use of in vitro fertilization was not a loving act but "an egotistical one."

Bishop Walter Sullivan of Richmond, Virginia, also echoed the Vatican's view. Frightened by the possibility that the Eastern Virginia Medical School might open an in vitro clinic, Sullivan spoke of "cultural schizophrenia" in which research concerning test tube babies goes on while at the same time "through legal abortion we deny life to possibly millions of babies each year." After raising a number of questions about in vitro fertilization, Sullivan said, "We live in an age which has great benefits but which also mechanizes family life, depersonalizes human relationships, disintegrates marriage and marital intimacy. Is the test tube baby but another step in the dehumanizing process by which the person becomes nothing more than a product in a create-and-discard society?"

Speaking on behalf of the National Conference of Catholic Bishops, Archbishop John May of St. Louis seemed to reflect the Pope's negative thinking on in vitro and surrogate motherhood while keeping his statement sufficiently ambiguous:

> I welcome the instruction on respect for human life and its origin and the dignity of procreation. I am grateful to the Congregation for the Doctrine of the Faith for presenting a clear and compelling exposition of Catholic teaching and its application to contemporary concerns of life and death significance. The instruction demonstrates that the Church's moral teaching has much to contribute to elucidation of the moral dimensions of experimentation and practices in the field of bioethics. I hope that, as a result of this instruction, such considerations will be given appropriate attention by scientists, researchers, ethicists and all concerned.

It would appear the archbishop was struggling to serve two masters: American Catholics and the Vatican.

May was not the only church leader who spoke ambiguously on the subject. Joseph Cardinal Bernardin of Chicago, confronted by reporters, tried to sidestep the issue by saying in effect that Catholics shall render the things to God that are God's and to Caesar the things that are Caesar's. He declared couples who are unable to have children must make their own decisions after prayer and reflection. He based his statement on his personal experience with infertile couples who yearn for a child. I am totally in agreement with the cardinal's philosophy, which serves a pluralistic society and a pluralistic religion well. As I read his statement, I could also sympathize with his insecurity, knowing that in some small measure he had opposed the dogmatic statement made by the Pope.

A member of the National Conference of Catholic Bishops Committee for Pro-life Activities, Cardinal Bernardin said in part, "I look forward to joining with others in our society to work for legislation that will protect the rights spoken of in the instruction of the Congregation for the Doctrine of the Faith on Bioethics and Procreation." The statement continued as follows, "Similarly its reasoned rejection of improper experimentation on human embryos of surrogate mothers, of in vitro fertilization and of artificial insemination *will provide Catholics and other people of good will with criteria for making sound moral judgments*."

The italics are mine, for the last half of that final sentence is clearly *not* an endorsement of the Vatican's position. On the contrary, Cardinal Bernardin is saying that people should know how the Pope feels, but then should consider their own feelings and make up their own minds on the subject.

The cardinal went on to say, "We must continue to minister to those who suffer the pain of infertility in marriage and to cooperate with medical sciences as they seek appropriate remedies for infertility."

Once again, the cardinal's words appear to move him a considerable distance away from the Pope's position. Many members of the clergy took similar positions, and the Vatican was soon under siege by a group of theologians who are, as pointed out previously, brilliant, visionary, empathetic, and compassionate. They strongly support these new fertility techniques. There is no unanimous opinion on assisted reproductive technology. Archbishop Daniel E. Pilarczyk of Cincinnati and theologians at the Pope John Paul II Medical-Moral Research and Education Center near Boston approved the low tubal ovum transfer (LTOT). It confirms my opinion that Catholics must be guided by their conscience in making a decision about this issue.

How should the laity respond to this unresolved division in the Church? Should they share in the joy of previously infertile mothers or should they join the Vatican in its condemnation of in vitro fertilization and surrogate motherhood? The truth is, American Catholics are ill prepared to evaluate these technologies. How could it be otherwise when the Church is already so divided on other matters relating to human reproduction? The Vatican denounces every realistic method of birth control, yet Catholics use the pill or the condom or other contrivances in precisely the same percentages as non-Catholics.

It is, in fact, the Vatican's position on birth control that is the basis for its denouncement of the new fertility technologies. When Pope Paul VI in his encyclical *Humanae Vitae* condemned all artificial conception because it deliberately deprives the conjugal act of its openness to procreation, he laid the cornerstone for the Vatican's response to in vitro: The marital sexual act must not be tampered with for any reason; sexual intercourse and procreation must remain united in each marital act so that "lovemaking and babymaking" are never separated.

Although the Catholic Church has stated that human beings rise above animals because of their spirituality and intellect, by demanding that procreation only take place through the conjugal act they are reducing husband and wife to the level of a thoroughbred racing horse. There can be no artificial insemination of a thoroughbred racing horse. A colt can be conceived only through an act of a stallion and a mare. It is a shame that this intellect and ability to create life that God in his infinite wisdom has given to mankind cannot be used for procreation.

Based on this argument, no technological intervention in the sexual act could be approved, no matter how grand its results. All of the Vatican's arguments against artificial contraception are reiterated and applied so as to condemn any procedure that separates, even temporarily, the functions which "naturally" occur together. Thus, all reproduction by in vitro fertilization or third-party surrogacy is deemed immoral and the only possible stance toward the new technologies is condemnation.

I have been unable to find any concrete and logical support for this argument in Scripture or other Church teaching. It is arbitrary and has been self-perpetuating. Without trying to be facetious, let me ask this question: If God were so intent upon connecting connubial bliss and delivery, why did he separate them by forty weeks?

Sexual intercourse is not the only loving act in marriage. Procreation is not only the result of parents' coitus, but also the fruit of the parents' intangible love. What act could be more loving than to employ all the methods available—regardless of cost or difficulty—to achieve pregnancy?

The aim of in vitro fertilization and surrogate motherhood is the complete opposite of contraception and abortion. While contraception and abortion seek to prevent life or take it, these new technologies seek to save "life" that would otherwise be lost. Yet the Vatican packages them all together, as if the encyclical *Humanae Vitae* had hoisted the Church on its own petard.

The absurdity of the Vatican's position is demonstrated by its response to some of the fertilization methods that have been achieved since the success of in vitro. One method, gamete intra-fallopian transfer (GIFT), involves extracting an ovum, placing it near sperm cells in a catheter, and then inserting both into the fallopian tube. Conception follows inside the woman's body.

Although there has been no official word from Rome on GIFT, many Catholics have judged the technique acceptable provided masturbation is not involved in the collection of the sperm. Instead of masturbation, a perforated condom is used during intercourse, and sperm is retrieved from the condom afterward. If this method of sperm collection is followed, it is believed that GIFT and related methods of fertilization will be approved by the Pope. Why?

First, fertilization takes place inside the woman rather than inside a dish—even though the ovum and the sperm will have been placed there artificially. Second, masturbation will not be used. And third, the condom used to collect the sperm will have been perforated so that the act of coitus was "open" to fertilization, even though there was not one chance in a billion of that happening!

Perhaps one could start a discussion about how large the perforation in the condom needs to be in order to make this charade acceptable, and then the Church could return to the same kind of arguments it enjoyed when trying to determine how many angels might be balanced on the head of a pin.

Consider the truth of this matter: The married couples seeking in vitro fertilization or surrogate motherhood to create life do *not* deprive the conjugal act of its "openness" to procreation, nor do they disassociate the goods and meanings of marriage. As a matter of fact, most of them in desperation have extended themselves physically over and above the limits of those who seek intercourse merely for carnal pleasure. They are a despairing group pleading for help and often finding it difficult to retain their faith in God because he has denied them the one thing they want most—a baby.

On numerous occasions, I have seen the wonderful transformation that takes place in a marriage when a couple so long hungry for offspring share the joy of having brought forth a child. The couple may have a selfish motive, but they also are carrying out the command of God when he said go forth and procreate and populate the world. Mutual love is expressed in the suffering of the wife in the harvesting of her eggs and in the husband in the production of his sperm.

Scientific medical paradigms—as well as theological paradigms—change. Human search and discovery find deeper insights into the workings of nature. New medical discoveries and methodologies can be utilized to relieve suffering and are mediated by the physician as gifts of a loving creator. Even the Congregation for the Doctrine of Faith in its instruction paradoxically admits that the child who is a product of in vitro fertilization and embryo transfer must still be considered a gift from God.

I have heard some argue that man should not intervene with those who are infertile, for their condition may be punishment from God. In this argument, the point is made that except for congenital anomalies and adhesions secondary to surgery, venereal disease resulting from promiscuity is the chief cause of blocked tubes. The infertility is then considered justice or retribution for violating arbitrarily established human values, and "the punishment fits the crime."

This philosophy defames the 20 percent of monogamous women who, despite a virtuous life, have been condemned to infertility. It also defames the best known sensual sinner of all, Mary Magdalene, who was not only accepted by Christ, but was raised to the dignity of potential sainthood. Her lifestyle undoubtedly left her with blocked fallopian tubes. It is the height of human kindness to offer a second chance to these women—those who have always been monogamous, as well as those who have at some time been promiscuous—by helping them deliver a baby that belongs both to them and their husbands.

If the extraordinary use of organ transplantation from one human to another can be accepted, why not in vitro fertilization and surrogate motherhood? Organ transplantation improves the quality of physical life, and the ability to bear a child improves the quality of psychological life. The analogy seems obvious. And what about artificial insemination? For years this scientific development has been known by the Church without being condoned. Yet isn't this process really far less "natural" than having a baby by in vitro or surrogate motherhood? These babies can be the product of the wife's egg and the husband's sperm. The innuendoes of adultery raised in regard to artificial insemination do not apply here. The new technologies fulfill the one approved aim of marriage—that of procreation—and they do not exclude connubial bliss.

I am not one who subscribes to the belief that if something is technologically possible, it is automatically morally right. That over-simplifies complex problems that cross medical, moral, ethical, political, and social boundaries. The question that must always be answered is whether the good of a new discovery or technology out-weighs the alleged or possible evil. With the technology at hand—in vitro fertilization and surrogate motherhood—I feel they represent a wonderful gift to humanity.

That is not to deny that there are reasons for concern. With surrogate motherhood, for example, there are financial implications that may lead some women to ignore the intangible benefits simply for monetary gain and thereby suffer emotionally. Without well-structured guidelines, a surrogate mother might be placed in a position of deliberately bearing and selling a baby. This could have a devastating effect on the woman and on her other children, damaging the concept of bonding and the relationship between child and family.

But the answer to this potential problem is not to denounce the new technology and toss out the baby with the bath. Rather we must engage in open dialogue to clarify gray areas and offer solid guidelines for the preparation of laws and contracts that will prevent social and psychological harm.

As for in vitro fertilization, there was concern about "unforseen ramifications" that might make the cure worse than the problem. In 1980 the general secretaries of the U.S. Catholic Conference, the National Council of Churches, and the Synagogue Council of America issued a statement that said in part:

> History has shown us that there will be those who believe it appropriate to correct our mental and social structures by genetic means, so as to fit their personal vision of humanity. This becomes more dangerous when the basic tools to do so

are finally at hand. Those who would play God will be tempted as never before.

At the time this statement was made, there were legitimate concerns about the potential for abuse and the possibility of creating deformed babies. But time has proven that both of these worries were without basis. There has been no increase in the number of deformed babies due to these new technologies, and the medical profession and scientists have shown great restraint.

Recently, I received a letter from a colleague who asked a very thoughtful question: "If the Pope could hold Louise Brown, the little English girl who was artificially conceived, do you think he would— or could—look those parents straight in the eye and say their daughter should never have existed?"

I, for one, do not think so.

TWELVE

Euthanasia

I n a materialistic, technologically oriented society, the dying patient is often ignored as a human being. Most people do not fear
death per se, but do fear pain, loss of dignity, abandonment, and
isolation. For those of us who are Catholic physicians and who seek
to make life easier and more comfortable for our patients, treatment
for the terminally ill can lead to many morally troubling questions.

Although seldom discussed three decades ago, euthanasia and
related subjects, such as assisted suicide, are much in the news today:
a book at the top of the bestseller list, a doctor with a "suicide
machine" greatly in demand throughout the nation, a suicide assistant for AIDS patients explaining his "technique" on television. Euthanasia is being discussed today much as abortion was discussed
forty years ago. Organizations have been formed to urge the practice
and legalization of euthanasia, and only recently Washington very
nearly became the first state in the nation to make some form of it
legal.

This is a subject with extraordinarily complex implications that
strike at the most cardinal premises of biblical revelation. They affect
almost every facet of personal and social existence and they emphasize with stark clarity the need for sound Christian principles if the
very foundations of human civilization are to remain intact. For
example, due to the world's rapidly increasing population and the
resulting shortage of food and air and space, questions are being
raised worldwide about the management of helpless invalids, bedridden cripples, and "unproductive" aged people. Should they be
quietly ("mercifully") phased out of existence? And if not, why not?

On a subject so deserving of religious guidance, the institutional

[139]

Church has been disturbingly silent, and when the theological inquiry inspired by Vatican II finally led to some meaningful positions, the hierarchy managed to silence the great theologians, thus effectively closing off further Catholic discussion on this vitally important subject. Why?

There are many reasons, but one of the most obvious is the Church's recognition of its own vulnerability on this subject. How can a worldwide organization such as the Catholic Church speak authoritatively on a question that touches on problems due to overpopulation while the Pope travels from nation to nation admonishing the people not to practice any form of birth control?

So the Church sits idly by, preventing its theologians from discussing euthanasia and pretending that Catholic positions on the subject are sufficient to guide Catholic physicians and other members of the Church, as well as to offer direction to legislators. Are they? Let us see.

WHAT IS EUTHANASIA?

The news media often confuse euthanasia with mercy killing, but they can be very different. For one thing, euthanasia may be God-given or man-made, while mercy killing is always man-made. Although the Euthanasia Society of America defines euthanasia as "the termination of human life by painless means for the purpose of ending severe physical suffering," this definition is dated and much too narrow. In the August 1988 *Bulletin of the American College of Surgeons*, Dr. David C. Thomasma (director of the medical humanities program at Loyola University School of Medicine in Maywood, Illinois) offers these guidelines on the ever-widening range of euthanasia:

> The word comes from the Greek for "good" or "merciful" death. It is the act of painlessly putting to death persons suffering from incurable conditions or diseases. Current usage requires the distinction to be made between active and passive euthanasia (although some prefer a distinction between positive and passive euthanasia). Active euthanasia is an intentional act that causes death. Passive euthanasia is an intentional act that avoids prolonging the dying process.
> Euthanasia in its purest terms can be distinguished from

murder on the basis of motive. Murder would be killing someone for reasons other than kindness, while euthanasia, both
active and passive, aims at a merciful death.

Euthanasia should not be confused with state-sanctioned killings
such as capital punishment or killings that occur during war. These
deadly acts cannot be termed euthanasia since the intent was to kill
and/or punish, not to make the process of dying easier. In the same
way, the Nazi termination of the lives of others for eugenic or economic reasons could not be classified as euthanasia.

Following are some of the most commonly discussed forms of
euthanasia and some of the questions they raise:

1. Killing by family members: Every few months there is an article
   in the paper about a family member who killed his or her relative out of love and compassion because the family member
   was suffering from an incurable disease. Others who have the
   sole responsibility for the care of an invalid, sometimes a
   hopelessly brain-damaged person, realize that they themselves
   are going to die and therefore kill the person they have been
   taking care of so that the person will not be left to the mercy of
   the world. These are cases of active euthanasia that do not
   involve health care professionals, unless they assist in some
   way.
2. Injections: These are sometimes given to put patients out of
   their misery, and in most instances this is done without the
   consent of the patient. Obviously, this procedure is an active
   form of euthanasia. If caught, the persons administering the
   injections are tried for murder. There is another group of
   patients who have *requested* to be relieved of pain and suffering. If these patients are suffering a great deal and request
   euthanasia, is it homicide or an act of mercy? It must be
   remembered that in any discussion of euthanasia, death is not
   considered to be an enemy; rather it is considered to be a
   friend of the patient.
3. Assisted suicide: Sometimes death can be brought about by
   indirectly assisting patients in taking their own lives. For example, with the knowledge of those caring for them, patients may
   have sleeping pills, morphine, or potassium cyanide in a place
   where they can reach it. Is this passive or active euthanasia?

When a health professional taking care of a terminal patient he or she has been following for some time offers the patient a great deal of pain medicine and tells the patient to take as much as he wants, is this murder or is it a mercy killing?

4. Court-ordered removal of life-sustaining treatment: This act raises the question of whether the physicians in hospitals are being forced into practicing euthanasia. When the patient requests the withdrawal of life-sustaining medical care, doctors have a *legal* right to refuse the request. But do they have the *moral* right to do so?

5. Double-effect euthanasia: Many physicians may be guilty of this type of euthanasia, that is, the administration of increased doses of morphine or pain medication to control pain with the knowledge that such a massive dosage will decrease respiration to the extent that the patient may die. This is a very difficult decision and one for which there are *no* guidelines from the Church. If the medication is ordered to be given every four hours and the patient has tremendous pain at three hours and is screaming for medication, but his respiration is depressed, should the doctor administer the pain medicine? Which is the humane position to take, and is this necessarily the moral or religious position? Where is the fine line between murder and euthanasia?

6. Transferring to die: Health care professionals often transfer patients in a terminal state as a means of providing passive euthanasia. Death may occur when the patient is taken from the intensive care or coronary care unit to an intermediate area or to a routine area of treatment. Patients are often sent to hospices. Is this a form of passive euthanasia?

7. Tragic surgical choices: This is a very difficult situation for many physicians to face. At the time of surgery, they find a hopeless situation. For instance, should they resect large areas of dead bowel knowing that the patient will have to be on hyperalimentation (a method for giving proteins, fat, carbohydrates, minerals, and vitamins intravenously) and eventually die, perhaps after a lingering illness, or should they merely close the abdomen and keep the patient comfortable with pain medicine? Here again, the Church offers no guidelines.

8. Withholding and withdrawing: There are situations where crossroads of life have been reached with no demands from

patient, family, or court. The question is, should there be a withholding and withdrawing or not? For the doctor in such cases, the distinction between ordinary and extraordinary care has taken on a normative character not originally intended: Ordinary now means obligatory and extraordinary now means optional. How is the doctor to choose? The kind of euthanasia that can be honorable and may be defined as death with dignity involves the use of "ordinary" care and "ordinary" remedies, but this is a tenuous concept requiring subjective as well as objective criteria. The decision may represent the point at which the science of medicine fails and the art of medicine assumes control.

Questions concerning the practice of euthanasia have increased in number and intensity since 1975, when the parents of comatose Karen Ann Quinlan obtained court authorization to remove her from a life-supporting respirator. Subsequent rulings in New Jersey and elsewhere have permitted the removal of nutrition-hydration tubes, as well as life support systems, from seriously ill persons, some of whom were *not* terminally ill. Cases included those of Nancy Ellen Jobes, Hilda M. Peter, Elizabeth Bouvia, Beverly Requena, Hector Rodas, and Paul E. Brophy, people reported in the media who requested euthanasia.

Decisions in these cases were based on grounds related to quality of life criteria and the supremacy of right of privacy. These grounds, however, are not the only norms of judgment, especially in terms of religious morality. Christian thought about life and death has tried to hold in balance two basic truths: first, that there must be a great respect for life and the need to preserve life, but second, that death is not the greatest evil in the world and one does not have to avoid it at all costs. A technically precise theological statement of this attitude is that we have an obligation to use *ordinary* means to preserve life, but we have no obligation to use *extraordinary* means.

The Church has stated its opposition to the use of any active measures that will lead to death, even if these measures are to be used just hours before the so-called "natural" time for death, yet— very confusingly for the physician—there is support in the Church for the withdrawal of life support systems in instances where they are no longer in the best interest of the sick person, or where the patient has been declared incurably ill as opposed to gravely ill, or where the means to continue life have been declared extraordinary as opposed to ordinary.

These last two words—ordinary and extraordinary—have given rise to a great deal of controversy. What exactly do they mean?

1. Ordinary care is described as providing all medications, treatments, and procedures that offer reasonable hope of benefit to the patient and can be obtained and used without excessive pain, expense, or other inconvenience.
2. Extraordinary care means providing all medicines, treatments, and operations that cannot be obtained without excessive expense, pain, or other inconvenience or that if used would not offer reasonable hope of benefit.

However explicit these definitions may seem, they leave the Catholic physician with a greater latitude than he would like to have. Perhaps the most influential factor in determining the kind of care dispensed is the suffering of the patient. Should the aim be to eliminate all discomfort? Before you answer yes, remember that suffering has special significance for the Christian as an opportunity to share in Christ's redemptive suffering. Is it wrong to try to relieve someone's suffering; could this interfere with other moral and religious duties? For example, is it permissible in the case of terminal illness to use painkillers that carry the risk of shortening life, so long as the intent is to relieve pain rather than to cause death?

The Church has tried to sidestep direct confrontation with such issues by using "the double effect." The double effect is the Catholic principle that says it is morally allowable to perform an act that has at least two effects, one good and one bad, under the following conditions:

1. The act to be done must be good in itself or at least morally indifferent—and by the act to be done is meant the deed itself, taken independently of its consequences.
2. The good effect must not be obtained by means of the evil effect; the evil must be only an incidental by-product and not an actual factor in accomplishment of good.
3. The evil effect must not be intended for itself but only permitted; all bad must be excluded from the act.
4. There must be proportionately grave reason for permitting the

evil effect. At least the good and evil effect should be nearly equivalent.

All four of these conditions must be fulfilled. If any one of them is not satisfied, the act is morally wrong. Can you imagine what it is like for a Catholic physician to try to review this criteria when he or she is caring for a terminal patient in great pain?

Daniel C. Maguire, a professor at Marquette University, has written a book, *Death by Choice*, which has been updated and expanded. It provides a kinder and gentler idea about dying. He states that his son, Danny, had Hunter's disease, a degenerative brain disease. He mentions this, he says, to note that the theory of his book was tested in life and in death and not only in library research. Professor Maguire writes that he and his wife permitted Danny to die peacefully in their own home, sparing him extraordinary measures that would have prolonged his final vegetative state.

Professor Maguire wrote about the statements of Georgetown University's Robert Veatch: "I am even prepared to concede that here may be exceptional circumstances where active killing for mercy is morally acceptable." In addition, he presented a statement by Fordham University's Stephen Rowntree, who can now accurately observe, "The prohibition against direct taking of innocent human life is eroding." He stated, "My original thesis was that in the words of my ninety-two-year-old Irish mother, 'There are worse things than dying'!" At times, allowing death, or in extreme situations, encouraging it, may be the best that life offers.

Dan and Marjorie Maguire gave a eulogy at the funeral of Danny. It is beautiful and tells how they and everyone around Danny ministered to his every need but spared him the agony of extraordinary measures. It is a lesson in life and death and what love and trust in God can achieve. It gave me a great sense of appreciation for their devotion and sensitivity toward Danny. It gave me a sense of humility.

THE CATHOLIC POSITION

"Acts of euthanasia do great dishonor to the Creator of all life forms," says the Church. "All human beings should try to reach for ways to safeguard and respect the lives of others."

Granted, this is a very moral statement, but it does little to come to grips with the complex questions of morality, law, and medicine this subject involves. Yet this was virtually the only kind of "instructional" material offered by the Church on the subject of euthanasia until Pope John XXIII and Vatican II. As in many other important areas, this council encouraged Catholic theologians to discuss and explore the subject of euthanasia. Some such as Charles Curran became so popular and persuasive as author-lecturers that they literally forced the Church to present a position of some sort on euthanasia.

In 1980 the Vatican offered a "Declaration on Euthanasia." This and other Church documents of the same period set forth the following principles defining a "stewardship of life" ethic:

1. The Second Vatican Council condemned crimes against life, including euthanasia or willful suicide. Grounded as it is in respect for the dignity and fundamental rights of human persons, this teaching cannot be rejected on the grounds of political pluralism or religious freedom.
2. As human life is the basis and necessary condition for all other human goods, it has a special value and significance; both murder and suicide are violations of human life.
3. Euthanasia is an action or an omission that, of itself or by intention, causes death in order that all suffering may be eliminated. It is an attack on human life that no one has a right to make or request. Although individual guilt may be reduced or absent because of suffering or emotional factors which could soothe the conscience, this does not change the objective wrong of the act. It should also be recognized that an apparent plea for death may really be a plea for help and love.

On November 10, 1984, the Committee for Pro-life Activities, National Conference of Catholic Bishops, still under pressure from the theologians, offered "Guidelines for Legislation on Life-Sustaining Treatment." Not surprisingly, these guidelines show a considerable difference of opinion. In large part, they say the following:

The Judeo-Christian heritage celebrates life as the gift of a loving God who respects the life of each human being because each is made in the image and likeness of God. As Christians, we also celebrate the fact that we are Redeemed by Christ and called to share eternal life with him. In these roots the Roman

Catholic tradition has developed a distinctive approach to fostering and sustaining human life. Our tradition not only condemns direct attacks on innocent life, but also promotes a general view of life as a sacred trust over which we can claim stewardship, not absolute dominion. As conscientious stewards we see a duty to preserve life while recognizing certain limits to that duty, as was reiterated in the Vatican's "Declaration on Euthanasia." Based on this Declaration, the Committee offers the following recommendations concerning legislation for life-sustaining treatment:

1. Recognize the fundamental right to life of every human being, including the disabled, the elderly and the terminally ill. In general, phrases which seem to romanticize death, such as a "right to die" or "death with dignity," should be avoided.
2. Recognize that the right to refuse medical treatment is not an independent right but a corollary to the patients' right and moral responsibility to request *reasonable* treatment.
3. Avoid granting unlimited power to document (living will) or proxy decision-makers to make health care decision on a patient's behalf. The right to make such decision in one's own behalf is in itself not absolute and, in any event, cannot be fully exercised when a patient has had no opportunity to assess the burdens and benefits of treatment in a specific situation. Laws which allow a decision to be made on behalf of a mentally incompetent patient are in accord with responsible medical practice.
4. Reaffirm public policy against homicide and assisted suicide. Medical treatment legislation may clarify procedures for discontinuing treatment which only secures a precarious and burdensome prolongation of life for the terminally ill patient, while not condoning or authorizing any deliberate act or omission designed to cause a patient's death.
5. Recognize the presumption that certain basic measures such as nursing care, hydration, nourishment and the like must be maintained out of respect for the human dignity of every patient.
6. Protect the interest of innocent parties who are not competent to make treatment decisions on their own behalf.

Life-sustaining treatment should not be discriminatorily withheld or withdrawn from mentally incompetent or retarded patients.

7. Provide that life-sustaining treatment should not be withdrawn from a pregnant woman if continued treatment may benefit her unborn child.

No credit whatsoever goes to the Congregation for the Doctrine of the Faith for these guidelines. They were brought about by pressure from the great moral theologians who worked so diligently to prepare the institutional Church for the twenty-first century. Unfortunately, some of these theologians have been silenced now and the Church's "guidelines," although far better than the blank page previously offered, are already in need of updating. Many tough new questions have arisen since these guidelines were formulated and many more lie just ahead. For example:

1. Cryonics: This includes people who are near death and have their body frozen in hopes that someday they will be brought back to life. If someone assists with cryonics, is it euthanasia or homicide or neither?

2. Selective abortion: Many have considered abortion a form of active euthanasia because it takes innocent lives without the victim's consent. But now there are infertility patients who, having received fertility drugs, are found by ultrasound to have five or six fetuses. It is obvious that if nothing is done, the woman will go into premature labor and possibly lose all of the fetuses. There are ways today of aborting some of these fetuses while allowing the others to continue on to maturity. Is this euthanasia or good medicine?

3. Organ donation: Organ donation is rapidly increasing. In the present climate, the standards require that the patient can no longer participate in this decision and must be brain dead. But allowing natural death to occur when an organ is being sought to save the life of someone in need of that organ may result in too long a delay, with irreversible damage done to the donor organ. If an anencephalic patient (congenital absence of the cranial vault with cerebral hemispheres completely missing or reduced to small masses attached to the base of the skull) is maintained on a respirator so that organs can be harvested for

another human and then the respirator is turned off so that the organs can be obtained, is this euthanasia, murder, or an act of kindness?

4. Social euthanasia: There are more than 50 million people in the United States who cannot gain access to health care simply because they are uninsured or underinsured, and there are no signs that this situation is about to change. Is this a form of *social euthanasia*?

As stated earlier, questions are also being raised on secularist grounds about the management of "unproductive" people: the helpless invalids, bedridden cripples, the very aged. It has been stated that they are useless to society and to themselves, and since they face continual pain and suffering, they should be phased out of this life. Should there be a mandate by public authority for euthanasia? At present, the public answer is no.

However, if the population explosion continues unabated there will surely come a point when struggle on this planet to get enough food and water and air for existence will cause the question of euthanasia to take on new meaning. What is morally proper will be weighed against the suffering of billions of so-called healthy people who have the potential for improving the lot of their fellow human beings. Today, still in a time of relative plenty, it is easy to supply an answer about such an extension of euthanasia. But in a world struggling to survive, answers will not come so readily.

If the seriousness of such questions is doubted, we should remember that the prevailing philosophy in this nation has long been against murder and killing. Yet when the survival of this country was threatened by war, millions were taken into the army, navy, and marines and taught to kill. Those who killed most successfully were often made national heroes. Catholics were there with all the other Christians and Jews, applauding these acts of killing. Before a similar crisis occurs that demands the killing of those who are "useless," firm religious leadership with rational answers must be supplied and the apparatus for continuing dialogue established.

Mankind has gained a sense of mastery of the universe, from control over human life in planning conception to deciding who shall live and for how long. In doing so, however, humans have regrettably developed an indifference to whatever lies beyond the experience of man's life on earth. This has allowed euthanasia to emerge as a force that must be reckoned with in a thorough and knowledgeable manner.

In a complex society that may have 10 billion people early in the next century, it is essential for the Church to consider—openly and with wide discussion—the full range of questions surrounding euthanasia. Without forceful religious leadership, where will the world turn? And since the Vatican has seen fit to silence some of the Church's greatest theologians, where will that leadership come from?

Catholic theology has traditionally condemned euthanasia because human beings do not have full dominion over their lives. Catholics for generations have accepted that God is the creator and giver of life and that we are stewards of the gift that has been given. Today modern medical advances have given human beings much more control and power over their lives and death than ever before.

This power to control our destiny raises the question whether there is an intrinsic moral difference between acts of omission (such as failure to use extraordinary means) and acts of commission (positive methods to bring about death). There is a practical question that arises, i.e., if it is legitimate and acceptable for a Roman Catholic to dissent on contraception and sterilization, is it also legitimate to dissent on abortion and euthanasia? As a Catholic physician, I am troubled by these questions and the controversy they raise. I can only say that at present, I accept that there are new thoughts on death that are not only thinkable, but are also to be seriously considered.

THIRTEEN

Liberation Theology

L iberation theology is spreading across the world: In West Africa, priests are initiated into the confraternity of healers or witch doctors, and they struggle to correlate the healing power of Jesus with traditional healing rites. In Sri Lanka, a Christian lives among the Buddhists and rethinks his Christian identity. One of the foremost black theologians finds his conscious thinking profoundly influenced by his experience among the Minjung theologians of Korea. In Nicaragua, near the Honduran border, a small Christian community of poor campesinos gathers to read the Bible together and discuss what it means to turn the other cheek when they are attacked by soldiers.

For Catholics, liberation theology has been one of the most distinctive developments in the post–Vatican II period. This theology comes out of the struggle for liberation of the economically, politically, and socially oppressed people of South America, just as black theology or feminist theology developed in North America. Why should I, as a Catholic, care about the people of South America or any other oppressed area except the one in which I live? Because in the Christianity of this rapidly shrinking world, we must look not only at ourselves and those around us but beyond. As the Spanish philosopher José Ortega y Gasset wrote, "I am I and my circumstances, I am I and all that is around me. And today more than ever our circumstances embrace the planet."

Liberation theology takes on increased importance for the Church because the Third World—the nations where many of the socially oppressed people live—accounts for an increasing percentage of the

Catholic population. In 1900, 77 percent of all Catholics lived in the industrialized world of the wealthy north and 23 percent in the countries referred to now as the Third World. At the end of this century, 70 percent of all Catholics will be living in the countries of the Third World and only 30 percent in Europe and the United States of America. This social location of Catholicism among the less privileged acquires deeper significance in a global context. In the future, the bulk of the Christian population of the world will be black, brown, and yellow rather than white, poor rather than affluent, and on the revolutionary side of struggles over global military and economic power.

The theology seeks to reflect on the exploitation and oppression of people in the Third World, to translate the Christian message, and to give a credible and authentically Christian answer as to how these people may be "liberated." Obviously, then, this theology will be decisive for the future of the Church in the Third World and yet, sadly, the Vatican has made one attempt after another to crush the movement. Liberation theology is a manifestation of a worldwide movement for human emancipation.

Instead of incorporating the theology into the overall teaching plan of the Church, the Vatican turned these compelling beliefs upside down so that anyone who committed himself or herself on behalf of improving justice and human rights in South America was branded a Communist. Although the collapse of Communism in Eastern Europe and the Soviet Union should have lessened the Pope's fear of Marxism, the Vatican continues its negative attitude toward liberation theology, perhaps because it is hated by such a broad coalition in the hierarchy, extending from the Roman Congregation for the Doctrine of the Faith and its prefect, Cardinal Ratzinger, to the Roman Commission for Latin America and its Latin American Bishops' Conference, CELAM, to conservative reactionary and even totalitarian political forces in the Church. This theology is considered threatening and dangerous, while it should be recognized as an awesome force that must be studied, understood, and incorporated into the teachings of the Church.

How can the Pope and the princes of the Church speak so passionately about the importance of human rights, yet at the same time attack liberation theology, which seeks to bring human rights to the oppressed? What is there about this theology that so frightens and infuriates the Vatican? Let us look backward for a moment.

Theology is the field of study, thought, and analysis that deals with God, his attributes, and his relation to the universe. In a Catholic context, theology concerns the truths of faith, real and theoretical, and their application. Theology literally means the "science of God" as used by the Stoics in the third century B.C. to describe a reasoned analysis of deity. Earlier uses were more naturalistic. Thus, Plato in the *Republic* and Aristotle in his *Metaphysics* called Homer, Hesiod, and Orpheus "theologians" because they first determined the genealogies and attributes of the gods.

With the advent of Christianity, theology came to mean what its etymology suggested (Latin *theologia*, from Greek *theo*, "God," plus *logia*, "knowledge") and was defined by St. Augustine as "reasoning for discourse about the divinity." Through the patristic age to the period of the Schoolmen this definition remained the acceptable generic meaning. Peter Abelard (1079–1144) is credited with first having used the term in its modern connotation, but it was St. Thomas Aquinas (1225–1274) who defended theology as a science because it investigates the contents of belief by means of reason enlightened by faith (*Fides, quaerens intellectum*) in order to acquire deeper understanding or revelation.

Aquinas also distinguished theology proper from natural theology, or what Gottfried Leibniz later called "theodicy," which studies God as knowable by reason alone and independent of divine authority. Since the thirteenth century, the term *theology* has been applied to the whole study of revealed truth and gradually replaced its rival synonyms.

The Second Vatican Council, in its constitution on revelation, made the following declaration about theology and its relation to divine revelation:

> Sacred theology rests on the written word of God, together with sacred tradition, as its primary and perpetual foundation. By scrutinizing in the light of faith and all truths stored up in the mystery of Christ, theology is most powerfully strengthened and constantly rejuvenated by the word. For the sacred Scriptures contain the word of God and, since they are inspired, really are the word of God; and so the study of the sacred pages is, as it were, the soul of sacred theology.

Pope John Paul II, addressing theologians on November 1, 1982, at the Pontifical University of Salamanca, noted that theology, which is necessary for "creative as well as faithful" renewal of the Church, must flow from faith because "doing theology is a task exclusively proper to the believer as believer; it is a task vitally aroused and sustained at every moment of faith." Pope John Paul II has stated that Christian faith is ecclesial. One cannot believe in Christ without believing in the Church, "the body of Christ"; one cannot believe with Catholic faith within the Church without believing in its magisterium, which is above challenge. The Pope called theology "ecclesial science at the service of the Church" and said it must be "dynamically integrated to the Church's mission. Thus, the theologian's task is in the character of an ecclesial mission, as a participation in the Church's evangelizing mission and as outstanding service to the ecclesial community. This is where the theologians' grave responsibility rests."

History of Liberation Theology

In the past, theology has been divided into five fields: dogmatic theology, including Christology and soteriology (Christ and the doctrine of the work of the Redeemer), moral theology, pastoral theology, ascetic theology (the practice of virtue and means of attaining holiness and perfection), and mystical theology (higher states of religious experience). But in 1973, after Gustavo Gutierrez first spoke about liberation theology, the study group Liberation and Church was founded in Peru and became a legitimate division of theology supported by other liberation theologians such as Leonardo Boff and Juan Segundo.

The subject of liberation theology is not theology but liberation. Classical theology aims at a deeper understanding of faith whereas liberation theology aims to transform the world. The reforms live by the dictum that the task of philosophy is not to understand but to change the world. Liberation theology is certainly one of the most significant developments of the last several years. It may create more changes than those brought about by Martin Luther. If one were to look for prophetic leaders among contemporary churchmen, one would have to name Helder Camera of Brazil, Ernesto Cardenal of Nicaragua, or Desmond Tutu of South Africa, rather than any figure emerging from the white First World.

Where did liberation theology come from? Liberation theologians count themselves part of a long and rich heritage. Among the first liberation theologians were those Old Testament writers who told the story of Exodus, the liberation of the Hebrews from the harsh oppression as slaves from Egypt. Although the Latin American Church has too often been in league with the pharaohs of its continent, there has always been a strong liberation tradition as well. For example, the Dominican friar Bartolomé de Las Casas (1474–1566) is affectionately remembered as the defender of the Indians for his courageous protest before the Spanish crown against cruel exploitation by the gold-hungry conquistadors.

Liberation theology also owes something to two non-Catholic theologians from the past, John Frederick Denison Maurice (1805–1872) and Dietrich Bonhoeffer (1906–1945). Although they lived a century apart, they spoke with equal sharpness to the present situation, and despite the fact that they had no direct influence on one another, there is amazing congruence in their liberation thoughts. They offer a healthy counterbalance to modern liberation theology because they spoke more in the indicative than in the imperative.

Maurice was a highly unorthodox English theologian whose teachings and writings were concerned with putting Christianity to work to improve the daily lives of ordinary men and women. He helped found the Working Men's College, as well as the Queen's College for Women. It was his teaching that, more than any other single force, produced Christian Socialism, which opposed laissez-faire individualism and demanded political or economic action in the interest of *all* the people.

Bonhoeffer, one of the first German theologians to be marked as an enemy of the Nazi regime, was a modern Christian martyr, hung by the Germans before he was forty years of age. Bonhoeffer's writings, most of them completed in prison, outline a highly individual interpretation of biblical concepts in a world that he felt had come of age and in which neither metaphysical nor psychological categories were adequate. His work showed the way to a revolution in the understanding of Christian belief, not in a separate "religious" realm, but in a dialectical identity with this world and with Christ as one who is, in suffering, very much *for* this world. Bonhoeffer believed that theologians should make the transition from theory to physically improving the lives of human beings, and this was much like the Christian Socialism of John Frederick Denison Maurice, which was much like the liberation theology of today.

Despite the Vatican's present attitude, important inspiration for liberation theology also came from the great social encyclicals of the Church. *Rerum Novarum* (Pope Leo XIII, 1891) concerned capital and labor, specifically in the context of the poor conditions of the working person and the right of the worker to organize labor unions. *Quadragesimo Anno* (Pope Pius XI, 1931), on reconstruction of the social order, was issued to mark the fortieth anniversary of Rerum Novarum. Addressed to the world, *Mater et Magistra* (Pope John XXIII, 1961) cited the needs of the underdeveloped countries, the depressed state of agriculture, and the pressures of an expanding population and stressed the obligation of wealthy nations to assist nations less fortunate. The document thus broadened previous papal social encyclicals, which had dealt principally with industrial relations and distributive justice in developed industrial countries. Another great encyclical, *Populorum Progressio* (Pope Paul VI, 1967), concerned the development of people and the need to take drastic action to close the growing imbalance between rich and poor nations.

Quadragesimo Anno was particularly important as an antecedent to liberation theology. This encyclical was issued by Pius XI in the midst of the terrible world depression. Together with his other pronouncements on social issues, it indicated how social Catholicism had developed into a coherent social philosophy, more than able to hold its own against its chief rivals, materialistic Marxism and materialistic liberal capitalism. It condemned the control of worldwide finance and credit by a small number of financiers who thus supply, "so to speak, the life blood to the entire economic body—so that no one can breathe against their will. As a result the state has become a slave, bound over to the service of human passion and greed."

This pronouncement clearly supplied some of the foundation for the new liberation theology, but it was not until theologians in Latin America began to apply these socialist teachings of the Church to the wretched conditions there that modern-day liberation theology was born. Gustavo Gutierrez, a Peruvian, was sent to study in Europe and watch the preparation for Vatican Council II. When he returned to Peru, he stated that he had discovered that poverty was destructive and not accidental. He also declared that poor people were a social class. With his understanding that poverty was something to be fought against, that poverty was structural, and that poor people were a class and could organize, it became clear to him that in order to serve the poor, one had to move into *political* action.

In the 1960s Gutierrez began a long process of both reinterpreting and refocusing the Scriptures from the perspective of the poor. His desire and mission was to articulate in the light of the Christian tradition the faith-filled experiences of those struggling for liberation. A parish priest in Lima, Peru, he insisted he was first a pastor and only secondarily a theologian. His writings address the North American–influenced spirituality as excessively spiritualized, individualistic, interior, elitist, and romantic. Gutierrez is a brilliant thinker whose seminal ideas have helped develop and influence the whole movement known as liberation theology. He finds his strength and inspiration in his solidarity with the poor and the oppressed whom he serves. He is the father of liberation theory. I see in his writings the influences of the four encyclicals that I just reviewed.

Liberation theology comes in many varieties because it grows out of the conviction that theology does not belong to the realm of abstract thought and that it must start from honest reflection on the reality in which one lives. Thus there is black liberation theology, Latin American liberation theology and feminist liberation theology, to cite just a few examples. But from whatever perspective liberation theologians begin, they all condemn that "suburban captivity" of the Church that all too often makes church meetings virtually indistinguishable from the Rotary or Elks clubs. The voices of contemporary liberation theologians have contributed greatly to current thought about what the Church really is called to be and to do. They are among the most important and most creative voices in theology today.

Although everyone recognizes that the North American experience is different from the South American experience, there has been much talk about what liberation theology would look like in the North American context. But in a way, even beyond efforts for women and blacks, that question has already been answered. I refer to the community organization approaches developed by Saul D. Alinsky in the 1930s and 1940s. An agnostic Jew who held a variety of jobs, Alinsky had been attracted by the labor union organizers of the CIO. Later he even wrote a biography of John L. Lewis. But his main focus had always been the neglected person in society, and in the late 1930s, he organized the "Back of the Yards" area in Chicago, which had been the scene of Upton Sinclair's book *The Jungle*. This movement launched his lifelong work in community organization which carried through the Industrial Areas Foundation that he began in 1940.

The purpose of Alinsky's community organization would enable the powerless and the have-nots to participate in their destiny. Alinsky referred to himself as a radical in his earlier writings, but in the early 1960s he described himself as a *"realistic* radical" to distinguish himself from the radicals of the New Left. Alinsky defines a true radical (a realistic radical) as a person to whom the common good is the greatest personal value. A true radical wants a world in which the worth of the individual is recognized, where all human beings are economically, politically, and socially free. According to Alinsky, a true radical is passionately devoted to democracy.

With his own person, Alinsky illustrated the importance he attached to irreverence as a primary virtue in the organizer, a quality that has not endeared him to the Vatican. In his discussions, he often refers to his irreverence as a purposeful tendency to polarize issues by using hyperbole to infuriate his opponents. According to Alinsky, liberals like people with their heads, while radicals like people with their heads and hearts. Liberals are well balanced, impartial, and objective; whereas radicals are passionate partisans for the poor and the victims of injustice.

Alinsky also pointed out that the issue of power constitutes a fundamental difference between radicals and liberals. Liberals fear power. Radicals use power. Liberals often agree with goals, but will never use conflict and power tactics to achieve these goals. Radicals use conflict and power and actually precipitate the social crisis for their actions. There are as many clear lines between radicals and liberals as there are between liberals and conservatives. It is obvious that Alinsky often found himself at odds with liberals. They agreed with him at least in theory about the existence of the problems and the goals to be achieved, but they strongly disagreed with his tactics.

In selecting issues, Alinsky gave succinct advice: "Pick the target, freeze it, personalize it and polarize it." In reality, nothing is 100 percent good or bad, but in organizing, says Alinsky, one must act as if the issue is so. Through such tactics the organizer goads the enemy into a response. The response often involves a tactical blunder on the part of the establishment that helps both the organizer and the incipient community organization.

There are many similarities between Alinsky's community organization approach and liberation theology. An important one concerns a basic understanding of sociology and epistemology. Like Alinsky, liberation theology reacts against value-free sociology with its claim of arriving at totally objective truths and its emphasis on quantitative analysis. A value-free approach by its very nature tends to identify and reinforce the status quo. Knowledge is not objective and independent of human involvement as a classical understanding of one's thought. Epistemology reminds us that all knowledge is situational and subject to prejudice. As Alinsky so frequently pointed out, one must approach all existing reality and thought patterns with some ideological suspicion.

Saul Alinsky and the Industrial Areas Foundation have had more impact on grass-roots Catholic work for social justice than any other person or group in the United States in the last several decades. Yet surprisingly, although there has been significant discussion about Alinsky's approach to community organization in Protestant literature, the theological and ethical communities of the Catholic Church have not reflected on this phenomena, perhaps because, as alluded to earlier, Alinsky often tweaked the nose of the establishment, including the Roman Catholic Church.

LIBERATION THEOLOGY AND THE VATICAN

In the beginning, the Vatican did not seem to be particularly concerned with this new liberation theology. It was looked upon as something of a passing fad, but it did not pass. Instead, this new view gained strength and effectiveness, eventually playing a major role in international politics. At times, it was portrayed by those representing a certain trend in U.S. policy toward Latin America as highly dangerous. These politicians and organizations recognized at the very beginning that the theology of liberation posed a serious threat to this nation's self-centered policy of intervention and manipulation in Central and South America. This threat was witnessed by the "Rockefeller Report" of 1969 and an analysis written that year by members of the Rand Corporation in Santa Monica, California, entitled *Latin America Institutional Development: The Changing Catho-*

lic Church, as well as by a secret paper prepared by the CIA for the Bolivian military regime.

As if taking its cue from the CIA, the Vatican now began to criticize liberation theology, criticism that sharpened markedly in 1983 and 1984, due primarily to the actions of Joseph Cardinal Ratzinger, Rome's prefect of the Congregation for the Doctrine of the Faith. In March 1983, Cardinal Ratzinger presented to the Peruvian Bishops Conference ten critical questions directed to Gustavo Gutierrez's liberation theology. In September of that year, Ratzinger delivered a lecture, in the presence of the Pope, on the dangerous theoretical aspects of liberation theology. On January 23, 1984, the Peruvian magazine *Oiga* published an article by Cardinal Ratzinger, *Presupuestos, Problemas y Desafios de la Teologia de la Liberacion (Presuppositions, Problems, and Defects of the Theology of Liberation)*. An Italian translation of the article appeared on March 3, 1984, in *Thirty Giorni*, an Italian magazine, and a somewhat abridged version was published in the August 1984 issue of *Die neue Ordnung*. It read in part, "An analysis of the phenomenon of liberation theology reveals a fundamental threat to the Church."

So the Vatican sees liberation theology as a threat. The only question is, a threat to whom in the Church? Does the Vatican fear it will lose its own personal power of Papal authority due to this new theology and the continued growth and independence of the Third World Church? Karl Rahner, the great German theologian, has already posed the rhetorical question: "Do not the Roman congregations still have the mentality of a centralized bureaucracy which thinks it knows best what serves the kingdom of God and salvation of souls throughout the world, and such decision take the mentality of Rome or Italy in a frighteningly naive way as a self-evident standard?"

According to Rahner, the Roman domination of Christianity has reached an end, and he sees this as the beginning of the World Church. He divides Church history into three epochs. The first epoch was the short period of Jewish Christianity during which the gospel was proclaimed in Israel and to it. The second epoch was that of gentile Christianity when the gospel was preached and churches established within the relatively homogeneous Hellenistic-European cultural world. This second epoch lasted from the first century into the twentieth.

The third epoch is that of World Christianity, which Rahner dates, very roughly, from the time of the Second Vatican Council. From this time, churches outside the North Atlantic center have begun in a significant way to articulate their faith in their own terms, to speak from their own faith experience. European nations had their colonies and the European churches had their missions. All of the philosophies and approaches to a stereotyped religion have begun to change in the years following Vatican Council II.

Churches of Asia, Africa, and Latin America have begun to speak from their own experience. No longer do they always look to the sending churches before they reach their views. Their theology and religious reflection is no longer totally derivative. In the words of Gustavo Gutierrez, "They drink from their own wells." When the churches outside the North Atlantic countries began to think for themselves, they thought about liberation, and one of the ways they speak is through liberation theology.

Notwithstanding Vatican intentions to the contrary, the initiative has begun to pass from Europe to the Third World, from the second epoch of Rahner to the third epoch. Rome may be the bureaucratic center of the Church, but it is no longer the *vital, mystical center*. That center has passed from Rome to São Paulo; and the Vatican, which is the Holy See of the Church of the second epoch, is not letting go gracefully.

In discussions of liberation theology and religious education, the term *praxis* ("established practice") is often used. It involves action and the practice of theology that follows reflection and discussion. Liberation theology leads to additional prayerful, critical reflection on the Good News for a better way of living and freedom from oppression. Liberation theology is concerned with living faith and the ongoing mission of the people of God. It seeks the renewal and restructuring of society and culture so as to bring about human rights and liberation for all, authentic social justice, and the dynamic development of the kingdom of God. Praxis in religious education helps link the theory about being a Catholic Christian to real-life, faithful concerns of being a Christ follower.

The Brazilian Franciscan theologian Leonardo Boff, one of the great supporters of liberation theology in the World Church, was called to Rome to defend his views before the Congregation for the Doctrine of the Faith. In his writings, he had criticized the Vatican's arbitrary use of centralized power as dangerous. So he was summoned to meet with Cardinal Ratzinger, who at Boff's request allowed two Brazilian cardinals to be present. The major significance of their presence testified to the ecclesiastical character of the liberation theology that was being developed in Brazil. That theology may contain ambiguities. It may even contain errors, but it strives to be a theology within the Church and to the benefit of the Church. Ambiguities can be explained and errors corrected. Neither deprive liberation theology of its legitimate place in the pilgrim journey of the Catholic Church. Leonardo Boff amply established a completely different way of translating the idea of church office into reality. Nevertheless, he was ordered not to speak openly nor to publish any of his work for at least a year.

In their endeavor to crush liberation theology and silence any criticism of the Pope's misuse of power, the Vatican's moves may have backfired. The summoning of Boff to Rome produced enormous public interest in the theology of liberation. All of a sudden this theology seemed to "hit the streets." For the first time, one could hear it discussed in cafés, the marketplace, and living rooms. The wide debate provoked by the Ratzinger-Boff dialogue plus the publication by the Congregation of the Doctrine of the Faith of "Instruction on Certain Aspects of the Theology of Liberation" produced publicity that Boff could not possibly have generated on his own.

Thomas Aquinas, whose name became synonymous with traditional Roman Catholic theology, taught in his *Summa Theologica* that "in extreme necessity all goods are common; that is, all goods are to be shared." In light of this statement, how can a Catholic theologian such as Cardinal Ratzinger fight liberation theology? It is obvious that (1) he does not understand it and (2) he has no idea that it is going to be one of the great forces that will change the Catholic Church forever. Liberation theology will not go away. It is as enduring as people's struggle for freedom.

Cardinal Ratzinger may try to stop liberation theology, but he might as well go chasing moonbeams or try to light a penny candle from a star. Boff himself criticized the perspective of the Ratzinger instruction mentioned above, stating that it did not represent the Latin American perspective, but the European opinion. It was, in other words, the Third World as seen from the palace window.

The Catholic Church can survive only if it recognizes the legitimacy of the complexities and the particular values of different theologies, theologians, legal and liturgical forms, and organizational structures. The Europe-centered Roman Church must become a conciliar Church—many-faceted and pluralist—and theology must be a liberation theology, a *working* theology. It is no longer accept-able to subscribe to a theology that stifles the guidance of conscience and imposes dogmatic definitions rather than human needs. Orga-nized Christianity must lead to freedom.

It is the Church's duty to prevent the future exploitation of people. This duty will not be fully undertaken until the Vatican openly recognizes that the Church exists for the people. Pope John XIII referred to human beings as the "people of God." This will be fulfilled when human beings become aware of themselves and find the primacy of liberating activity in Christian life.

FOURTEEN

Church and State

Political pronouncements from Rome have been contradictory and despotic. On the one hand, Third World clergy who encourage the overthrow of oppressive totalitarian regimes are vilified and silenced or otherwise punished. Meanwhile, clergy in the democratic nation of the United States are directed to disobey and obstruct the law and to encourage others to do likewise. So insistent is Rome's call for disobedience here that the mandatory retirement age of bishops (seventy-five) is ignored for conservatives hewing to the party line, while liberal bishops are immediately retired and replaced with conservatives. What strange motives drive a Pope to condemn rebellion in dictatorships while demanding it in a democracy?

We have already discussed the Vatican's Communist-phobia and its concern over growing Third World power within the Church, both of which have contributed to the hierarchical fear of liberation theology, but what is it that precipitates precisely the opposite attitude in the United States? Here, where the separation of church and state is clearly demanded by one of our most cherished amendments to the Constitution, the Vatican has repeatedly sought to obtain state funds for parochial schools, has asked Catholics to lie down in the street to block a woman's way to a legal abortion clinic, and has insisted that the heads of state-licensed, tax-benefiting Catholic colleges and universities take steps to "insure the school's Catholic character," even though such measures would inevitably lead to repression of academic freedom. All the while the Vatican has threatened to excommunicate any office-holding Catholic who admits to a pro-choice stance on abortion (ironically, God gave us free will, which is synonymous with freedom of choice or pro-choice).

[164]

Such conduct not only endangers the separation of church and state in this nation, it also threatens the tax-free status of the Catholic Church. Should that status be changed, the results would be catastrophic—for parochial schools, for Catholic colleges, even for the assembly buildings of the Church. Why then does the Vatican continue to encourage and even demand civil disobedience and obstruction of laws of which it disapproves? Is there basic disagreement with this government's separation of church and state? Does the Vatican wish church and state to be one and the same? I can tell it that it will never happen here, and my advice is to observe the laws of the land.

According to John L. McKenzie in *The Roman Catholic Church*, it is impossible to understand the "character" of Catholicism without some reference to the historical relations between the Church and civil societies.

HISTORY

Two contrasting types of church-state arrangements have appeared in history. One is a divorce between the two, either spelled out or understood. The second is a joining together of forces for mutual benefit. Both have been relatively common. In ancient Egypt, religion and state were one and the same. But Hinduism, Buddhism, and Confucianism, although greatly influential in their nations of origin, never developed the centralized and ecclesiastical organizations necessary to produce a long-term joining with the government.

In some places where church and state were joined, contention arose as to *which* church should rule. When Henry VIII of England broke with Rome in 1534, he created the Church of England and became a "Protestant" ruler, but when the throne passed to his daughter Mary in 1553, she married Philip of Spain and reestablished Roman Catholicism. But Mary was succeeded by Elizabeth in 1558, who made England's religion Protestant again. So in twenty-seven years, the people of England changed their religion three times.

By far the longest and strongest alliance between church and state was forged by the early Christian Church and the Roman Empire. It is a fact, as delineated by Fernand Mourret in his *History of the Catholic Church*, that this very special union has dominated most Roman Catholic thought and action on the relations of church and state into the twentieth century. How did the Church and the Roman Empire become one?

During the first three centuries after Christ, if there could be said to be any relationship between church and state, it would have to be labeled hostile. The Christian community of that day produced no clear position relative to the government and vice versa, but Christianity was rapidly—almost miraculously—becoming the faith of the majority of those who lived in the Roman Empire. On the eve of Constantine's fateful battle with Maxentius, Constantine had a vision of Christ, who told him to ornament the shields of his soldiers with the Savior's monogram—the Greek letters chi and rho. Constantine obeyed and in the ensuing battle was victorious. The era of persecutions of Christians ended when Emperor Constantine converted to Christianity in 312, and Christianity became the religion of the empire. This meant major changes for both government and religion, which are sill felt in the Church even today.

The Roman government had always exercised some degree of control over religion, and neither Constantine nor his successors felt that this should change simply because the new state religion was Christianity. Constantine repealed the legislation of Augustus that penalized celibates, legalized bequests to the Church, and gave validity to manumission—the emancipation from slavery—which may be the forerunner of liberation theology.

Emperor Constantine also gave powers of jurisdiction to bishops, allowing either party in a civil suit to transfer jurisdiction to a bishop, whose verdict would be final and carried out by the civil authority. Constantine also made Sunday a public holiday following Christian practice. He used the bishops as experts on religious issues, but it was the emperor who selected the bishops and even heard appeals on their decisions, taking whatever action he saw fit.

The Church accepted this important measure of state control in return for the protection and support the state offered. Soon leaders of the Church agreed that it was the responsibility of the state to *keep order* in the Church. This view seemed innocent enough, but almost immediately created problems. If the emperor kept order in the Church, then it must be the emperor who, in the final analysis, decided religious arguments between different Christian groups when such arguments could not be settled. This is precisely what happened in the case of the Arian sect, and it was the impetus for the calling, by the emperor, of the First Council of Nicaea in 325, described in Chapter 5.

But now that such matters were in the hands of the emperor rather than the Church fathers, the fortunes of schisms like Arianism rose and fell with the change of emperors. Thus, when Constantine died in 337, Arianism came to the fore again under the new emperor, eventually requiring a revision of the Nicene Creed—which remained in effect until the second ecumenical council (381) met at Constantinople, where Arianism was again denounced and still another revision of the Nicene Creed was approved. The Council of Nicaea II, 787, also condemned iconoclasm, condemned the belief that Christ was the son of God by adoption rather than nature, and regulated the veneration of holy images. In the full text of the council, the Lord's prayer originates.

Christian beliefs and practices could now change with the crowning of a new emperor, who in effect had replaced the Pope as the head of the Church. This would create serious problems for the clergy during the centuries that followed. In the sixth century, for example, Emperor Justinian undertook to rule on the competing orthodoxy of Monophysite Christians, who rejected the two natures of Christ, divine and human, and argued instead for a single composite nature, and Nestorian Christians, who denied the unity of the divine and human natures in Christ. The schism became so divisive that the emperor felt obliged to take the Pope captive in A.D. 548 and *force* him to concur in the emperor's decision.

Four centuries later, Emperor Henry IV, with a group of bishops loyal to him, declared the election of Pope Gregory VII to be void, but Pope Gregory would not budge. Instead, he excommunicated Henry, who now fearing the loss of his throne, submitted to the Pope, waiting for three days outside the papal gate, barefoot in sackcloth in the snow-filled courtyard of Countess Mathilda of Canossa, until the Pope absolved him. Three years later, Henry returned to Rome with an army, captured the city, and installed an antipope. Pope Gregory, out of power, died a year later.

Despite such conflicts as these, the union of church and state worked far more often than it failed, and those centuries of Roman "Christiandom" are seen by the Vatican as the most successful in the history of the Church. "The Popes could summon European kings to the Crusades," explains Father McKenzie. "Bishops could turn heretics over to the State to be burned, since heresy was a breach of civil as well as ecclesiastical order. On the other hand, kings could expect the Popes and Bishops to support their wars and to inflict ecclesiastical penalties for civil disorder."

The state-supported power of the Church continued in one form or another until the sixteenth century. Then, with the rebellion of Martin Luther in 1517 and King Henry VIII of England in 1534, the iron grip of the Catholic Church was broken. It would never be so strong again, but not for want of trying.

AMERICA

The Reverend Pat Robertson, the television evangelist who sought the Republican presidential nomination in 1988, recently commented on TV that in terms of separation of church and state, this nation has fallen into a terrible condition. He had just learned of a federal judge's opinion that any lawyer who quoted the Bible as an authority in his closing argument might be offering grounds for appeal. "How can this be?" asked Robertson. "We are a nation founded by Christians and now we can't even quote the Bible as an authority. I think that's a shame."

Is it? The evangelist seems to have overlooked what this nation might be like if the founding fathers had not been wise enough to add the First Amendment to the Constitution. It is true that America's early settlers were very dogmatic Christians. The Puritans came to America not to found a state where human beings could practice religion in whatever way they chose, but rather to found a state where Christianity was both the government and the religion, and not just any Christianity, but the Puritans' particular variety. The Puritans would punish dissenters by putting their feet in stocks, cutting off their ears, lashing their backs, or sending them into the wilderness. Robertson would not have been allowed to preach his religious beliefs via the airwaves had the Puritans won the day and founded a Puritan United States.

Of course, the Puritans were not the only religious group to try to make their beliefs a state religion in America. Each of the thirteen colonies, with the possible exception of Rhode Island, began with a government that fostered a particular religion, but it was difficult for the establishment of one system of beliefs to take hold because there were so many other sects, primarily Protestant, and because followers moved so freely from one settlement to another—Baptists went to Anglican Virginia, Catholics arrived in Maryland, Jewish immigrants landed in New York, and so on. This mixture of religions made state establishment of any one of them virtually impossible.

During the 1700s, much of the fiery rivalry between the various Protestant sects subsided. These sects moved closer to the credo that Martin Luther had both preached and exemplified: the liberty of every man to think out his own relation to God. One reason for this growing emphasis on freedom of religion may have been Protestant fear of Roman Catholicism gaining in America the kind of hold it enjoyed in Europe. Samuel Adams, for example, stated that "much more is to be dreaded from the growth of Popery in America than from the Stamp Act." After declaring independence in 1776, the colonies repealed most of the legislation that had once supported a particular religion, and this led to the first clause of the First Amendment to the Constitution adopted in 1791: "Congress shall make no law respecting an establishment of religion, or prohibiting the free exercise thereof . . ."

Since the adoption of this amendment two hundred years ago, there have been serious challenges to the separation of religion and government in this nation, both at the state and federal level. Most have involved the issue of funds for private, that is religious, schools, and most of these challenges have involved the Catholic Church.

The importance of parochial schools to the Church dates far back. Although there was no formal school education in the early centuries of the Church, many Catholics viewed the parochial school system as the fulfillment of Matthew 28:19, where the risen Jesus commissions his disciples to "go and teach all nations."

The attitude of the Church toward nonparochial schools has always been hostile. Catholic directives state that education at any level should include religious instruction and that Catholic students should *not* attend schools where Catholic instruction is not provided. Until recently, many dioceses enforced the rule against public school attendance. "It is more than coincidental," says Father McKenzie, "that in much nineteenth century European fiction, the public schoolmaster is the village atheist."

In the United States, where the parochial school system has become the largest in the world, education is the major nonecclesiastical work of the Church. But over the years, costs for school construction and maintenance have grown increasingly burdensome and the hierarchy of the Church, as if blind to the importance in this nation of the separation of religion and government, has tried again and again to make state or federal government supply funding for Catholic schools. It was not until 1947 that the Supreme Court gave the Church some hope. In the case of *Everson v. Board of Education*, the Court, by a narrow five-to-four vote, upheld a New Jersey law that allowed the state, under its general welfare powers, to pay for the busing costs for parochial as well as public schools. But as if to forewarn religious leaders not to take this as an invitation to further blur the line between church and state, the Court offered this highly influential dictum:

> The "establishment of religion" clause of the First Amendment means at least this: Neither a state nor the Federal Government can set up a church. Neither can pass laws which aid one religion, aid all religions or prefer one religion over another. Neither can force nor influence a person to go to or to remain away from church against his will or force him to profess a belief or disbelief in any religion. No person can be punished for entertaining or professing religious beliefs of disbeliefs, for Church attendance or non-attendance. No tax in any amount, large or small, can be levied to support any religious activities or institutions, whatever form they may adopt to teach or practice religion. Neither a state nor the Federal Government can, openly or secretly, participate in the affairs of any religious organizations or groups and vice versa. In the words of Jefferson, the clause against establishment of religion by law was intended to erect "a wall of separation between church and state."

These strong words may have discouraged many religious leaders, but not all. One Catholic saw the *Everson* decision as the opening of a door, and he immediately began pushing to force the adoption of other measures, such as subsidies for parochial textbooks and public aid for Catholic health care and other services. This was the man author John Cooney called "the American Pope," Francis Cardinal Spellman. He was the archbishop of New York, the most important Catholic see in the world other than Rome.

When Spellman was named archbishop in 1939, one of the mandates given him by Pope Pius XII was to obtain aid for parochial schools. Spellman was so determined to accomplish this mandate that when the favorable court decision was finally won in 1947, the cardinal harshly condemned any critics of the Supreme Court's ruling in the *Everson* case, stating that they were "mainly the intolerant who in their failure to win a victory in the court of law seek recourse in the shady corners of bigotry." That would become one of Spellman's chief weapons against those who opposed his efforts to knock down the wall separating church and state: accusing them of bigotry or Communism.

Spellman even attacked Eleanor Roosevelt when in 1949 she stated in her newspaper column "My Day" that public taxes should *not* be used to support private or religious schools. For this "offense," Cardinal Spellman accused the former First Lady—her work for minorities already legendary—of bigotry. He also accused her of having Communist sympathies and even impugned her role as a mother. The furor was so great that Spellman was forced eventually to apologize, and his attack on Mrs. Roosevelt served only to increase the strength of Other Americans United for the Separation of Church and State, an organization created specifically to stop Spellman.

Ex-Governor Herbert Lehman of New York expressed his surprise at the cardinal's attack in a long statement in the *New York Times*. Catholics and non-Catholics deplored the ill-advised and unwarranted accusation. I remember talking to the Reverend George Barry Ford, chaplain to Catholic students at Columbia University and pastor of Corpus Christi Church, about Cardinal Spellman's attack on Eleanor Roosevelt. Father Ford was a great admirer of Mrs. Roosevelt and considered her the "First Lady of the World." He was deeply upset by the attack on his dear and respected friend. He was also upset by the damage it had done to ecumenism and the relationship between Catholics and other religious groups.

Later the cardinal made a courtesy call on Mrs. Roosevelt at Hyde Park in a rather obvious attempt to soften the public feeling against him stimulated by his attack on her. As always, Eleanor Roosevelt greeted him with the gentle dignity and courtesy that had made her loved throughout the world. However, as a Catholic, I knew that it would take years to convince Americans that Cardinal Spellman spoke only for himself and his selfish interest and not for all Catholics in the United States.

Gaining state aid for Catholic schools was not the only way Spellman sought to reverse the principles of Thomas Jefferson regarding church and state. With the cardinal's blessing in 1952, a Catholic hospital in Poughkeepsie, New York, fired several highly qualified doctors simply because they were supporters of Planned Parenthood. When the *New York Post* deplored the fact that a hospital with such an obviously biased position on birth control, due to religious beliefs, received public funds, Cardinal Spellman first invited the *Post*'s publisher, Dorothy Schiff, into his home and then loudly berated her for "attacking the Poughkeepsie hospital." Spellman also punished the *Post* with a concerted campaign to keep major department stores from advertising in that newspaper.

Each year the costs for New York Catholic schools increased alarmingly. In just the four years from 1955 to 1959, Spellman spent $168 million for new buildings in New York, most of which went to the construction cost of ninety-four new schools. As soon as the post–World War II boom slowed, Spellman was unable to raise or provide the money to keep the parochial system viable. Despite the tax-free status of the Church, there were simply not enough funds to support this overexpanded school system along with all the other responsibilities—including the annual donations by the American Catholic Church to the Vatican—faced by the U.S. Church. The cost of new construction, repairs, utilities, and interest had spiraled. In addition, a shortage of the Church's traditional schoolteachers, nuns and priests, who had worked for a pittance, forced the Church to replace them in many cases with lay teachers demanding a commensurate wage. In 1967, for the first year since World War II, the number of new elementary parochial schools opening in New York did not increase over previous years, and Spellman's high schools for that year lost $1.8 million.

On April 4, 1967, New York held a convention to discuss streamlining and modernizing the state constitution. Spellman sought to have the convention change the one existing amendment, called the Blaine Amendment, that prohibited "direct or indirect aid to private schools." To achieve this end, the political organization sponsored by the cardinal, Citizens for Educational Freedom, proposed the idea that Catholics were being forced to pay twice for education—first for public schools that they did *not* use and second for their own—and said the state should give them assistance.

The approach ignored this nation's separation of church and state, as well as the fact that Catholic parents themselves *chose* to send their children to parochial school. It also ignored a most embarrassing practice that I saw firsthand at Catholic grammar school in Erie. The pupils who failed or created problems at our school, even though they were Catholics, were transferred to the public school system. Of course, public schools had no choice but to accept these failures and misfits.

By the time the convention met, Spellman was confident of victory. "A majority of the 186 delegates chosen for the 1967 Constitutional Convention are pledged to work for the removal of the Blaine Amendment," the *Catholic Tablet* reported on November 10, 1966.

A $2-million advertising campaign had accompanied Spellman's personal efforts. He had managed to win the support of such names as Robert Kennedy, Jacob Javits, and Anthony J. Travia, the Speaker of the New York State Assembly and the president of this constitutional convention. He also had the support of Governor Nelson Rockefeller, a political leader Spellman had cultivated in 1962 when Rockefeller divorced his wife of thirty years, embroiling him in a scandal that almost destroyed his public career. With all the other religious leaders condemning Rockefeller for his divorce (adultery was then the only allowed grounds), Spellman saw a chance to put a powerful man in his debt. So, despite the Church's strong opposition to divorce, Spellman stepped forward and publicly endorsed Rockefeller. Now, in 1967, he had Rockefeller's support for repeal of the Blaine Amendment, putting New York parochial schools on the same footing as public schools. This would have consequences far outside New York, for it was expected that this new charter would serve as a model for other states for generations to come.

Organizations like Americans United for Separation of Church and State were appalled, but they appeared powerless. The Church, through its lobbying and advertising, seemed to make the results inevitable. Even Convention President Travia was willing to admit, "I feel that repeal of the Amendment was a foregone conclusion even before the Convention opened."

On August 15, the delegates voted 132 to 49 to "replace the words of the Amendment with looser language," and the Spellman forces had won. But then the cardinal made a mistake. He allowed Speaker Travia to lump this amendment in with other controversial matters, including assumption by the state of welfare and court costs and elimination of voter referendums on new bond issues, all of which would be decided on as one package by the public in a general referendum on the new Constitution in November. Allies of the cardinal, including Governor Rockefeller, urged Travia to put the repeal of the Blaine Amendment in its own special place on the November ballot, but Spellman was certain this was unnecessary. Thanks to the cardinal's egotistical stubbornness, the entire package was rejected by a margin of three to one. It was perhaps the closest any state in this union has come to destroying the separation between church and state.

BROKEN PROMISES

If, as indicated by Samuel Adams's statement concerning his fear of "Popery," the Catholic Church was partially responsible for the First Amendment to the U.S. Constitution, it was far more responsible for the separation of religion and government in the European nations that overthrew their monarchies after the American Revolution. Statements issued from Rome at that time left no doubt that the Vatican felt the years when Catholicism was dominant were the ideal years for the world. In *The Roman Catholic Church*, Father McKenzie writes, "The intolerance that accompanied some Catholic pronouncements on this subject led Protestants to fear that the Church looked to a restoration of the medieval Church in which dissenters were not tolerated and the Roman practice in some countries seemed to support this fear."

Clearly, it was because of this fear that many Protestant leaders in those nations newly emerging from monarchy included constitutional provisions that church and state would always be separate. But none of these rebuffs to the Church produced a change in the hierarchical attitude toward the "ideal" relationship between church and state. Nor did more recent changes, including those brought about by the 1946 adoption of the new constitution in Italy, which stated, "The State and the Catholic Church are each, in its own order, independent and sovereign" (Article 7).

Change in the Church's attitude did not begin until twelve years later when Pope Pius XII, the Pope who had urged Francis Spellman to amend the U.S. Constitution, died and was succeeded by Pope John XXIII. "The Pope of Power had been replaced by the Pope of Peace," wrote John Cooney.

It was perceived by most Catholics who followed the careers of Pope John XXIII and Francis Cardinal Spellman that the cardinal was not one of Pope John's strong supporters. From reports in the media it was apparent that Cardinal Spellman lacked enthusiasm for the

Second Vatican Council's decision to "recognize the modern pluralistic state as a legitimate form of society and to work no more for political support for ecclesiastical ends." As a practicing Catholic, I wish that the male hierarchy of the Catholic Church would follow the decision of Vatican Council II.

This new Church attitude expounded by Vatican II was carried forward by Pope Paul VI, successor to John XXIII, and despite religious leaders like Cardinal Spellman, the new approach produced some truly impressive results in this nation, especially in terms of higher education. In 1967 Notre Dame became the first and largest religious university in the world to turn over its board of trustees to lay control. When this happened, there were many who said "There goes the Catholic character of the university," but just the opposite proved to be true. The lay board and the hierarchy learned to work together, raised money, built buildings, and expanded programs and now have one of the most progressive schools in the world. This is clearly a credit to Father Theodore Hesburgh of Notre Dame, but it is also a credit to the concept of academic freedom and the separation of church and state.

Other colleges—Georgetown, Boston College, Villanova, and many more—have prospered by following the example of Notre Dame, and there is no doubt that these changes and their results were of paramount importance in 1971's extraordinary case of *Tilden v. Richardson.* Here the U.S. Supreme Court, by a narrow five-to-four vote, decided that Catholic colleges and universities, in contrast to secondary schools, *were* eligible for public funding. This decision was based on the majority conclusion that Catholic colleges and universities were no longer engaged in indoctrination and, I might add, no longer tightly controlled by the hierarchy of the Church. It is a decision that has immeasurable importance for every Catholic college and university in the United States, for federal funding in today's times is almost certainly vital for the viability of these institutions.

In the face of such incontrovertible facts, what has been the Vatican's attitude? In its most recent proposals in this area (1986), the Vatican under John Paul II sought to authorize American bishops to "make sure the Catholic character of [universities] is preserved and Catholic doctrinal principles served." No wonder the presidents of Catholic colleges and universities were stunned. Such proposals would not only lead to loss of federal funding, they are contrary to

American values of both academic freedom and due process, both of which were written into most university statutes and protected by civil and constitutional law.

Says Father Hesburgh of Notre Dame: "Obviously if a power outside the University can dictate who can teach and who can learn, the University is not free and, in fact, is not a true University where the truth is sought and taught. It is rather a place of political or religious indoctrination. The latter is perfectly fitting for a Catechetical center, but not for a University."

If the Pope's proposals should prevail—and the colleges have thus far refused to comply—Father Hesburgh warns that the best Catholic institutions would be faced with a durable dilemma: "They would have to choose between being real universities and being really Catholic, when in fact they are both."

Sister Alice Gallin, executive director of the Association of United States Catholic Colleges, agrees with Hesburgh. "The proposals would be disastrous for colleges and universities of our country. The very life of our colleges and universities is one of academic freedom and self-regulation by the academic community . . . A university is a place for an intellectual journey towards truth, not a place where one receives the truth already packaged."

She also stated that any attempt to subvert academic freedom would result in the diminishment of influence Catholic institutions of higher learning have on the total higher education community and ultimately in Catholic colleges and universities being excluded from the community of teachers and scholars.

Brother Patrick Ellis, head of La Salle College in Philadelphia, stated that the way the Vatican proposals read made it look as if "the boom is being lowered." Its empowering of an authority off campus would be a denial of freedom for independent Catholic universities.

These educators were embarrassed by the way the persons of other faiths were dealt with in the Vatican document, which called for such educational goals as offering non-Catholics the message of salvation. Fortunately, most Catholic universities respect religious pluralism and seek to explore the meaning of religious experience for society as a whole and within diverse cultural groups. They accept new members of the faculty for their commitment to the goals of the university, not their religious affiliation, so the proposal by the Vatican to authorize bishops to make certain the Catholic doctrinal principles are served is not possible. Under accrediting standards, the Church-related campuses *have* to offer well-rounded teaching unbound to religious prescription.

How well does Pope John Paul II understand the place of theology in higher education? He has made statements that on the surface appear to have credibility. He has stated, "Every Catholic university must show itself to all not only as a scientific workshop but also as a solid rock of Christian principles to which scientific activity can be anchored." Few Catholic educators would quarrel with that ideal.

But this assertion begs an important question: Who determines the Catholic character of such institutions? The Vatican schema assigns this responsibility to the Catholic hierarchy in general and to the local bishop in particular (and, given the schema ecclesiology, ultimately to the Pope). This is a total refutation of Vatican II and, if followed, will almost certainly cost the universities and colleges their federal funding. As a Catholic, I regretfully agree that this is justice in our heterogeneous and pluralistic society.

Sadly, this is only one of many areas in which the promises of Vatican II have been broken by the rigid, conservative regime of Pope John Paul II. As pointed out in Chapter 6, the Vatican's loss on abortion rights in Catholic countries like France, Italy, and Spain has caused it to focus all its attention, funds, and manpower on the one dominant country where, thanks to the Church's partnership with the White House and fundamentalists, abortion might be outlawed.

This obsession with abortion in the United States has not only caused the Vatican to encourage Catholics to physically prevent women from exercising their legal right to an abortion, it has also caused the Church to leap headlong into U.S. politics, thereby breaking the law and risking its tax-exempt status. Section 501(C)(3) of the U.S. Tax Code guarantees First Amendment separation of church and state by prohibiting any tax-exempt religious group from supporting or attacking political candidates, yet the Church has done so repeatedly.

As pointed out in Lawrence Lader's book *RU486*: "The official newspaper of the archdiocese of San Antonio, Texas, not only listed its favored candidates in an editorial, but taunted the IRS in its headline: 'TO THE IRS NUTS!!!' Dozens of other official newspapers since then, from St. Cloud, Minnesota, to Jackson, Michigan, to Vienna, Virginia, have published lists of candidates to support or attack based on their stand on abortion."

The Church has counted on its influence with Presidents Reagan and Bush to keep the IRS from bringing suit, and when this worked, political intervention due to Vatican influence became even more pronounced: The bishop of San Diego stated that he would deny communion to an assemblywoman running for the state senate because she was pro-choice. The archbishop of Guam announced his intention to excommunicate any Catholic legislator who failed to vote for a bill restricting abortion, and John Cardinal O'Connor of New York City (the Pope's American alter ego) threatened to excommunicate any Catholic officeholder, including Governor Mario Cuomo, who refused to reverse his pro-choice identity.

"In effect," says Lawrence Lader, "the Catholic Church was tearing apart the two-hundred-year-old principle of Church-State separation . . . It was saying that Catholic officeholders had to sacrifice their own convictions and often the consensus of a majority of their constituents in order to obey the Bishops."

U.S. Senator Patrick J. Leahy, a Democrat from Vermont, was outraged. Although a Catholic himself, he warned the Vatican that its conduct was "not acceptable in a country based on the First Amendment."

THE FUTURE

If the tax-free status of the Catholic Church should be lost in the United States, members of the Vatican would suffer not at all, but Church members and institutions in this nation would suffer dramatically. The focus of the Church must be changed. The Vatican must be made to see that our Constitution with its First Amendment emphasis on separation of church and state cannot be ignored, that the obstruction of women's rights and threats against those in political office or seeking such office must cease.

The Vatican should not encourage the breaking of laws. Catholic doctrine firmly recognizes the need of secular human society of the common good. Thus, Catholics, like everyone else, have an obligation to obey the secular authority. Religious claims cannot make Catholics incapable of fulfilling their civil obligations, since both are ultimately from one God.

"In their own spheres," says Vatican Council II, "the political community and the Church are mutually independent and self-governing. Yet by a different title each serves the social and personal vocations of the human beings" (Constitution on the Church in the Modern World, section 75).

The principle of rendering "to Caesar the things that are Caesar's and to God the things that are God's" (Matt. 22:21) recognizes the autonomy of the two communities. Vatican Council II stated explicitly that "the Church does not lodge its hope in privileges conferred by civil authorities. Indeed it stands ready to renounce the exercise of certain legitimately acquired rights if it becomes clear that their use raises doubts about the sincerity of its witness or if new conditions of life demand some other arrangement."

Thus, the Church must not only refrain from breaking the law of the land, it must even refrain from taking advantage of rights that are perhaps no longer best for all concerned. In turn, said the Vatican II documents, the Church demands the right to "preach the faith with true freedom, to teach its social doctrine, and to discharge its duty among men without hindrance."

Pope John Paul II must be brought back to this promise made in the grand beginning of Vatican II. Those in the Church who support the Pope's rigid conservatism must cease building new Catholic secondary schools in the United States and phase out those now in operation. The reasons are many.

First, the construction and maintenance of such schools is not, as once thought by some, the fulfillment of Scripture. We have long known that the original translation of Matthew 28:19 was in error. Interpreting from the Greek, the command of the risen Christ to his disciples was not "go and teach all nations," but "go and make disciples." The building of schools is clearly not the proper response to this command and it may not even be the most effective way to build membership.

"Child control may not be the best way to develop convinced adults," says Father McKenzie, "and there is reason to suspect that the conviction is often more shallow the greater the effort expended. Possibly the existence of the school system has allowed clergy and parents to evade their own responsibilities in the education of the young."

Second, from almost every standpoint, Catholic schools are "un-American." Not only do they violate the spirit of the Constitution, their high costs encourage men like Cardinal Spellman to violate the letter, as well as the spirit, of that document. Moreover, the Catholic people who pay for these schools do not own or control them.

When the first Catholic schools were established, the members wanted to control the physical property through trustees or boards of their own choosing in the same fashion as those ultimately in charge of schools belonging to other church groups. The Catholics had absorbed the independent American spirit. They did not wish to have their money and their effort used to erect buildings that would be owned by priests who in turn would be subject to the Vatican. But the Church had no place in its system for this kind of American rebellion. After brief flurries of revolt in Philadelphia and other cities, Church members were defeated by the Catholic hierarchy.

So, even today, Catholic people in America do not own and cannot assume control over a single brick or board in their schools. American Catholics would never tolerate such a system of ownership for their *public* schools. Public school buildings belong to the people of each district and the people, as voters, have final say as to their use. This system of democratic educational control is so well established in American tradition that no one thinks of questioning it, yet it is violated by Catholic schools.

Catholics are not even given the opportunity to decide whether a school should be erected in their parish. The decision is made for them. In 1884 the Third Plenary Council of Baltimore laid down the rule that *every* parish, regardless of size or affluence, must have a Catholic school attached to the Church. Actually, the school was often built before the church, temporary quarters being used for worship until the school was complete. Says Father McKenzie, the emphasis on Catholic school construction came about because the hierarchy feared the "perversion of Roman Catholic children in the public schools of the United States."

Today, this mammoth duplication of the public school system has placed an impossible drain on the resources of the Church in America, especially with the inflation of maintenance costs and the growing shortage of nuns, brothers, and priests to serve in the schools. As far back as 1964, Mary Perkins Ryan asked the right question in her book, *Are Parochial Schools the Answer?* Her conclusion—they are not. Father James Kavanaugh concurred in *A Modern Priest Looks at His Outdated Church*.

"There is no modern folly to match that of the Catholic Bishops who continue to erect Catholic schools," writes Kavanaugh. "The Catholic school system has drained the revenue of every parish, stolen the majority of religious vocations to staff its offices and classrooms, absorbed our energies and consumed our time. To sustain it, we have neglected our parishes, ignored the poor, delayed renewal and alienated our non-Catholic friends."

Kavanaugh agrees that the system should be phased out and he concluded somewhat sadly, "Long enough have we equated religion with education and lost our vision for the vast works that have not been done. Once we ran the hospitals, the orphanages, the homes for lepers and the schools for children. Now man has matured sufficiently to recognize his responsibility as man. Can we not be grateful that it is difficult to recognize a Christian in our society since so many men and women do Christian work? Is there no work for a parish without fences, for a church without schools?"

The Vatican must be convinced that education is not a tool of the Church. "That the cause of the Church is noble does not mean that the Church can distort learning," says Father McKenzie. "The nobility of the cause is conditioned by the integrity of the men in whose hands the cause is placed. The type of control which many of the hierarchy seem to desire should not be granted to anyone, because that type of control will render education impossible."

FIFTEEN

Changing the Church

It really looks as if God has lavished upon me his most tender and motherly care; he has led me out of so many difficulties and, through countless acts of kindness, he has brought me here to Rome. It must be for some particular purpose of his; there can be no other reason for my master's infinite generosity.

—Written by Angelo Giuseppe Roncalli
(Pope John XXIII) at age twenty

Today there are conversations, books, TV programs, and seminars that clearly demonstrate that American Catholics want to change their Church. According to research conducted by George Gallup, Jr., and Jim Castelli, a majority of Catholics support:

- greater lay participation in parish decision-making (77%)
- more influential roles for women in parishes (78%)
- allowing parishes to help choose the priests who come to serve them (55%)
- full-time lay parish administrators (55%)
- full-time lay religious educators and liturgists (68%)
- ordination of women (52%)
- birth control (68%)
- married priests (63%)
- remarriage after divorce (73%)
- lay marriage and personal counselors (79%)

Numerous conversations that I have had with a variety of Catholics from all walks of life indicate that they have respect for Church leaders, but want a hierarchical structure within which lay people will exercise greater leadership. It is my opinion that Catholics want more lay leadership within the Catholic Church, but they do not want to change it to a Protestant church.

At the same time, nuns have let it be known that they resent their male bosses in the Vatican telling them they cannot wear blue jeans or work on skid row; husbands and wives are fed up with the Pope's endless "thou-shall-nots"; the divorced and remarried want their Church's wholehearted acceptance; theologians are seeking the right to speak freely; and some brave bishops are showing open rebellion at the insensitivity of Vatican bureaucrats.

In the Sunday edition of the *New York Daily News*, September 6, 1987, Maria Shriver, a member of a prominent Catholic family, was quoted as saying she disagrees with Pope John Paul II on almost everything, but she does not feel this makes her any less Catholic. She stated that many Catholics, like herself, want to see the Church change, but they want to make changes by staying in the Church, not by leaving it. She shares the philosophy of Desiderius Erasmus (died 1536), who tried to reform the Church from within.

American Catholics are far from alone in this thinking. For example, the Italian Basic Christian Community Movement has started something it calls "reappropriation theology." It aims to reappropriate the ministry of the Word, the sacraments, and the service that has been falsely alienated from the people by the ecclesiastical "ruling class." Reappropriation theology means a basic spiritual revolution in people's consciousness that puts their lives at the center of the meaning of the Church, rather than seeing themselves at the periphery, banging on locked doors and asking permission to enter from those who seem to own the conduits of the Spirit.

The *people* do not exist for their *Church*; the *Church* exists for billions of *people*, no two identical. The ways of being Catholic must multiply and the Church must be made more diverse; pluralism in religious expression must increase. The Vatican must begin to look forward again, fulfilling the vision of Pope John XXIII, instead of looking backward to safe theories and models.

Few Catholics know much about the central government of the Church. Rather, they relate to their parish priests and, in a more distant way, to their bishop and to the Pope. This much we all understand: priest to bishop to Pope. Normally, the parishioner has little need for greater knowledge about Church government. But more must be understood if structural changes are to be brought about.

What follows is certainly not a course in Church organization. It is simply a brief summary to help in understanding what needs to be restructured and why. It should be pointed out at the very beginning that when we discuss the government of the Church, we do not begin with a written document, such as the Constitution of the United States, but simply the tradition the Church has accepted. Nevertheless, for our purposes we can compare the government of the Church with that of the United States. Although there are meaningful differences in the two structures, these differences will aid us in pointing out some of the most basic problems with the Church hierarchy.

THE POPE

The Pope can be compared to the president of the United States. While the president is chosen by the electoral college, the Pope is chosen by the far less representative College of Cardinals. In the past, the method of electing the Pope, that is, the Bishop of Rome, proved far more democratic, as we shall see later. Moreover, the power of the Pope, now virtually absolute, was once similar to the power bestowed on presidents.

There have been many great and saintly Popes, as well many who were nonentities and even worthless, but the office has almost always been better than the man, which explains its survival. The Papacy is the only institution that has continued to survive from the early Roman Empire.

For many, the Pope is the symbol of Roman Catholicism. It is he who most closely connects the Church to Christ. According to Catholic belief, each Pope is the successor to Peter and the importance of this succession is pointed up by the fact that Peter was the Apostle to whom Christ assigned the founding and leadership of the Church. This belief is based upon several passages in the New Testament, the best known being Matthew 16:18–19, where Christ speaks to Peter:

> "And I tell you, you are Peter, and on this rock I will build my church, and the powers of death shall not prevail against it. I will give you the keys of the kingdom of heaven, and whatever

you bind on earth shall be bound in heaven, and whatever you loose on earth shall be loosed in heaven."

Unfortunately, this passage is found nowhere else in the Scriptures— omitted where it might be expected to appear in Mark and Luke. For this reason, many critics do not accept it as an authentic saying of Christ; however, Simon Peter's leadership is also supported by Luke 22: 31–32, where Christ again speaks to Peter:

> "Simon, Simon, behold. Satan demanded to have you that he might sift you like wheat, but I have prayed for you that your faith may not fail; and when you have turned again, strengthen your brethren."

Peter's special place is also demonstrated in John 21: 15–17, where Christ tells Peter, "Feed my lambs" and "Tend my sheep."

In Catholic belief, the papacy is a legitimate *continuous* develop-ment of the powers Christ granted to Peter and the other Apostles, authorizing them to preach the gospel, administer the sacraments, and rule the Church. Just as no one but Jesus could have given this authority to the Apostles, no one but the Apostles could pass it on to others. Therefore, no individual in today's Church could perform apostolic functions if he could not trace his appointment through legitimate succession back to one of the Apostles—and Catholic belief accomplishes this by way of the Pope, successor to Peter, by whom all episcopal appointments are made.

The claim of continuity from Peter to the current Pope is based on the succession of the Pope as Bishop of Rome. Thus, it is vital to this argument that Peter held that position—not actually a bishop, for no such title or office was used by the early Christians, but Peter must have been the head of the Church in Rome. This claim of Peter's stewardship is based on some highly questionable evidence, includ-ing the possibility of Peter's burial in St. Peter's Basilica, evidence that eminent historians such as Joselyn M. C. Toynbee challenge. Was Peter the head of the Roman Church? "It must be said that the question has no entirely convincing answer from strictly historical evidence," admits Father McKenzie in *The Roman Catholic Church*.

But in terms of individual Catholic faith, this discussion has no great importance. The question of Peter's leadership in Rome as the basis for continuous papal succession is a point more suited to arguments over which church is the "true" Church or to the days when cities other than Rome fought for the right to be the center of the Church or when the Pope argued with other monarchs over his right to the property that encompasses the Vatican. In terms of Catholic faith, it is enough to know that:

1. Peter was the leader of the Apostles and thus the leader of the first Christian "Church." (This is made clear in Acts 1–12.)
2. This structure continues today with the Pope as a member of and the leader of the College of Bishops and thus the leader of the Catholic Church.

No matter how the succession is traced, one thing is certain: The powers of modern Popes go far beyond the powers of Peter. The best knowledge we have of the role this first Church leader played comes from the aforementioned chapters of Acts. From this source we know that in exercising his leadership, Peter spoke on behalf of the entire group, suggested courses of action, and made decisions.

But it is clear that he exercised this leadership as one of the Apostles, as part of the group. Important decisions were always the decisions of the *College* of Apostles. For example, in the baptism of Cornelius, Peter's action was discussed and ratified by the Twelve Apostles. This was the very important decision Peter made to extend the teaching of Christianity to the Gentiles. Even though the impetus for Peter to enter the "unclean" house of a Gentile, Cornelius, was a visitation from God, Peter nevertheless *sought the approval of the other Apostles*.

Thus, it is clear that the Pope did not make important decisions without consulting the other Apostles. It is also clear that he was not always resolute in his decisions since, well after the meeting with Cornelius, Peter refused to sit down with the Gentile Christians at Antioch until Paul convinced him to do so.

If, then, the papacy is a continuation of the leadership first demonstrated by Peter, why has the nature of that leadership changed so drastically? When and how did the Petrine legacy cease to be a shared responsibility and become instead a dictatorship? Certainly it did not happen in the early Church.

Little change is evident until the time of the emperor Constantine. When Constantine became a Christian, the Bishop of Rome became the emperor's bishop, and when the all-powerful emperor dealt with the Church, he did so through his bishop. The very fact that the First Council of Nicaea in 325, called by Constantine, was presided over by the legates of the Bishop of Rome is proof of increased power for this officer. The Bishop of Rome was now almost certainly accepted as the most important single officer of the Church.

Here, then, was the soil in which the seed of the Pope's power was sown—the imperial kingdom of Rome. The power bestowed upon the Pope was the emperor's sword.

This continuing growth in power was finally defined and codified at the First Vatican Council in 1870. According to this council, the Pope has the supreme and full power of jurisdiction over the entire Church, both in matters of faith and morals and in matters of discipline and government. This power is subject to no one in the Church, and there is no area or person within the Church not subject to a direct command from the Pope.

The papacy had become a religious dictatorship, complete with all the excesses and corruption that inevitably flow from absolute power.

BISHOPS

As originally conceived, the College of Bishops might be compared to the U.S. Congress, each bishop chosen by and representing the people of his diocese in the same way that a congressman is chosen by and represents the people of his state or district. In addition, the College of Bishops in its infancy served more as a partnership with the Pope, as Congress does with the president and as the other Apostles did with Peter.

Bishops are in charge of the diocese at the local level with no ecclesiastical superior other than the Pope. In his own diocese, a bishop has powers comparable to those of the Pope for the worldwide Church, and like the Pope, the bishop has his own local staff or curiae, as well as advisory bodies.

In Catholic belief, today's bishops are the successors to the Apostles, those whom Christ commissioned to proclaim the gospel throughout the world. This is not an individual but a group succession. No bishop can be said to be equivalent to one of Christ's Apostles, but the worldwide group of bishops is equivalent to the group of Apostles. Succession is maintained by filling vacancies in the College of Bishops and increasing the number of bishops in line with Church growth.

Bishops are not the subjects of the Pope in the same sense that other Catholics are his subjects. The bishop is a member of a college, of which the Pope is also a member, and its leader as Peter was the Apostles' leader. So bishops have the right to deal with the Pope as his colleagues rather than as his subjects.

In the early centuries of Christianity, a bishop was elected by the whole local Church—initially the parishioners and later the clergy. The election result was announced to the bishops of the region, who signified their acceptance or approval by granting the new bishop communion. Today, unfortunately, this democratic procedure has disappeared. All episcopal appointments are made by the Pope.

Election of bishops by laity or clergy was not perfect. On occasion politics were invoked by ambitious clergy and laymen who sought to elect a bishop whom they could control. But discontinuing elections in favor of papal appointment has not eliminated these dangers. Instead, more serious problems have emerged.

What does the Pope look for in a candidate for the episcopacy? According to Father McKenzie, "One may say that *cooperation* is the major qualification." He refers, of course, to cooperation with the Pope and his curia. It is this cooperation that, more than any other element, assures a candidate that he will be chosen bishop.

Is this any way to produce great prelates? As a Catholic, I say no. Since cooperation is the key qualification, learning can be a detriment. A theologian of distinction is almost never chosen as bishop. On the other hand, nearly every new bishop has spent time in Rome, which allowed him to press the flesh and advance his candidacy with members of the curia.

Perhaps most tragic of all is the fact that the selection of bishops by papal appointment has virtually eliminated the only possible check and balance on the power of the Pope. The late Karl Rahner, one of the greatest of all Catholic theologians, provided a firm theological foundation for the bishops' independent claim to ecclesiastical authority, a claim that should render today's monarchial or dictatorial model of the Papacy obsolete and have the College of Bishops work in partnership with the Pope in the governing of the Church. But what good is such a foundation if the bishops continue to owe their appointment to the Pope? Can one reasonably expect bishops to rise up and oppose a Pope to whom they owe their positions?

The Pope and his curia tend to appoint only those who agree with their ideas. "The one qualification is that he is safe," says John

McKenzie, and he defines "safe" as maintaining positions that enjoy long experience and general acceptance rather than reaching toward new points of view. This means papal appointment of bishops saddles the Church with leaders who live in the past instead of the present or the future, hardly the sort of men who might act as a balance for the archaic ideas of Pope John Paul II.

Papal appointment of bishops also means that the property paid for by the Catholics of any diocese is owned and controlled by a man whose first allegiance is to the Vatican, not to the people who continue to pay for the property's upkeep, as well as the bishop's income. In most of the United States, the bishop is a *sole corporation*, meaning that he owns all Church property—land, buildings, schools, factories—within his diocese. There is no board of directors to control his activities. He possesses all this property in precisely the same way that the ordinary citizen can his own home. For the bishop, this is an extraordinary power base, and it has been used more than once to force "cooperation" with Rome from reluctant congregations. For example, bishops have been known to threaten the demotion of their church if parishioners refuse to do as asked. Such conduct is fully within the bishop's power!

CARDINALS

Unlike the titles "Pope" or "bishop," the title "cardinal" is purely honorary, carrying with it no ecclesiastical jurisdiction. Nevertheless, the College of Cardinals is the most powerful group within the Church, first because it is its responsibility to elect the Pope and second because members are either bishops of some of the most important sees in the world or holders of the most important offices in the curia.

In its loftiest responsibility, the College of Cardinals might be compared to this nation's electoral college. But this comparison was far more accurate in the early centuries of the Church than it is today. Back then, the Pope, who was after all the Bishop of Rome, was elected like a bishop of any other diocese, by the entire Catholic population of the areas or, later, by the clergy who acted as an electoral body for the laity. Due to disputes, sometimes even bloodshed, it was soon accepted that the newly elected candidate should not take office until he had been confirmed by the emperor. The disputes did not end. When the emperor was away, rival factions sometimes had Popes empowered who had not won an election, some of whom were later deposed or poisoned or thrown into prison.

Such conduct was eliminated by Pope Nicholas II and his Bull of 1059, which reserved the Pope's selection process to the members of the higher clergy, the cardinals. This process empowered the cardinals to hold the election wherever they saw fit, in case there was trouble in Rome, and empowered the newly elected Pope to act immediately should anyone try to halt his enthronement. Although this procedure helped eliminate bloody disputes over the Papacy, it also removed all remnants of a democratic election process for the Bishop of Rome. Moreover, despite all the safeguards experience has forced upon the College, the cardinals are not free from pressure. True, so far as historians can determine, scandalous procedures have not succeeded in electing a Pope since the eleventh century, but such conduct has prevented good men from being elected and that is a matter of great importance.

Today, both Catholics and non-Catholics make jokes about papal elections—the closeting of the cardinals, the food rationing to force a quick decision, the smoke signals to announce the results—but thinking Catholics find all this matter much too serious for laughter. Since the cardinals are the personal choices of the Pope, the process is far closer to a monarchic system than that of a democratic society. While the Pope does not choose his successor, he does select the relatively small group of people by whom and from whom his successor will be chosen. Of course, the cardinals could look beyond their own number to choose a Pope. Any baptized male seven years or older is eligible, but the cardinals have never once gone outside their college.

Since the appointment to cardinal usually occurs after a longer career, most members of the College are much older than men working in business and state government. Thus, those who choose the Pope and who hold the top positions in Church government are well past their most productive years. Not surprisingly, all this makes the cardinals appear to the outside world as a doddering, self-perpetuating power group, which, in fact, they are, except for Pope John XXIII. He was old in body but young at heart, in mind, and in spirit, supported by a great vision of what had to be done to modernize the Catholic Church, and he started the process.

The Curia

Continuing the comparison of Church government with that of the United States, the curia might be compared to the president's cabinet. In effect, the cardinals who make up the curia are the Pope's personal assistants, doing the work that he gives them while having no authority except that which the Pope assigns. Beginning in the fourth century with a single office, the Apostolic Chancery, the curia has grown to a complex of worldwide agencies, including five offices, ten congregations, and three tribunals plus assorted councils and commissions, all of which, under the authority of the Pope, administer the affairs of the universal Church at the highest level.

The chief of the five offices is the Secretariat of State, which in recent decades made its cardinal the most powerful man in the Pope's administration. The other offices are the Apostolic Chancery (preparing certain documents), the Apostolic Datary (handling appointments to many posts), the Apostolic Camera (administering affairs in the period between Popes), and the Secretariat for Latin (overseeing proper use of the language in documents).

Over the years, there were sometimes questions of overlapping jurisdiction among the offices of the curia. When this situation occurred, the Pope appointed a committee of cardinals to settle the question. The most important of these committees were called *congregations*. It is significant that once such congregations were formed, they were seldom discontinued, so that they have actually become the chief administrative units of the curia. The Congregation for the Doctrine of the Faith, for example, dates back to 1542 when it was known as the Inquisition, the watchdog over faith and morals. Other important congregations include the Congregation of the Bishops, supervising dioceses, including appointment of bishops; and the Congregation of the Clergy, supervising ecclesiastical property and revenues, all in strictest secrecy.

Although dioceses around the world have their own judicial structure, appeals may be made to the curia. Many appeals are handled by the appropriate congregation; otherwise cases come before one of the curia's three tribunals—the Sacred Penitentiary (questions of individual conscience), the Rota (various cases of religious law, especially matrimony), and the Apostolic Signature (a kind of ecclesiastical supreme court, but not comparable to that of our nation).

The shortcomings of the curia are not really surprising. Aside from the endless bureaucracy, most of the cardinals in these key positions, due both to advanced age and the source of their appointment, make up a cabinet of yes-men. While some cabinet officers in the United States have resigned in opposition to the direction chosen by their President, it would be difficult to find comparable cases where members of the curia have quit their Pope. The cardinals in Rome are best known for doing what they believe is expected, not what they believe is right.

Moreover, a cloak of secrecy hangs over much of the curia's work. For example, as mentioned in chapter 10, the Congregation for the Doctrine of the Faith has been notorious in the way it has forbidden theologians to write or teach without making any specific charges of unsound doctrine, refusing to divulge, even to the censored, the reason for his punishment. Some of those forbidden to speak or write have even been forbidden to reveal the fact that they were forbidden.

Secrecy is also involved in the selection of bishops. The only essential qualifications for a prospective bishop are that he must be at least thirty years of age and have served five years as a priest. Aside from the curia's rumored insistence on "cooperation," as mentioned earlier, we have no way of knowing what criteria are used to determine a candidate's potential. The process by which these appointments are made is one of the most closely held secrets in the Church. Once, the entire community of the diocese participated in the selection process, which has now been given to the Pope and his assistants. Not only have members of the diocese lost the opportunity to participate in the selection of their bishop, they are even denied the right to know how the choice was made.

Then there are the "experts." If those outside the curia raise questions about any kind of controversial decision, the response is always the same: The decision was based on testimony from experts. But when the names or credentials of these experts are requested, the curia hides behind its curtain of secrecy.

So often is the right to secrecy invoked that the press has a tried-and-true method for getting its stories at the Vatican. Reporters find a member of the curia staff willing to make a deal about secret information. Thus, newspaper or TV stories are peppered with "according to an unnamed Vatican source." Father McKenzie has stated, "When secrecy is normal, the irresponsible journalistic leak also becomes normal." What a terrible image for the curia—a body that provokes dishonesty among "religious" people.

No part of the Papacy is handled more secretly than the treasury. Although the world knows that the pontifical administration disposes of enormous sums, in cash as well as investments and property, no one knows how much or when or where, for no public statement is made. Even members of the Church, who donate to the organization week after week, have no idea of the true extent and location of the Church's holdings. It should not be surprising, then, that the Church is faced with embarrassing stories like the $2-billion Banco Ambrosiano scandal, which brought grief and devastation to many families and for which the Pope and his curia have never apologized nor even tried to explain. In these affairs, as in affairs of the spirit, the Pope answers to no human authority.

Insofar as it concerns money and property and investments, the secrecy and scandal surrounding the wealth of the Church is made all the more deplorable by the Vatican's insistence on full ecclesiastical pomp. Such ostentation costs a fortune. Perhaps in the days when a Pope or a bishop competed with kings and emperors, the necessity for a powerful, formidable appearance did not seem unreasonable. But today, when all men and women of goodwill seek to relieve the suffering of the weak and starving and wretched, this is no time for the display of a monarchial style of life.

No one would suggest that the Pope should appear in rags and travel by bus. All Catholics want to feel proud when they see their Pope. Adequate provision for the papacy is essential, but imperialistic pomp and the accumulation of wealth for wealth's sake is another matter entirely. Catholic legends of saints are filled with stories of holy bishops and priests selling the trappings of pomp to provide money to the poor. Catholics love and admire these kinds of religious leaders. I believe that full financial disclosure should be a must for the curia. If this proves the Church to be as rich as most suspect, steps should be taken to turn a large share of these assets into assistance for the needy of the world.

The Catholic Church has always been associated with pomp, power, and wealth. Its wealth was related to its paintings and sculptures by great artists and to real estate around the world. However, the Church temporarily changed from being property rich to one with a limited supply of cash. The event that transformed the Catholic Church into a world-rich corporation occurred in 1929. The Vatican abandoned the Catholic Popular Party when it was evident that this party had little interest in reestablishing the power and privileges to the Vatican. The Lateran agreements in 1929 with Mussolini gave the Catholic Church what it had failed to achieve through popular democratic movements. Mussolini settled the long-standing Roman questions relating to the confiscation of Papal states by the Italian government by paying the Pope a high indemnity of 750 million lire and bonds worth one billion lire. This was wisely and judiciously invested in the international stock market. Overnight the Papacy and the Vatican became a major capitalist corporation.

The story becomes more involved and shows how connivingly a secret and corrupt corporation operates. Francesco Pacelli, brother of Eugenio Pacelli who became Pope Pius XII in 1939, carried out the negotiations with the Fascists. Their uncle Ernesto Pacelli was the aggressive head of the Bank of Rome. The Concordat of 1929 restored many of the powers that had once been lost by the Vatican. The result was that Italy was again made a Catholic confessional state.

The Vatican was not content to deal with one dictator but, having won a major victory over Mussolini, searched for more power. In 1933, Eugenio Pacelli, the Papal Nuncio to Germany, was the architect of a Concordat with Hitler. The Catholic Church by this concordat was assured freedom to practice Catholicism, appoint clergy, have the freedom of internal communication and publication. The German state, similar to the Concordat with Mussolini, had the right to veto papal appointments of bishops. The clergy had to take a loyalty oath to Germany and in return the state would pay the subsidy for the Catholic clergy. The Catholic Church had been effectively tied to the fascist states by these two concordats. The silence of Pope Pius XII about genocide and atrocities has repeatedly been condemned over the years. We as Catholics reluctantly accept the Vatican's defense that speaking out would have doomed Catholics in these two fascist states. The power of the Papacy in speaking out against the evils directed by Hitler and Mussolini would have had great power in galvanizing worldwide opposition. In a dream world, rhetoric will sustain an image no matter how false, but in the real world of the twentieth century, I must assume that the Pope was unwilling to jeopardize the privileged status gained by the two concordants. I must assume that power and wealth, according to Vatican standards, are the worthiest of goals. Hypocrisy can be raised to empathy for humanity when money is involved. This must be changed if the Church is to serve as a leader. It is in a critical position of becoming a major global institution that links the former Communist, Capitalist, and Third Worlds.

Andrew Greeley, in *Confessions of a Parish Priest*, writes, "With the papacy in mind, as a sociologist, I would refine the dictum: power without accountability corrupts, and absolute power without any accountability corrupts absolutely."

THE AMERICAN CHURCH

Like the rest of the world, the United States is divided into Catholic dioceses, a division that changes from time to time and is decided by the Pope. Contiguous dioceses are formed into provinces, and one of the dioceses within a province, usually the oldest or largest, may be called the *metropolitan see*. The bishop of this see is an archbishop. He is empowered to conduct visitations or inspections of the dioceses within his province and to inform the Pope if he observes abuses. The archbishop also presides over councils of the bishops in his province, but he does *not* have jurisdiction over these bishops and in no sense is he their superior.

Cardinal Spellman became the most famous and powerful archbishop in the history of the United States. At the peak of his influence, he enjoyed tremendous power with many American bishops as the titular head of the Church in the United States, but in no real sense did he become the American Pope.

The bishops of the United States have organized themselves into the National Conference of Catholic Bishops. This provides them with an opportunity to meet on a regular basis in order to share their insights and experiences. Through its various committees, the conference can exercise the national pastoral office of "bishop," but not in any official sense so far as the Church government in Rome is concerned. There is only one head of the U.S. Church, and he is the Pope.

Historically, Catholics in the United States have always wanted the Church to reflect the spirit of the new nation. The Vatican, on the other hand, has often been suspicious and fearful that the American Catholic Church would become *too* American and in the process break away from the domination of Rome.

Back in the eighteenth century, as mentioned briefly in chapter 14, the young Catholic Church in the United States attempted to incorporate some American ideas into the life of the Church. John Carroll, who was the superior of the Church's U.S. Mission in 1785, asked Rome to grant to the Church in the United States that ecclesiastical liberty which the temper of the age and of the people required. The Catholics of that period fully supported the concept of separation of church and state. They even went so far as to institute a democratic process in the Church, electing lay trustees who presided over the government of the parish and temporal matters and who could handle property ownership. Like John Carroll, many Catholics then believed that English rather than Latin should be used in the liturgy.

Rome brought tremendous pressure on Carroll and those around him to end the Americanization of the Church. By the time Carroll was anointed bishop in 1789, he had turned his back on such "brazen ideas." However, the dream of a better, more American Catholic Church did not die. It simply slept and waited.

Meanwhile, Catholic membership in this new nation grew at a rate enjoyed nowhere else in Church history. In the century from 1790 to 1890, the number of Catholics in the United States increased from thirty thousand to an astonishing 7 million. And in the 1890s, the dream of Americanizing the Church was rekindled.

Many American Catholics believed that the Church should adjust its doctrines, especially regarding morality, to the culture of the people. These men wanted the Church to emphasize the active virtues of social welfare and democratic equality more than the passive values of humility and obedience to ecclesiastic authority. The argument was not unlike the one the Church would have many years later in that of liberation theology. American Catholics did not deny the importance of faith and grace. They simply suggested that the Church's emphasis was wrong. Instead of putting all its energy into helping the faithful find freedom and joy in heaven, the Church should also help those people on earth gain freedom from the chains of poverty and inequality.

The challenge, known as "Americanism," sent shock waves through the curia with its reactionary cardinals and Pope, and on January 22, 1899, Pope Leo XIII condemned Americanism in an apostolic letter, *Testem Benevolentiae*. "It is hard to understand," said the Pope, "how principles can place the natural ahead of the supernatural virtues." What the Pope failed to appreciate is that to the starving man, gruel is more important than grace, and to the slave, equality on earth is more important than equality in heaven. The letter went on to deny the right of the U.S. Church to implement suggestions made by this doctrine of Americanism, threatening offenders with excommunication. Once again, the American Catholic dream was denied.

But now, another hundred years have passed and the membership of the Church is quite different from what it was a century ago. During the 1800s and much of the 1900s, the Church hierarchy could feel secure in dealing with U.S. Catholics, most of them uneducated immigrants. But today those immigrants have worked hard and prospered, educated their children, and found success both intellectually and financially in massive numbers, whether they are Irish or German, Italian or Polish, or, more recently, of many other nationalities.

Unprepared to deal with an educated Catholic population—expecting the childish obedience that had so long kept the Church in the twelfth century—the Vatican seemed at a loss as to how it should proceed. Then came the miracle that was Pope John XXIII. When Pope Pius XII (elected in 1939) died in 1958, the fifty-one cardinals (only seventeen were Italians) met to elect the next Pope. They were almost evenly divided between those who felt the need for a definite break with Pope Pius's triumphalist Church and those in favor of continuing it.

After a three-day struggle, a compromise was reached. Angelo Roncalli, the seventy-six-year-old patriarch of Venice, reputed to be moderate and conciliatory, was elected. It is doubtful if anyone on either side had an inkling of the revolutionary ideas percolating behind the old man's peasant face as they met to do him homage. The first surprise came when he chose the name John—a name that had not been taken since the notorious antipope John XXIII had been deposed at the Council of Constance (1414–1418). He soon showed that he would not be intimidated by the Vatican protocol or inhibited by the memory of his predecessor.

The cardinals unknowingly had elected a Pope who would change the Catholic Church forever. The curia lost control for the first time in its history. It is clear that this great Pope could feel the pulse of the American Catholic movement. Aware of the unrest among *all* Catholics, he called the Second Vatican Council. A window was opened.

The council launched a series of internal reforms, which included strong support for religious freedom and cooperation with other Christians, committing the Church to involvement on behalf of social justice *here on earth*, a wider role for the laity, and the celebration of Mass in everyday spoken languages rather than Latin.

The seeds for other reforms were also sown, but since the selection of Pope John Paul II, Vatican curia offices have reasserted control over the day-to-day business of the American Church. They have sought to stamp out the seeds of progress in America and return the clergy of the United States to the role of total obedience that they played for almost two centuries. Progressive bishops are moved out the moment they reach retirement age and rigid, conservative yes-men replace them. Those chosen cardinal need meet only that vital curia requirement of being "safe."

The result is more and more leaders like New York's John Cardinal O'Connor and Boston's Bernard Cardinal Law, whose ideas on the use of condoms and universal catechism, respectively, are in total opposition to the Americanization of the Church. However, they maintain their positions because they are puppets who mimic the Pope and blindly follow his dictates. It disturbs me as a Catholic to have the feeling that they do this to maintain their positions rather than from deep personal convictions.

THE CRISIS WE FACE

Suppose the president grew so strong that he managed to do away with popular elections for members of Congress, and instead of the people choosing their representatives, the president appointed them himself or left the selection to other members of his administration. Obviously, if members of Congress owed their appointment to the president rather than to the people, it is unlikely that they would disagree with any legislation the president proposed. The president would then have a free hand to disregard the rights and wishes of the people.

An analogous situation has occurred in the Church. There is no person or group to stand against the Papacy, and the current Pope not only uses the dictatorial powers codified in 1870, he goes beyond them. The code of canon law describes the Pope's power as full and supreme, but he may *not* reject the decision of an ecumenical council once promulgated. Yet that is precisely what Pope John Paul II and his curia have attempted to do with the decisions made at Vatican II.

As Leon Cardinal Suenens, Primate of Belgium, one of the architects of Vatican II, has said, "The Pope should no longer act as though he were outside the Church and above the Church." But the message goes unheeded. What can we do? Some say we must wait and hope for a loving, progressive man like Pope John XXIII. I do not agree. The American Catholics united have the power to change the dictatorial power of the Church. They can withhold giving money to the Vatican until a dialogue is initiated.

When a Pope dies, especially if his Papacy has been a long one, like John Paul II's, one can logically assume the cardinals will select a candidate who reflects the values and beliefs of the fallen Pope. Most cardinals at the conclave of 1958 hoped to select someone whom they could control. They came expecting to be part of the election of Archbishop Siri of Genoa, a man cast in the rigid, conservative mold of Pope Pius XII. Fortunately, the arrival of Cardinal Wyszyski, the only cardinal from a communist country, helped to inspire the progressive cause, producing a deadlock between Cardinal Siri and the progressive candidate Archbishop Montini of Milan.

When neither candidate could muster the necessary votes, the cardinals agreed to move to a compromise candidate. The conservatives saw this new candidate as only a brief interim Pope, while they strengthened their forces for the next conclave. For this role, they wanted a man who did not have long to live. They chose Cardinal Angelo Giuseppe Roncalli, whom Cardinal Spellman would later say did not deserve to be pope, but should instead be selling bananas, a smiling, dumpy, seventy-seven-year-old (no cardinal over seventy had been chosen Pope in more than two hundred years).

Cardinal Roncalli became John XXIII, chosen because of a deadlock and because he seemed malleable. He was not expected to live long. However, in the five years given to him as Pope, he did more for his Church than perhaps any other Pope in history.

If Pope John XXIII had the vision and will and strength—working even as he knew he was dying of cancer—to open that window on the Church, can we not find the strength to fight the Vatican's efforts to close it?

We cannot simply wait and hope. We must fight to take advantage of modern communication systems by having the Pope chosen in a far more democratic manner, an election in which all members of the College of Bishops will vote. The American and German Catholics keep the Vatican viable through their generous gifts of money. Their combined voices and the withholding of funds could bring the

Vatican to its knees, and it would accept change. Imagine what a difference this would make in Church leadership and envision what opening up elections to public scrutiny would make to how the Church is viewed by the outside world.

More important, now that developments in communication make such an election possible, we are able to move far closer to the workings of the early Christians. After all, without Christ here on earth to make the choice, who better to select the leader of the apostles than the apostles themselves—the College of Bishops in consultation with concerned Catholics.

We must fight also to democratize the selection of bishops, not just in the United States, but throughout the world, and allow the Catholics of each diocese to have input through responsible Catholics in choosing their own bishops. In selecting bishops, the Church has had experience both with elections and with appointments by the Pope. Perhaps neither is perfect, but as Father John McKenzie points out, "Election is urged because it does meet certain problems inherent in centralized appointment, because the things which compelled its abandonment do not seem to be clear and present dangers now and because election is more in harmony with the democratic government which modern Western man, at least in theory, still professes to be best for him."

Today, most bishops feel that their main duty is to protect the establishment and "cooperate" with those to whom they owe their appointment. Election by members of the diocese will cause the new bishop to feel greater responsibility toward his constituents and will also cause the laity to feel more of a compulsion to support the Bishop. It is obvious that American Catholics must join together to have lay boards that judge the qualifications of their leaders.

New Catechism for Catholics

This catechism defines sins of the modern world. As I read about this story in the *New York Times*, my mind wandered back to the time that I entered Holy Rosary School in Erie, Pennsylvania, and received my first catechism. The story of the new catechism brought back a wave of nostalgia for those wonderful happy days that I spent there. The world has turned over many times since then and my childlike altruism has been replaced with a more mature searching of conscience for what is best for the world, for human beings, and for myself. In order to describe the impact of the new catechism, I shall briefly outline the history of the catechism as I know it.

Pope Paul III, who died in 1549, convoked the Council of Trent that opened on December 13, 1545, in the northern Italian city of Trent, with some thirty bishops in attendance. It took eighteen years for the council to complete its work, from 1545 to 1563, although it was in actual session for only a little more than three of these years. The trend of the council was extremely conservative; the liberals were not given much of a hearing. Thus, in requiring seminaries for the future training of priests, the bishops made sure that the training given would be highly traditional, and they paid little heed to the progress in biblical studies made by the humanists.

They also reaffirmed tradition as regards the structure of the Catholic Church. A most important measure, no doubt, was acknowledging peoples' supremacy and so laying to rest the ghost of Constance. By submitting its decrees to the Pope for confirmation and entrusting to him the task of carrying out its incomplete work, the council further strengthened the hold of the Pope over the Church. Under the papal autocrat they placed episcopal autocrats by giving the bishops absolute control over their diocese. And they left no room for participation by the laity in the administration of the Church. In sum, they bequeathed to modern Catholics a highly authoritarian, centralized structure that was still basically medieval.

The one positive outcome for the Council of Trent was the pivotal event of the Catholic reformation. It defined the key doctrines of the Church; and it set the whole Church on the path of reform. This can be appreciated in retrospect, but at that time pessimists, given the history of the previous reform councils, might well have wondered whether all these decrees might simply remain dead letters. However, in the time of crisis some Roman popes with outstanding leadership rose to the occasion. The first and greatest of these reform popes was Pius V, who died in 1572. He had previously been known as a relentless inquisitor; he set such a high standard of papal morality that it has never again suffered any serious relapse. An ascetic, mortified man, who loved nothing more than prayer, he transformed the Vatican by vigorous measures and examples into a kind of monastery. Throwing himself into the work of reform with indefatigable energy, he published the Catechism of the Council of Trent, a clear, concise summary of Catholic beliefs and practices and also the previously mentioned *Missale Romanum*, or Revised Roman

Missal, which imposed the uniform liturgy on the whole Catholic world.

It was from this beginning that the Baltimore Catechism, which I grew up with, had its beginnings. With childlike faith I and the members of my class learned the catechism by heart and were quizzed daily on what it contained. It was a question and answer book that we all accepted as being the authentic word directly from God and must be accepted without any reservations. The new catechism is not written in the question-and-answer form that many people associate with the word catechism. Nor is it intended to replace other sources of church teachings, such as scripture, creeds, papal statements, and decrees of ecumenical councils.

The Baltimore Catechism was originally the "Catechism of Christian Doctrine, Prepared and Enjoined by Order of the Third Council of Baltimore." The Baltimore Catechism is a book containing the basic beliefs and teachings of the Catholic faith that have been used in the United States to instruct young people and adults. Teachers use it to impart the doctrines of Catholicism by using the question and answer method of instruction. We students at Holy Rosary School had a session every day on the Baltimore Catechism. It was our bible. My mother, a devout Catholic, was pleased when I won an award for having committed the Catechism to memory and being able to recite verbatim the answers to the questions contained in it. This was also a proud moment for me.

In November, 1884, the American bishops met for the Third Plenary Council of Baltimore, which was convened by Archbishop James Gibbons. During the final days of the two months' meeting, they commissioned Father DeConcilio to write a basic catechism that could be used for simple religious instructions. When this project was completed, the texts of the catechism were forwarded to the bishops. They suggested numerous changes and so a revision was undertaken in 1896. The text was completely revised by 1941.

This catechism was the most popular religious text in Catholic schools and religious education programs until the 1960s, when many Catholic educators began to consider it inadequate and outdated. Its theology had not been revised to reflect the developments in Church thinking after Vatican II. Also, the Baltimore Catechism's view of Western culture and modern living was not in total harmony with the Church's more recent teachings about the world and contemporary technology.

For the first time in more than four centuries the Roman Catholic Church, on Tuesday, November 17, 1992, issued a new, universal Catechism, a massive compendium of its teachings that reaffirms traditional tenets of faith, but also identifies a range of new sins that are products of modern society. Among the sins defined in the new Catechism are tax evasion, drug abuse, mistreatment of immigrants, financial speculation, abuse of the environment, artificial insemination, and genetic engineering. Most of these are admirable statements but there are some, such as artificial insemination and genetic engineering, that may be subject to debate and disagreement at the grass roots of the Catholic Church.

The news accounts of the new Catechism focused almost entirely on the concrete and catchy sections dealing with modern forms of ancient sins, like tax evasion and drunken driving, rather than the more abstruse but theologically important sections dealing with God, Jesus, the sacraments, Scripture, and the Church.

The Catechism was uppermost on the American bishops' minds during the four days that they met and debated a landmark document of their own, a proposed pastoral letter dealing with women's role in the Church and society. The debates in Washington moved on a question raised by the appearance of the Catechism, namely, how can the Church be an effective leader in a world of radically different cultures and dramatic social upheavals, where things as basic as the relationship between men and women are being rapidly transformed and where religious leadership must be exercised in the glare of media?

Although the news releases report that the Pope planned to release the Catechism in Rome in December 1992, news leaks of some of its contents to Italian and French newspapers prompted the move to bring forward the date of its release. It is my opinion that this was done to negate and draw attention from the debate going on in Washington among the U.S. bishops. The Pope obviously was informed that his stand on women was not well received and that there would not be a unanimous vote supporting his position.

The new Catechism is another attempt by the Vatican to smother dissent and centralize power in Rome. It is a betrayal of the gains of Vatican II. The Catechism has elicited new fears. In striving to restore doctrinal and administrative order, Pope John Paul II relied on a Vatican officialdom that had never much favored the Second

Vatican Council. Liberals worried that the Catechism would become a hard and fast substitute for the council's own documents, either ignoring the council's fresh understanding of Church teaching or giving them the most conservative interpretation possible.

The document is the result of six years' work by the commission headed by Joseph Cardinal Ratzinger of Germany, who is the prefect of the Congregation for the Doctrine of Faith. Pope John Paul II approved the new Catechism and even ordered last-minute changes in the section on morality. Since French was the working language of its drafting, the French edition has been published and the Italian edition was published on December 8, 1992. The English language version is scheduled for publication in spring 1993.

The Catechism addresses the ordination of women, theft, abortion, drunken driving, euthanasia, birth control, pornography, homosexuality, the Jews, and immigration. The Catechism appears to be designed to give the Pope and the curator power over all Catholics by making them feel guilty and even inferior. The section dealing with morality and ethics accounts for only 87 of the Catechism's 321 subchapters but undoubtedly will give rise to the greatest amount of debate.

. The other three sections cover the Church's beliefs, its liturgy, and its prayer. In most cases, they summarize existing dogmas and practice among Catholics. It feebly attempts to reach out with ecumenism by stating that the Church has no hesitation in allocating to Christians the greatest responsibility for Jesus' suffering, a responsibility that they too often attributed solely to the Jews.

Having been disappointed in the pronouncements coming from the Vatican, I had hoped when I read about the new Catechism that there would be something substantial that would truly be an update on the fundamental principles of the Church. Unfortunately, it is the work of the same old tired minds trying to preserve their autonomy without facing the realities of the twenty-first century. After reading it, I can only conclude that Pope John Paul II and Joseph Cardinal Ratzinger are the *original* and *true cafeteria Catholics*. They have picked what they wanted, coated it with a thin veil of sweetness but avoided what is essential. They have done nothing to stem the tide of revolt that is well underway in the Catholic Church.

When I look at the Roman Catholic Church throughout its long history, including the Church today, I am saddened by its scandalous record of power-mongering, special privileges for the rich, inappropriate and often deceitful explanations for positions which they have taken. Unfortunately, these are not accidental, private sins of individuals or the mistakes secondary to poor judgment. The power and wealth philosophy comes from an ideology and collective organization of hierarchial, patriarchial clericalism. Unless the Roman Catholic Church changes from being an outrageous institution to one that has a dialogue and collegiality with its members, it does not deserve our loyalty.

How can we bring about such major changes in the Church as the election of the Pope by all bishops and election of bishops by all Catholics in their diocese? It is clear that what is needed—what is essential—is Vatican III. The very thought of such a council will frighten the entrenched hierarchy of the Church and send a wave of despair, depression, and realization through the curia that a world revolution is taking place in the Catholic Church.

In order to fulfill the vision of Pope John XXIII and prepare the Church for the twenty-first century, the new council will have a formidable agenda. To summarize what has been discussed in the preceding pages, Vatican Council III must:

1. Reinstate the democratic selection of bishops through selection by all Catholics in the diocese.

2. Establish the election of the new Pope by the worldwide College of Bishops. This Pope will have a mandate to remodel the curia so that it focuses on poverty rather than pomp. It should be international in character, corporatelike rather than a gerontocracy, and open rather than secret in its method of operation.

3. Review and modernize Church positions on those subjects of greatest concern to Catholics around the world, including full and equal rights for women, their ordination to the priesthood, the worldwide need for birth control, new methods of childbirth, ecumenism, a personalist approach to moral issues and the use of biblical and historical criticism, improved conditions

for priests, optional celibacy, the vital need for openness and freedom with the Church's theologians, freedom of religion, redefined free will, liberation theology, theological and cultural pluralism, divorce, abortion, euthanasia, collegiality, and lay boards at all levels of the ministeries of the Catholic Church.

Sadly, few are ready to call for the Council. Indeed, no powerful voices will clamor for the convening of Vatican Council III unless the rigid, conservative hierarchy of the Church is made to feel a ground swell of rebellion. Only *you* can produce such a ground swell, just as Church members did in Holland, dissenting, demonstrating, and arguing until the bishops were forced to reform the decision-making process there. They set up the National Pastoral Council based on democratic and representative principles. Its delegates are elected by the people and charged with voting on proposals that often originate at the lowest level.

We must set out to produce worldwide the kind of pressure Catholics brought in Holland. It is not enough to hope and pray and read books. We must take meaningful steps designed to make the Vatican listen and move. We need study groups to decide upon the full list of measures to be taken, but here are some immediate suggestions:

1. *The Collection Basket.* No matter what else one may do to attract the attention of the Vatican, it is unlikely to produce the desired response unless it is coupled with a reduction of what seems to matter most to the curia—money. My personal suggestion is to reduce your usual Church contributions by two-thirds, including with each donation a small printed note stating that this is one-third your normal gift and is meant only for your local parish because you disagree with the Roman leadership and are working toward Vatican III to change it. The rest of your usual gift could be donated to your charity of choice or, once it is in place, donated to a world committee made up of laity and clergy for Vatican III. It cannot be controlled by the male hierarchy, which is done in setting up synods, electing bishops, and so on. The curia must be forced by the power of economics and public relations programs to accept the change.

2. *Speaking Out.* Talk to everyone in your parish who is interested in listening. This is not a matter of taking positions on

controversial subjects. You need not reveal your personal views on divorce, birth control, abortion, or whatever. You need only point out that the vision of Pope John XXIII is being dismantled, the window is being closed. You seek Vatican III so that the initial efforts made by Pope John and Vatican II will not be thwarted. You seek dialogue so that the Church leadership does not continue to do what it is forbidden to do—contradict the findings of an ecumenical council. Be prepared to speak to anyone, including the press, to say that you, like others, such as Maria Shriver, love your Church and have no intention of leaving it, but Vatican III is essential. I, for one, pledge my energy to preserve the Catholic Church by modernizing it.

3. *Action*. Be prepared to participate in action if the opportunity arrives to further the cause of preparation for Vatican III or to stop those who wish to halt it. Also, be prepared for open dissent, for demonstrations, for sit-ins. Be prepared to show the same kind of fight-for-rights displayed by the people of Holland. We must be articulate and vocal, but we must be respectful of the values of all human beings.

4. *Organizing*. We must build an international network to further the cause: a World Committee for Vatican III. Be prepared to help form your local chapter and to gather members from your parish. In an effort to assist in the launching of this Committee, I have authorized my publisher to donate to the World Committee for Vatican III a certain percentage of my profits from the worldwide sales of this book.

5. *Involving Women*. Vatican Council III must avail itself of the critical mass of women who in the wake of the reforms and socialization that Vatican Council II generated have reconstituted their way of life with remarkable developments in consciousness, lifestyle, and dedicated missions. They represent the largest single group of educated, articulate, bonded women the world has ever seen. There is a new solidarity emerging among Church women across continents, cultures, and ethnic groups. Unlike John Paul II, who has failed to harvest the gifts of women for the Church, Vatican III must give them a significant role in planning a stronger Catholic Church to meet the challenges of the next centuries. Catholics must grant the request made by Sister M. Teresa Kane in 1979 and include women "in all ministries of our Church."

Vatican Council III must have the input of the best minds of other churches and religions if it is to complete its agenda and reach decisions respected by the world. I believe one reason why Pope John XXIII had the ability to accomplish so much so quickly occurred because he appealed to the imagination of all men and women, no matter what their religion. As Eugene Kennedy stated in writing about Pope John XXIII: "When he died, people of other faiths went into mourning, referring to him as 'my Pope.' " God forbid that we, as Catholics, betray the dream of a great Pope!

If the Church is to attract new members in the twenty-first century, if it is to grow in the future as it has in the past, it must be respected throughout the world by Catholics and non-Catholics alike. This respect will be given only if, through Vatican III, the spiritual splendor of the early Church is restored, as envisioned by Pope John XXIII:

In this way shall be set before the eyes of the world an admirable spectacle of truth, unity and charity; and those who are separated from this Apostolic Chair may receive a gentle invitation to seek and find that unity for which Christ prayed so ardently.

We, the Catholics of the world, must join with all human beings of goodwill to bring this vision about. History will then judge us well and, looking back, will say, *"Finis coronat magnum opus. Gaudeamus igitur. Satis verborarum."* "The end crowns the great work. So let us be joyful. No more need be said."

Suggested Reading

Ashe, K. *Today's Woman Tomorrow's Church*. Chicago: Thomas More Press, 1983.

Benton, W. *Contemporary Civilization*. Parts 1 and 2. New York: Monarch Press, 1962, 1963.

Berryman, P. *Liberation Theology*. Pantheon Books. New York: Random House, 1987.

Blanshard, P. *American Freedom and Catholic Power*. Second ed. Boston: Beacon Press, 1958.

Bokenkotter, T. *A Concise History of the Catholic Church*. Revised ed. Garden City, NY: Image Books/Doubleday, 1990.

_____. *Dynamic Catholicism: A Historical Catechism*. Garden City, NY: Image Books/Doubleday, 1992.

Brennan, R. E. *Thomistic Psychology*. New York: Macmillan, 1941.

Brotherton, A. *The Voice of the Turtledove—New Catholic Women in Europe*. New York: Paulist Press, 1992.

Burtchaell, J. T. *The Limits of the Law: Reflections on the Abortion Debate*. Chicago: Americans United for Life, 1987.

Calow, J. T. *Catholics and Broken Marriage*. Notre Dame: Ave Maria Press, 1979.

Cambridge Women's Study Group. *Women in Society: Interdisciplinary Essays*. London: Virago Press, 1981.

Carr, A. E. *Transforming Grace: Christian Tradition and Women's Experience*. San Francisco: Harper & Row, 1988.

Cheatham, A., and Powell, M. C. *This Way Day Break Comes*. Philadelphia: New Society Publishers, 1986.

Chesterton, G. K. *Orthodoxy*. Garden City, NY: Image/Doubleday, 1959.

_____. Saint Thomas Aquinas "The Dumb Ox." Garden City, NY: Image/Doubleday, 1956.

Chittister, J., Sr. *Women, Ministry and the Church*. New York: Paulist Press, 1983.

Curran, C. E. *Catholic Higher Education, Theology and Academic Freedom*. Notre Dame: University of Notre Dame Press, 1990.

_____. *Directions in Catholic School Ethics*. Notre Dame: University of Notre Dame Press, 1985.

_____. *Issues in Sexual and Medical Ethics*. Notre Dame: University of Notre Dame Press, 1978.

———. *Tensions in Moral Theology*. Notre Dame: University of Notre Dame Press, 1988.

———, McCormick, R. A., eds. *Readings in Moral Theology*. No. 1. *Moral Norms and Catholic Tradition*. New York: Paulist Press, 1979.

Dalcourt, G. J. *The Philosophy of St. Thomas Aquinas*. New York: Monarch Press, 1965.

Daley, L. C. *The Writings of Saint Augustine*. New York: Monarch Press, 1965.

Deedy, J. *The Catholic Fact Book*. Chicago: Thomas More Press, 1986.

Dyer, G. J. *An American Catholic Catechism*. New York: Seabury Press, 1975.

Ekstrom, R. R., and Ekstrom, R. *Concise Catholic Dictionary for Parents and Religion Teachers*. Mystic, CT: Twenty-third Publications, 1982.

Fiorenza, E. S. *In Memory of Her—A Feminist Theological Reconstruction of Christian Origins*. New York: Crossroad, 1985.

Ford, G. B. *A Degree of Difference: Memories of George Barry Ford*. New York: Farrar, Straus & Giroux, 1969.

Foy, F. A., and Avato, R. M. *A Concise Guide to the Catholic Church*. Huntington, IN: Our Sunday Visitor, 1984.

———, eds. *1988 Catholic Almanac*. Huntington, IN: Our Sunday Visitor, 1988.

Gallup, G., Jr., and Castelli, J. *The American Catholic People: Their Beliefs, Politics and Values*. Garden City, NY: Doubleday, 1987.

Giles, M. E., ed. *The Feminist Mystic and Other Essays on Women and Spirituality*. New York: Crossroad, 1987.

———. *When Each Leaf Shines: Voices of Women's Ministry*. Denville, NJ: Dimension Books, 1986.

Glazier, M., ed. *Where We Are: American Catholics in the 1980s*. Wilmington, DE: Michael Glazier, 1985.

Greeley, A. M. *An Autobiography: Confessions of a Parish Priest*. New York: Simon and Schuster, 1986.

———. *The Final Planet*. New York: Warner Books, 1987.

———. *Unsecular Man: The Persistence of Religion*. New York: Schocken Books, 1985.

Groeschel, B. J., and Weber, T. L. *Thy Will Be Done—A Spiritual Portrait of Terence Cardinal Cooke*. New York: Alba House, 1990.

Haddad, Y. Y., and Findley, E. B. *Women, Religion and Social Change*. Albany, NY: State University of New York Press, 1985.

Hanson, E. O. *The Catholic Church in World Politics*. Princeton, NJ: Princeton University Press, 1987.

Hardin, M. E. *Women's Mysteries: Ancient and Modern*. New York: Harper Colophon Books, 1971.

Hardon, J. A. J. *The Catholic Catechism: A Contemporary Catechism of the Teachings of the Catholic Church*. Garden City, NY: Doubleday, 1974.

_____. *Pocket Catholic Dictionary.* Garden City, NY: Image/Doubleday, 1985.

Hellwig, M. K. *Christian Women in a Troubled World.* New York: Paulist Press, 1985.

_____. *Understanding Catholicism.* New York: Paulist Press, 1981.

Jancar, B. *Review Notes and Study Guide to the Philosophy of Aristotle.* New York: Monarch Press, 1964.

Jung, P. B., and Shannon, T. A., eds. *Abortion and Catholicism: The American Debate.* New York: Crossroad, 1988.

Kelly, K. T. *Divorce and Second Marriage: Facing the Challenge.* New York: Seabury Press, 1982.

Kennedy, E. *Tomorrow's Catholics—Yesterday's Church—The Two Cultures of American Catholicism.* New York: Harper & Row, 1988.

Kohmischer, M. F. *Catholicism Today: A Survey of Catholic Belief and Practice.* New York: Paulist Press, 1980.

Kolbenschlag, M., ed. *Women in the Church I.* Washington, D.C.: Pastoral Press, 1987.

Küng, H. *The Church.* Garden City, NY: Image/Doubleday, 1976.

_____. *Why I Am Still a Christian.* Nashville: Abingdon Press, 1986.

_____, and Swidler, L., eds. *The Church in Anguish.* San Francisco: Harper and Row, 1987.

Kuper, J., ed. *Key Thinkers, Past and Present.* London and New York: Routledge & Kegan Paul, 1987.

LoBello, N. *The Vatican Empire.* New York: Trident Press, 1968.

Luker, K. *Abortion and the Politics of Motherhood.* Berkeley: University of California Press, 1986.

Maguire, D. *The Moral Choice.* New York: Winston Press, 1979.

Mahoney, J. *Bioethics and Belief.* Westminster, MD: Christian Classics, 1984.

May, W. W., ed. *Vatican Authority and American Catholic Dissent: The Curan Case and Its Consequences.* New York: Crossroad, 1987.

McCarthy, D. G., Bayer, E. J., eds. *Handbook on Critical Sexual Issues.* Garden City, NY: Image/Doubleday, 1984.

McCormick, R. A. *Health and Medicine in the Catholic Tradition.* New York: Crossroad, 1987.

McKenzie, J. L., S. J. *The Roman Catholic Church.* New York: Holt, Rinehart and Winston, 1969.

Micks, M. H. *Introduction to Theology.* Revised ed. San Francisco: Harper and Row, 1983.

Moltman-Wendell, E. *The Women Around Jesus.* New York: Crossroad, 1987.

Nathanson, B., with Ostling, R. N. *Aborting America.* Garden City, NY: Doubleday, 1979.

Neuhaus, R. J. *The Catholic Moment.* San Francisco: Harper and Row, 1987.

Reuther, Rosemary Radford. *Contemporary Roman Catholicism: Crises and Challenges*. Kansas City, MO: Sheed and Ward, 1987.

Ripple, P. *The Pain and the Possibility: Divorce and Separation Among Catholics*. Notre Dame, IN: Ave Maria Press, 1987.

Sahakian, W. S. *History of Philosophy*. New York: Barnes and Noble Books, 1968.

Schillebeeckx, E. *On Christian Faith—The Spiritual, Ethical and Political Dimensions*. New York: Crossroad, 1987.

Segunda, J. L. *Theology and the Church: A Response to Cardinal Ratzinger and a Warning to the Whole Church*. Minneapolis: Winston Press, 1985.

Sheed, F. J. *Theology for Beginners*. Third ed. Ann Arbor, MI: Servant Books, 1981.

Sprague, J., ed. *An Andrew Greeley Reader*. Chicago: Thomas More Press, 1987.

Storkey, E. *What's Right With Feminism*. Grand Rapids, MI: William B. Eerdmans, 1986.

Taffe, T. P. *The Writings of the Early Church Fathers*. New York: Monarch Press, 1966.

Tracy, D. *Plurality and Ambiguity: Hermeneutics, Religion, Hope*. San Francisco: Harper and Row, 1987.

Tracy, D., Küng, H., and Metz, J. B. *Toward Vatican III*. New York: Seabury Press, 1978.

VanLierdo, P. C. (trans. by Msgr. James Tucek) *The Holy See at Work: How the Catholic Is Governed*. New York: Hawthorne Books, 1962.

Vorgrimler, H. *Understanding Karl Rahner—An Introduction to His Life and Thought*. New York: Crossroad, 1986.

Weakland, R. G. *All God's People: Catholic Identity After the Second Vatican Council*. New York: Paulist Press, 1985.

Weaver, M. J. *New Catholic Women: A Contemporary Challenge to Traditional Religious Authority*. San Francisco: Harper and Row, 1986.

Index